Lecture Notes in Computer Science 12007

More information about this series at http://www.springer.com/series/7408

Ekaterina Komendantskaya ·
Yanhong Annie Liu (Eds.)

Practical Aspects of Declarative Languages

22nd International Symposium, PADL 2020
New Orleans, LA, USA, January 20–21, 2020
Proceedings

 Springer

Editors
Ekaterina Komendantskaya
Heriot-Watt University
Edinburgh, UK

Yanhong Annie Liu
Stony Brook University
Stony Brook, NY, USA

ISSN 0302-9743   ISSN 1611-3349 (electronic)
Lecture Notes in Computer Science
ISBN 978-3-030-39196-6   ISBN 978-3-030-39197-3 (eBook)
https://doi.org/10.1007/978-3-030-39197-3

LNCS Sublibrary: SL2 – Programming and Software Engineering

This Springer imprint is published by the registered company Springer Nature Switzerland AG
The registered company address is: Gewerbestrasse 11, 6330 Cham, Switzerland

Preface

Welcome to the 22nd International Symposium on Practical Aspects of Declarative Languages—PADL 2020!

PADL is a well-established forum for researchers and practitioners to present original work emphasizing novel applications and implementation techniques for all forms of declarative programming, including programming with sets, functions, logic, and constraints. Declarative languages have been applied to increasingly more important and challenging real-world applications, ranging from database management to active networks to software engineering to decision support systems. Topics of interest to PADL include, but are not limited to:

– Innovative applications of declarative languages
– Declarative domain-specific languages and applications
– Practical applications of theoretical results
– New language developments and their impact on applications
– Declarative languages for software engineering
– Evaluation of implementation techniques on practical applications
– Practical experiences and industrial applications
– Novel uses of declarative languages in the classroom
– Practical languages/extensions such as probabilistic and reactive languages

PADL 2020 especially welcomed new ideas and approaches pertaining to applications, including design and implementation of declarative languages going beyond the scope of the past PADL symposia, for example, advanced database languages and contract languages, efficient symbolic reasoning methods, and automatic theorem proving methods.

Originally established as a workshop (PADL 1999 in San Antonio, Texas), the PADL series developed into a regular annual symposium; previous editions took place in San Antonio, Texas (1999), Boston, Massachusetts (2000), Las Vegas, Nevada (2001), Portland, Oregon (2002), New Orleans, Louisiana (2003), Dallas, Texas (2004), Long Beach, California (2005), Charleston, South Carolina (2006), Nice, France (2007), San Francisco, California (2008), Savannah, Georgia (2009), Madrid, Spain (2010), Austin, Texas (2012), Rome, Italy (2013), San Diego, California (2014), Portland, Oregon (2015), St. Petersburg, Florida (2016), Paris, France (2017), Los Angeles, California (2018), and Lisbon, Portugal (2019).

The 22nd installment of the symposium was co-located with the 47th ACM SIGPLAN Symposium on Principles of Programming Languages (POPL 2020), and took place during January 20–21, 2020, in New Orleans, USA.

PADL 2020 featured invited talks, an invited experience and direction session, presentations of full and short research papers, discussion panels, and a competitive programming experience session.

The program included two invited talks:

- Nikolaj Bjorner (Microsoft Research, USA),
  "Logical Engines for Cloud Configurations"
- Adnan Darwiche (University of California, Los Angeles, USA),
  "Symbolic Reasoning About Machine Learning Systems"

The invited experience and direction session included four invited talks:

- Molham Aref (RelationalAI, USA),
  "Relational Artificial Intelligence"
- Mayur Naik (University of Pennsylvania, USA),
  "Learning Interpretable Rules from Structured Data"
- Grant Passmore (Imandra Inc. and Cambridge University, UK),
  "An Introduction to the Imandra Automated Reasoning System"
- Philip Wadler (University of Edingburgh, UK),
  "We Are All Poor Schmucks: On the Value of Gradual Types"

and was chaired by David S. Warren (Stony Brook University, USA).

Research papers include 10 full papers and 4 short papers, selected from 24 submissions including 21 complete submissions. Each submission was reviewed by at least three Program Committee members and went through a five-day online discussion period by the Program Committee before a final decision was made. The selection was based only on the merit of each submission and regardless of scheduling or space constraints.

Research papers are grouped into five topics: (1) Logical Engines and Applications, (2) Answer Set Programming Systems, (3) Memory and Real-Time in Functional Programming, (4) Reasoning and Efficient Implementation, and (5) Small Languages and Implementation.

There were four discussion panels by invited speakers, presenters of research papers, and all participants, on (1) Programming with Logic for the Masses, (2) Memory and Real-Time Programming in Practice, (3) Reasoning for Machine Learning at Large, and (4) Experience and Direction.

The programming experience session offers a presentation by Neng-Fa Zhou on the programming problems written using PiCat that won the online track of the programming contest at the 35th International Conference on Logic Programming (ICLP 2019).

We thank the Association of Logic Programming (ALP) and the Association for Computing Machinery (ACM) for their continuous support of the symposium, and Springer for the longstanding, successful cooperation with the PADL series. We are grateful to the 21 members of the PADL 2020 Program Committee and the external reviewers for their timely and invaluable work. Many thanks to Marco Gavanelli, the ALP Conference Coordinator, and Brigitte Pientka, the POPL 2020 Chair, for their great help in steering the organizational details of the event; and to Yi Tong, Elmer van Chastelet, and Josh Ko for their important technical support.

We are happy to note that the conference paper evaluation was successfully managed with the help of EasyChair.

January 2020   Ekaterina Komendantskaya
                                                         Yanhong Annie Liu

Organization

Program Chairs

Ekaterina Komendantskaya   Heriot-Watt University, UK
Yanhong Annie Liu   Stony Brook University, USA

Program Committee

Christopher Brown	St. Andrews University, UK
William E. Byrd	University of Alabama at Birmingham, USA
James Chapman	IOHK, UK
Iavor Diatchki	Galois, Inc., USA
Gabriel Ebner	Vrije Universiteit Amsterdam, The Netherlands
Esra Erdem	Sabanci University, Turkey
Martin Gebser	University of Klagenfurt, Austria
Alex Gerdes	University of Gothenburg, Sweden
Manuel Hermenegildo	IMDEA Software Institute and T.U. of Madrid, Spain
John Hughes	Chalmers University of Technology, Sweden
Kristian Kersting	TU Darmstadt, Germany
Hsiang-Shang 'Josh' Ko	Institute of Information Science, Academia Sinica, Taiwan
Ramana Kumar	DeepMind, UK
Michael Leuschel	University of Düsseldorf, Germany
Francesca A. Lisi	University of Bari, Italy
Enrico Pontelli	New Mexico State University, USA
Francesco Ricca	University of Calabria, Italy
Enrico Tassi	Inria, France
K. Tuncay Tekle	Stony Brook University, USA
Toby Walsh	UNSW Sydney, Australia
Jan Wielemaker	Vrije Universiteit Amsterdam, The Netherlands

Publicity Chair

Yi Tong   Stony Brook University, USA

Additional Reviewers

Mario Alviano
Alexander Bentkamp
Bernardo Cuteri
Maximilian P. L. Haslbeck
Tran Cao Son
Jessica Zangari

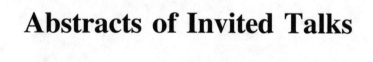

Abstracts of Invited Talks

Logical Engines for Cloud Configurations

Nikolaj Bjørner

Microsoft Research
nbjorner@microsoft.com
https://www.microsoft.com/en-us/research/people/nbjorner/

Abstract. Configurations form a basis for deploying infrastructure and custom instances in today's hyperscale cloud environments. Similar to conventional program analysis, configurations can be subjected to logical specifications and checked for correctness claims. In contrast to program analysis, the analysis relies on information from, and provides feedback on the health of, live systems.

This talk takes as starting point some of the experiences with using the SMT solver Z3 for checking declarative configurations in the Azure cloud. It then describes solving techniques applied for checking configurations, and SMT formulas in general. A theme characterizing these solving techniques is how they combine search for a model with deducing logical consequences. The talk provides exemplars of how search and consequence finding is integrated in Z3.

Biography. Nikolaj's main line of work is around the state-of-the-art SMT constraint solver Z3. Z3 received the 2015 ACM SIGPLAN Software System award and most influential tool paper in the first 20 years of TACAS, and the ETAPS test of time award. Leonardo and Nikolaj received the Herbrand Award at CADE 2019, in recognition of numerous and important contributions to SMT solving, including its theory, implementation, and application to a wide range of academic and industrial needs. A prolific application is around Network Verification as deployed in the Sec-Guru tool in Microsoft Azure. In previous work in the Windows File Systems Group, he developed the Distributed File System Replication, DFS-R, protocol. He studied at DTU, DIKU; and for his Master's and PhD at Stanford.

Symbolic Reasoning About Machine Learning Systems

Adnan Darwiche

University of California, Los Angeles
darwiche@cs.ucla.edu
http://web.cs.ucla.edu/~darwiche/

Abstract. I will discuss a line of work in which we compile common machine learning systems into symbolic representations that have the same input-output behavior to facilitate formal reasoning about these systems. We have targeted Bayesian network classifiers, random forests, and some types of neural networks, compiling each into tractable Boolean circuits, including Ordered Binary Decision Diagrams (OBDDs). Once the machine learning system is compiled into a tractable Boolean circuit, reasoning can commence using classical AI and computer science techniques. This includes generating explanations for decisions, quantifying robustness, and verifying properties such as monotonicity. I will particularly discuss a new theory for unveiling the reasons behind the decisions made by classifiers, which can detect classifier bias sometimes from the reasons behind unbiased decisions. The theory is based on a new type of tractable circuits, 'Reason Circuits,' introduced specifically for this purpose.

Biography. Adnan Darwiche is a professor and former chairman of the computer science department at UCLA. He directs the Automated Reasoning Group, which focuses on probabilistic and symbolic reasoning and their applications to machine learning. Professor Darwiche is Fellow of AAAI and ACM. He is a former editor-in-chief of the *Journal of Artificial Intelligence Research* (JAIR) and author of "Modeling and Reasoning with Bayesian Networks," by Cambridge University Press. His group's YouTube Channel can be found at: http://www.youtube.com/c/UCLAAutomatedReasoningGroup.

Abstracts of Invited Talks
for the Invited Experience
and Direction Session

Relational Artificial Intelligence

Molham Aref

RelationalAI
https://www.linkedin.com/in/molham/

Abstract. In this talk, I will make the case for a first-principles approach to machine learning over relational databases that exploits recent development in database systems and theory. The input to learning classification and regression models is defined by feature extraction queries over relational databases. The mainstream approach to learning over relational data is to materialize the results of the feature extraction query, export it out of the database, and then learn over it using statistical software packages. These three steps are expensive and unnecessary. Instead, one can cast the machine learning problem as a database problem, keeping the feature extraction query unmaterialized and using a new generation of meta-algorithms to push the learning through the query. The performance of this approach benefits tremendously from structural properties of the relational data and of the feature extraction query; such properties may be algebraic (semi-ring), combinatorial (hypertree width), or statistical (sampling). Performance is further improved by leveraging recent advances in compiler technology that eliminate the cost of abstraction and allows us to specialize the computation for specific workloads and datasets. This translates to several orders-of-magnitude speed-up over state-of-the-art systems.

This work is done by my colleagues at RelationalAI and by members of our faculty research network, including Dan Olteanu (Oxford), Maximilian Schleich (Oxford), Ben Moseley (CMU), and Xuanlong Nguyen (Michigan).

Biography. Molham Aref is the Chief Executive Officer of RelationalAI. He has more than 28 years of experience in leading organizations that develop and implement high value machine learning and artificial intelligence solutions across various industries. Prior to RelationalAI he was CEO of LogicBlox and Predictix (now Infor), Optimi (now Ericsson), and co-founder of Brickstream (now FLIR). Molham held senior leadership positions at HNC Software (now FICO) and Retek (now Oracle).

Learning Interpretable Rules
from Structured Data

Mayur Naik

University of Pennsylvania
mhnaik@cis.upenn.edu
https://www.cis.upenn.edu/~mhnaik/

Abstract. The problem of learning interpretable rules from structured data has important theoretical and practical ramifications in the fields of machine learning and program synthesis. Datalog, a declarative logic programming language, has emerged as a popular medium for studying this problem due to its rich expressivity and scalable performance. I will present search-based and constraint-solving techniques to learn Datalog programs from relational input-output data. The techniques address previously open problems as well as pose new challenges, spanning data-efficient learning, tolerating noise, supporting expressive features of Datalog, learning without syntactic bias, and scaling to very large search spaces.

Biography. Mayur Naik is an Associate Professor of Computer and Information Science at the University of Pennsylvania. His research spans programming languages related topics with the overarching goal of making software better, safer, and easier to build and maintain. His current focus concerns developing scalable techniques to reason about programs by combining machine learning and formal methods. He is also interested in foundations and applications of neuro-symbolic approaches that synergistically combine deep learning and symbolic reasoning. He received a PhD in Computer Science from Stanford University in 2008. Previously, he was a researcher at Intel Labs, Berkeley, from 2008 to 2011, and a faculty member at Georgia Tech from 2011 to 2016.

An Introduction to the Imandra Automated Reasoning System

Grant Passmore

Imandra Inc. and Clare Hall, Cambridge
grant.passmore@cl.cam.ac.uk
https://www.cl.cam.ac.uk/~gp351/

Abstract. Imandra (imandra.ai) is a cloud-native automated reasoning system powering a suite of tools for the design and regulation of complex algorithms. Imandra is finding exciting industrial use: for example, Goldman Sachs is now public with the fact that Imandra is used to design and audit some of their most complex trading algorithms.

Foundationally, Imandra is a full-featured interactive theorem prover with a unique combination of features, including: an "executable" logic based on a (pure, higher-order) subset of OCaml (in much the same way that ACL2's logic is based on a subset of Lisp), first-class computable counterexamples (with a proof procedure that is "complete for counterexamples" in a precise sense), a seamless integration of bounded model checking and full-fledged theorem proving, decision procedures for nonlinear real and floating point arithmetic, first-class state-space decompositions, and powerful techniques for automated induction (including the "lifting" of many Boyer-Moore ideas to our typed, higher-order setting).

In this talk, I'll give an overview of Imandra and we'll together work many examples. You can follow along and experiment with Imandra in the browser at http://try.imandra.ai/ and install Imandra locally by following the instructions at http://docs.imandra.ai/.

Biography. Grant Passmore is co-founder and co-CEO of Imandra Inc. (imandra.ai) where he leads the development of the Imandra automated reasoning system. Grant is a widely published researcher in formal verification and symbolic AI, with work ranging from nonlinear decision procedures in SMT to the analysis of fairness and regulatory compliance of financial algorithms. He has been a key contributor to safety verification of algorithms at Cambridge, Carnegie Mellon, Edinburgh, Microsoft Research, and SRI. He earned his PhD from the University of Edinburgh, is a graduate of UT Austin (BA in Mathematics) and the Mathematical Research Institute in the Netherlands (Master Class in Mathematical Logic), and is a Life Member of Clare Hall, University of Cambridge.

We Are All Poor Schmucks: On the Value of Gradual Types

Philip Wadler

University of Edinburgh
wadler@inf.ed.ac.uk
http://homepages.inf.ed.ac.uk/wadler/

Abstract. I always assumed gradual types were to help those poor schmucks using untyped languages to migrate to typed languages. I now realise that I am one of the poor schmucks. Much interest within the programming language community now centres on systems such as session types, effect types, and dependent types, which are not currently available in any widely-used language. To support migration from legacy code to code with these exotic type systems, some form of gradual typing appears essential.

(Adapted from *A Complement to Blame*, Philip Wadler, SNAPL 2015.)

Biography. Philip Wadler is Professor of Theoretical Computer Science at the University of Edinburgh and Senior Research Fellow at IOHK. He is an ACM Fellow and a Fellow of the Royal Society of Edinburgh, past chair of ACM SIGPLAN, past holder of a Royal Society-Wolfson Research Merit Fellowship, and winner of the SIGPLAN Distinguished Service Award and the POPL Most Influential Paper Award. Previously, he worked or studied at Stanford, Xerox Parc, CMU, Oxford, Chalmers, Glasgow, Bell Labs, and Avaya Labs, and visited as a guest professor in Copenhagen, Sydney, and Paris. He has an h-index of 70 with more than 25,000 citations to his work, according to Google Scholar. He contributed to the designs of Haskell, Java, and XQuery, and is a co-author of *Introduction to Functional Programming* (Prentice Hall, 1988), *XQuery from the Experts* (Addison Wesley, 2004), *Generics and Collections in Java* (O'Reilly, 2006), and *Programming Language Foundations in Agda* (2018). He has delivered invited talks in locations ranging from Aizu to Zurich.

Abstract for the Competitive Programming Experience Session

Competitive Programming with Picat

Neng-Fa Zhou

CUNY Brooklyn College and Graduate Center
zhou@sci.brooklyn.cuny.edu
http://www.sci.brooklyn.cuny.edu/~zhou/

Abstract. Picat (picat-lang.org) is a logic-based multi-paradigm programming language that integrates logic programming, functional programming, constraint programming, and scripting. Picat takes many features from other languages, including logic variables, unification, backtracking, pattern-matching rules, functions, list/array comprehensions, loops, assignments, tabling for dynamic programming and planning, and constraint solving with CP (Constraint Programming), MIP (Mixed Integer Programming), SAT (Satisfiability), and SMT (SAT Modulo Theories). These features make Picat suitable for scripting and modeling. Picat has been used in programming competitions, including ASP, Prolog, LP/CP, and Google Code Jam. For competitive programming, a language should be both expressive and efficient. With expressiveness, algorithms and models can be coded concisely and within the allowed time limit. With efficiency of the language system, programs can produce answers within the memory and time limits. I'll report on the solutions in Picat to the five problems used in the 2019 LP/CP Programming Contest.[1] The problems are all combinatorial, and all have practical application backgrounds, including code deciphering, resource allocation, auto-programming, game design, and operations research optimization. The problems require different modeling techniques and solvers. One of the programs employs the CP module, one uses the planner module, and three others rely on the SAT module. These solutions well illustrate the use of Picat's language constructs and solver tools, and, in hindsight, demonstrate the fitness of Picat for competitive programming. For each problem, I'll give a problem description, a program, and the underlying techniques used by the program. I'll also compare Picat, as a general-purpose language, with Prolog, Haskell, and Python, and, as a modeling language, with ASP, MiniZinc, and AMPL.

---

[1] The solutions are available at: http://picat-lang.org/pc/lpcomp2019.html. I won the online track of the contest with these solutions.

Contents

Logical Engines and Applications

Interactive Text Graph Mining
with a Prolog-based Dialog Engine

Paul Tarau[(⊠)] and Eduardo Blanco

Department of Computer Science and Engineering, University of North Texas,
Denton, USA
{paul.tarau,eduardo.blanco}@unt.edu

Abstract. On top of a neural network-based dependency parser and
a graph-based natural language processing module we design a Prolog-
based dialog engine that explores interactively a ranked fact database
extracted from a text document.

We reorganize dependency graphs to focus on the most relevant content elements of a sentence, integrate sentence identifiers as graph nodes
and after ranking the graph we take advantage of the implicit semantic
information that dependency links bring in the form of subject-verb-
object, "is-a" and "part-of" relations.

Working on the Prolog facts and their inferred consequences, the dialog engine specializes the text graph with respect to a query and reveals
interactively the document's most relevant content elements.

The open-source code of the integrated system is available at https://
github.com/ptarau/DeepRank.

Keywords: Logic-based dialog engine · Graph-based natural language
processing · Dependency graphs · query-driven salient sentence
extraction · Synergies between neural and symbolic text processing

1 Introduction

Logic programming languages have been used successfully for inference and planning tasks on restricted domain natural language processing tasks [1–4] but not
much on open domain, large scale information retrieval and knowledge representation tasks. On the other hand, deep learning systems are very good at
basic tasks ranging from parsing to factoid-trained question answering systems,
but still taking baby steps when emulating human-level inference processing on
complex documents [5,6]. Thus, a significant gap persists between neural and
symbolic processing in the field.

A motivation of our work is to help fill this gap by exploring synergies between
the neural, graph based and symbolic ecosystems in solving a practical problem:
building a dialog agent, that, after digesting the content of a text document
(e.g., a story, a textbook, a scientific paper, a legal document), enables the user
to interact with its most relevant content.

© Springer Nature Switzerland AG 2020
E. Komendantskaya and Y. A. Liu (Eds.): PADL 2020, LNCS 12007, pp. 3–19, 2020.
https://doi.org/10.1007/978-3-030-39197-3_1

We will start with a quick overview of the tools and techniques needed. Building a state-of-the art Natural Language Processing system requires inter-action with multi-paradigm components as emulating their functionality from scratch could easily become a 100-person/years project. In our case, this means integrating a declarative language module, focusing on high level text mining, into the Python-based **nltk** ecosystem, while relying on the Java-based Stanford CoreNLP toolkit for basic tasks like segmentation, part-of-speech tagging and parsing.

Overview of the System Architecture. Figure 1 summarizes the architecture of our system. The Stanford parser is started as a separate server process to which the Python text processing module connects as a client. It interfaces with the Prolog-based dialog engine by generating a clausal representation of the document's structure and content, as well as the user's queries. The dialog engine is responsible for handling the user's queries for which answers are sent back to the Python front-end which handles also the call to OS-level spoken-language services, when activated.

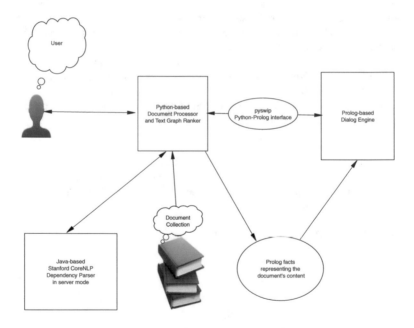

Fig. 1. System architecture

Today's dependency parsers [7–9], among which the neurally-trained Stan-ford dependency parser [7] stands out, produce highly accurate dependency graphs and part of speech tagged vertices. Seen as edges in a text graph, they pro-vide, by contrast to collocations in a sliding window, "distilled" building blocks through which a graph-based natural language processing system can absorb higher level linguistic information.

Inspired by the effectiveness of algorithms like Google's PageRank, recursive ranking algorithms applied to text graphs have enabled extraction of keyphrases, summaries and relations. Their popularity continues to increase due to the holistic view they shed on the interconnections between text units that act as recommenders for the most relevant ones, as well as the comparative simplicity of the algorithms. At close to 3000 citations and a follow-up of some almost equally as highly cited papers like [10] the TextRank algorithm [11,12] and its creative descendants have extended their applications to a wide variety of document types and social media interactions in a few dozen languages.

While part of the family of the TextRank descendants, our graph based text processing algorithm will use information derived from the dependency graphs associated to sentences. With help from the labels marking the edges of a dependency graph and the part of speech tags associated to its nodes, we will extract rank-ordered facts corresponding to content elements present in sentences. We pass these to logic programs that can query them and infer new relations, beyond those that can be mined directly from the text.

Like in the case of a good search engine, interaction with a text document will focus on the most relevant and semantically coherent elements matching a query. With this in mind, the natural feel of an answer syntactically appropriate for a query is less important than the usefulness of the content elements extracted: just sentences of the document, in their natural order.

We will also enable spoken interaction with the dialog engine, opening doors for the use of the system via voice-based appliances. Applications range from assistive technologies to visually challenged people, live user manuals, teaching from K-12 to graduate level and interactive information retrieval from complex technical or legal documents.

The paper is organized as follows. Section 2 describes the graph based Natural Language Processing module. Section 3 describes our Prolog-based dialog engine. Section 4 puts in context the main ideas of the paper and justifies some of the architecture choices we have made. Section 5 overviews related work and background information. Section 6 concludes the paper.

2 The Graph-Based Natural Language Processing Module

We have organized our Python-based textgraph processing algorithm together with the Prolog-based dialog engine into a unified system[1]. We start with the building and the ranking of the text graph. Then, we overview the summary, keyphrase and relation extraction and the creation of the Prolog database that constitutes the logical model of the document, to be processed by the dialog engine.

---

[1] Our implementation is available at https://github.com/ptarau/DeepRank.

2.1 Building and Ranking the Text Graph

We connect as a Python client to the Stanford CoreNLP server and use it to provide our dependency links via the wrapper at https://www.nltk.org/ of the Stanford CoreNLP toolkit [13].

Unlike the original TextRank and related approaches that develop special techniques for each text processing task, we design a unified algorithm to obtain graph representations of documents, that are suitable for keyphrase extraction, summarization and interactive content exploration.

We use unique sentence identifiers and unique lemmas[2] as nodes of the text graph. As keyphrases are centered around nouns and good summary sentences are likely to talk about important concepts, we will need to reverse some links in the dependency graph provided by the parser, to prioritize nouns and deprioritize verbs, especially auxiliary and modal ones. Thus, we redirect the dependency edges toward nouns with subject and object roles, as shown for a simple short sentence in Fig. 2 as *"about"* edges.

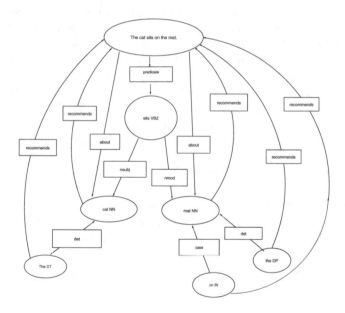

Fig. 2. Dependency graph of a simple sentence with redirected and newly added arrows

We also create *"recommend"* links from words to the sentence identifiers and back from sentences to verbs with *predicate* roles to indirectly ensure that sentences recommend and are recommended by their content. Specifically, we ensure that sentences recommend verbs with predicate function from where their recommendation spreads to nouns relevant as predicate arguments (e.g., having subject or object roles).

---

[2] A lemma is a canonical representation of a word, as it stands in a dictionary, for all its inflections e.g., it is **"be"** for "is", "are", "was" etc.

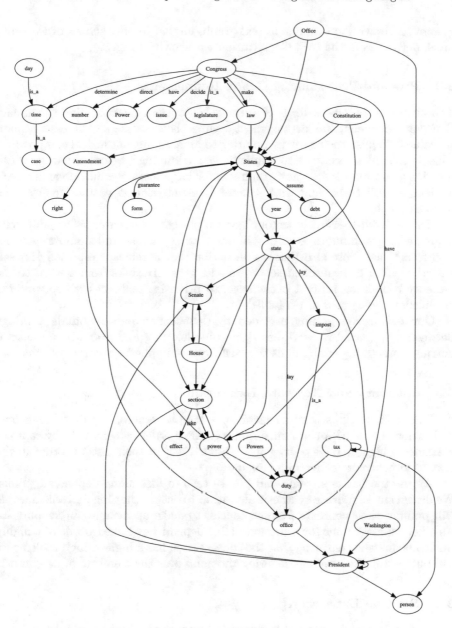

Fig. 3. Text graph of the highest ranked words in the U.S. Constitution

By using the PageRank implementation of the **networkx** toolkit[3], after ranking the sentence and word nodes of the text graph, the system is also able to display subgraphs filtered to contain only the highest ranked nodes, using Python's

---

[3] https://networkx.github.io/.

`graphviz` library. An example of text graph, filtered to only show word-to-word links, derived from the U.S. Constitution[4], is shown in Fig. 3.

2.2 Pre- and Post-ranking Graph Refinements

The algorithm induces a form of automatic stopword filtering, due to the fact that our dependency link arrangement ensures that modifiers with lesser semantic value relinquish their rank by pointing to more significant lexical components. This is a valid alternative to explicit "leaf trimming" before ranking, which remains an option for reducing graph size for large texts or multi-document collections as well as helping with a more focussed relation extraction from the reduced graphs.

Besides word-to-word links, our text graphs connect sentences as additional dependency graph nodes, resulting in a unified keyphrase and summary extraction framework. Note also that, as an option that is relevant especially for scientific, medical or legal documents, we add `first_in` links from a word to the sentence containing its first occurrence, to prioritize sentences where concepts are likely to be defined or explained.

Our reliance on graphs provided by dependency parsers builds a bridge between deep neural network-based machine learning and graph-based natural language processing enabling us to often capture implicit semantic information.

2.3 Summary and Keyword Extraction

As link configurations tend to favor very long sentences, a post-ranking normalization is applied for sentence ranking. After ordering sentences by rank we extract the highest ranked ones and reorder them in their natural order in the text to form a more coherent summary.

We use the parser's compound phrase tags to fuse along dependency links. We design our keyphrase synthesis algorithm to ensure that highly ranked words will pull out their contexts from sentences, to make up meaningful keyphrases. As a heuristic, we mine for a context of 2–4 dependency linked words of a highly ranked noun, while ensuring that the context itself has a high-enough rank, as we compute a weighted average favoring the noun over the elements of its context.

2.4 Relation Extraction

We add subject-verb-object facts extracted from the highest ranked dependency links, enhanced with "is-a" and "part-of" relations using WordNet via the `nltk` toolkit. We plan in the future to also generate relations from conditional statements identified following dependency links and involving negations, modalities, conjuncts and disjuncts, to be represented as Prolog rules. Subject-verb-object (SVO) relations are extracted directly from the dependency graph and an extra

---

[4] Available as a text document at: https://www.usconstitution.net/const.txt.

argument is added to the triplet marking the number of the sentence they originate from.

"Is-a" relations are extracted using WordNet [14] hypernyms and hyponyms[5]. Similarly, "part_of" relations are extracted using meronyms and holonyms[6]. As a heuristic that ensures that they are relevant to the content of the text, we ensure that both their arguments are words that occur in the document, when connecting their corresponding synsets via WordNet relations. By constraining the two ends of an "is-a" or "part-of" edge to occur in the document, we avoid relations derived from synsets unrelated to the document's content. In fact, this provides an effective word-sense disambiguation heuristic.

3   The Prolog-Based Dialog Engine

After our Python-based document processor, with help from the Stanford dependency parser, builds and ranks the text graph and extracts summaries, keyphrases and relations, we pass them to the Prolog-based dialog engine.

3.1   Generating Input for Post-processing by Logic Programs

Once the document is processed, we generate, besides the dependency links provided by the parser, relations containing facts that we have gleaned from processing the document. Together, they form a Prolog database representing the content of the document.

To keep the interface simple and portable to other logic programming tools, we generate the following predicates in the form of Prolog-readable code, in one file per document:

1. keyword(WordPhrase). – the extracted keyphrases
2. summary(SentenceId, SentenceWords). – the extracted summary sentences sentence identifiers and list of words
3. dep(SentenceID, WordFrom, FromTag, Label, WordTo, ToTag). – a component of a dependency link, with the first argument indicating the sentence they have been extracted
4. edge(SentenceID, FromLemma, FromTag, RelationLabel, ToLemma, ToTag). – edge marked with sentence identifiers indicating where it was extracted from, and the lemmas with their POS tags at the two ends of the edge
5. rank(LemmaOrSentenceId, Rank). – the rank computed for each lemma
6. w2l(Word, Lemma, Tag). – a map associating to each word a lemma, as found by the POS tagger
7. svo(Subject, Verb, Object, SentenceId). – subject-verb-object relations extracted from parser input or WordNet-based is_a and part_of labels in verb position

---

[5] More general and, respectively, more specific concepts.
[6] Concepts corresponding to objects that are part of, and, respectively, have as part other objects.

8. `sent(SentenceId, ListOfWords)`. – the list of sentences in the document with a sentence identifier as first argument and a list of words as second argument

They provide a relational view of a document in the form of a database that will support the inference mechanisms built on top of it.

The resulting logic program can then be processed with Prolog semantics, possibly enhanced by using constraint solvers [15], abductive reasoners [16] or via Answer Set Programming systems [17]. Specifically, we expect benefits from such extensions for tackling computationally difficult problems like word-sense disambiguation (WSD) or entailment inference as well as domain-specific reasoning [3,4,18].

We have applied this process to the *Krapivin document set* [19], a collection of **2304** research papers annotated with the authors' own keyphrases and abstracts.

The resulting 3.5 GB *Prolog dataset*[7] is made available for researchers in the field, interested to explore declarative reasoning or text mining mechanisms.

3.2   The Prolog Interface

We use as a logic processing tool the open source SWI-Prolog system[8] [20] that can be called from, and can call Python programs using the `pyswip` adaptor[9]. After the adaptor creates the Prolog process and the content of the digested document is transferred from Python (in a few seconds for typical scientific paper sizes of 10–15 pages), query processing is realtime.

3.3   The User Interaction Loop

With the Prolog representation of the digested document in memory, the dialog starts by displaying the summary and keyphrases extracted from the document[10]. One can see this as a "mini search-engine", specialized to the document, and, with help of an indexing layer, extensible to multi-document collections. The dialog agent associated to the document answers queries as sets of salient sentences extracted from the text, via a specialization of our summarization algorithm to the context inferred from the query.

As part of an interactive *read/listen, evaluate, print/say* loop, we generate for each query sentence, a set of predicates that are passed to the Prolog process, from where answers will come back via the `pyswip` interface. The predicates extracted from a query have the same structure as the database representing the content of the complete document, initially sent to Prolog.

---

[7] http://www.cse.unt.edu/~tarau/datasets/PrologDeepRankDataset.zip.

[8] http://www.swi-prolog.org/.

[9] https://github.com/yuce/pyswip.

[10] And also speak them out if the `quiet` flag is off.

3.4   The Answer Generation Algorithm

Answers are generated by selecting the most relevant sentences, presented in their natural order in the text, in the form of a specialized "mini-summary".

Query Expansion. Answer generation starts with a query-expansion mechanism via relations that are derived by finding, for lemmas in the query, WordNet hypernyms, hyponyms, meronyms and holonyms, as well as by directly extracting them from the query's dependency links. We use the rankings available both in the query and the document graph to prioritize the highest ranked sentences connected to the highest ranked nodes in the query.

Short-Time Dialog Memory. We keep representations of recent queries in memory, as well as the answers generated for them. If the representation of the current query overlaps with a past one, we use content in the past query's database to extend query expansion to cover edges originating from that query. Overlapping is detected via shared edges between noun or verb nodes between the query graphs.

Sentence Selection. Answer sentence selection happens by a combination of several interoperating algorithms:

- use of *personalized PageRank* [21, 22] with a dictionary provided by highest ranking lemmas and their ranks in the query's graph, followed by reranking the document's graph to specialize to the query's content
- matching guided by SVO-relations
- matching of edges in the query graph against edges in the document graph
- query expansion guided by rankings in both the query graph and the document graph
- matching guided by a selection of related content components in the short-term dialog memory window

Matching against the Prolog database representing the document is currently implemented as a size constraint on the intersection of the expanded query lemma set, built with highly ranked shared lemmas pointing to sentences containing them. The set of answers is organized to return the highest-ranked sentences based on relevance to the query and in the order in which they appear in the document.

We keep the dialog window relatively small (limited to the highest ranked 3 sentences in the answer set, by default). Relevance is ensured with help from the rankings computed for both the document content and the query.

3.5   Interacting with the Dialog Engine

The following example shows the result of a query on the US Constitution document.

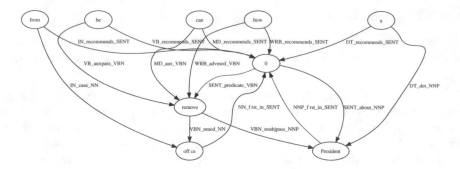

Fig. 4. Graph of query on the U.S. Constitution

>>> talk_about('examples/const')
?-- How can a President be removed from office?

59: In Case of the Removal of the President from Office, or of his Death, Resignation, or Inability to discharge the Powers and Duties of the said Office, the same shall devolve on the Vice President, and the Congress may by Law provide for the Case of Removal, Death, Resignation or Inability, both of the President and Vice President, declaring what Officer shall then act as President, and such Officer shall act accordingly, until the Disability be removed, or a President shall be elected.
66: Section 4 The President, Vice President and all civil Officers of the United States, shall be removed from Office on Impeachment for, and Conviction of, Treason, Bribery, or other high Crimes and Misdemeanors.
190: If the Congress, within twenty one days after receipt of the latter written declaration, or, if Congress is not in session, within twenty one days after Congress is required to assemble, determines by two thirds vote of both Houses that the President is unable to discharge the powers and duties of his office, the Vice President shall continue to discharge the same as Acting President; otherwise, the President shall resume the powers and duties of his office.

Note the relevance of the extracted sentences and resilience to semantic and syntactic variations (e.g., the last sentence does not contain the word "remove"). The dependency graph of the query is shown in Fig. 4. The clauses of the query_rank/2 predicate in the Prolog database corresponding to the query are:

```
query_rank('President', 0.2162991696472837).
query_rank('remove', 0.20105324712764877).
query_rank('office', 0.12690425831428373).
query_rank('how', 0.04908035060099132).
query_rank('can', 0.04908035060099132).
query_rank('a', 0.04908035060099132).
query_rank('be', 0.04908035060099132).
query_rank('from', 0.04908035060099132).
query_rank(0, 0.0023633884483800784).
```

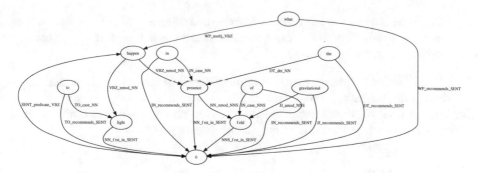

Fig. 5. Graph of query on Einstein's book on Relativity

Our next example uses an ASCII version of Einstein's 1920 book on relativity, retrieved from the Gutenberg collection[11] and trimmed to the actual content of the book (250 pages in `epub` form).

>>> talk_about('examples/relativity')
?-- **What happens to light in the presence of gravitational fields?**
611: In the example of the transmission of light just dealt with, we have seen that the general theory of relativity enables us to derive theoretically the influence of a gravitational field on the course of natural processes, the laws of which are already known when a gravitational field is absent.
764: On the contrary, we arrived at the result that according to this latter theory the velocity of light must always depend on the co-ordinates when a gravitational field is present.
765: In connection with a specific illustration in Section XXIII, we found that the presence of a gravitational field invalidates the definition of the coordinates and the time, which led us to our objective in the special theory of relativity.

The query graph is shown in Fig. 5. After the less than 30 s that it takes to digest the book, answers are generated in less than a second for all queries that we have tried. Given the availability of spoken dialog, a user can iterate and refine queries to extract the most relevant answer sentences of a document.

On an even larger document, like the Tesla Model 3 owner's manual[12], digesting the document takes about 60 s and results in 12 MB of Prolog clauses. After that, query answering is still below 1 s.

>>> talk_about('examples/tesla')
?-- **How may I have a flat tire repaired?**
3207: Arrange to have Model 3 transported to a Tesla Service Center, or to a nearby tire repair center.

---

[11] https://www.gutenberg.org/files/30155/30155-0.txt.
[12] https://www.tesla.com/sites/default/files/model_3_owners_manual_north_america_en.pdf.

3291: Note: If a tire has been replaced or repaired using a different tire sealant than the one available from Tesla, and a low tire pressure is detected, it is possible that the tire sensor has been damaged.

The highly relevant first answer is genuinely useful in this case, given that Tesla Model 3's do not have a spare tire. Being able to use voice queries while driving and in need of urgent technical information about one's car, hints towards obvious practical applications of our dialog engine.

4 Discussion

Ideally, one would like to evaluate the quality of natural language understanding of an AI system by querying it not only about a set of relations explicitly extracted in the text, but also about relations inferred from the text. Moreover, one would like also to have the system justify the inferred relations in the form of a proof, or at least a sketch of the thought process a human would use for the same purpose. The main challenge here is not only that theorem-proving logic is hard, (with first-order classical predicate calculus already Turing-complete), but also that modalities, beliefs, sentiments, hypothetical and contrafactual judgements often make the underlying knowledge structure intractable.

On the other hand, simple relations, stated or implied by text elements that can be mined or inferred from a ranked graph built from labeled dependency links, provide a limited but manageable approximation of the text's deeper logic structure, especially when aggregated with generalizations and similarities provided by WordNet or the much richer Wikipedia knowledge graph.

Given its effectiveness as an interactive content exploration tool, we plan future work on packaging our dialog engine as a set of Amazon Alexa skills for some popular Wikipedia entries as well as product reviews, FAQs and user manuals.

Empirical evaluation of our keyphrase and summarization algorithms will be subject to a different paper, but preliminary tests indicate that both of them match or exceed Rouge scores for state of the art systems [23].

5 Related Work

Dependency Parsing. The Stanford neural network based dependency parser [7] is now part of the Stanford CoreNLP toolkit[13], which also comes with part of speech tagging, named entities recognition and co-reference resolution [13]. Its evolution toward the use of Universal Dependencies [24] makes tools relying on it potentially portable to over **70** languages covered by the Universal Dependencies effort[14].

---

[13] https://stanfordnlp.github.io/CoreNLP/.
[14] https://universaldependencies.org/.

Of particular interest is the connection of dependency graphs to logic elements like predicate argument relations [25]. The mechanism of automatic conversion of constituency trees to dependency graphs described in [9] provides a bridge allowing the output of high-quality statistically trained phrase structure parsers to be reused for extraction of dependency links.

We analyze dependency links and POS-tags associated to their endpoints to extract SVO relations. By redirecting links to focus on nouns and sentences we not only enable keyphrase and summary extraction from the resulting document graph but also facilitate its use for query answering in our dialog engine.

Graph Based Natural Language Processing. In TextRank [11,12] keyphrases are using a co-occurrence relation, controlled by the distance between word occurrences: two vertices are connected if their corresponding lexical units co-occur within a sliding window of 2 to 10 words. Sentence similarity is computed as content overlap giving weights on the links that refine the original PageRank algorithm [26,27]. TextRank needs elimination of stop words and reports best results when links are restricted to nouns and adjectives. In [10] several graph centrality measures are explored and [28] offers a comprehensive overview on graph-based natural language processing and related graph algorithms. Graph-based and other text summarization techniques are surveyed in [29] and more recently in [30]. Besides ranking, elements like coherence via similarity with previously chosen sentences and avoidance of redundant rephrasings are shown to contribute to the overall quality of the summaries. *The main novelty of our approach in this context is building the text graph from dependency links and integrating words and sentences in the same text graph, resulting in a unified algorithm that also enables relation extraction and interactive text mining.*

Relation Extraction. The relevance of dependency graphs for relation extraction has been identified in several papers, with [8] pointing out to their role as a generic interface between parsers and relation extraction systems. In [31] several models grounded on syntactic patterns are identified (e.g., subject-verb-object) that can be mined out from dependency graphs. Of particular interest for relation extraction facilitated by dependency graphs is the shortest path hypothesis that prefers relating entities like predicate arguments that are connected via a shortest paths in the graph [32]. To facilitate their practical applications to biomedical texts, [33] extends dependency graphs with focus on richer sets of semantic features including "is-a" and "part-of" relations and co-reference resolution.

The use of ranking algorithms in combination with WordNet synset links for word-sense disambiguation goes back as far as [34], in fact a prequel to the TextRank paper [11]. With the emergence of resources like Wikipedia, a much richer set of links and content elements has been used in connection with graph based natural language processing [8,35,36].

We currently extract our relations directly from the dependency graph and by using one step up and one step down links in the WordNet hypernym and meronym hierarchies, but extensions are planned to integrate Wikipedia content, via the **dbpedia** database[15] and to extract more elaborate logic relations using a Prolog-based semantic parser like Boxer [37].

Logic Programming Systems for Natural Language Processing. A common characteristic of Prolog or ASP-based NLP systems is their focus on closed domains with domain-specific logic expressed in clausal form [1–4], although recent work like [18] extracts action language programs from more general narratives.

As our main objective is the building of a practically useful dialog agent, and as we work with open domain text and query driven content retrieval, our focus is not on precise domain-specific reasoning mechanisms. By taking advantage of the Prolog representation of a document's content, we use reasoning about the extracted relations and ranking information to find the most relevant sentences derived from a given query and the recent dialog history.

6   Conclusions

The key idea of the paper has evolved from our search for synergies between symbolic AI and emerging machine-learning based natural language processing tools. It is our belief that these are complementary and that by working together they will take significant forward steps in natural language understanding. We have based our text graph on heterogeneous, but syntactically and semantically meaningful text units (words and sentences) resulting in a web of interleaved links, mutually recommending each other's highly ranked instances. Our fact extraction algorithm, in combination with the Prolog interface has elevated the syntactic information provided by dependency graphs with semantic elements ready to benefit from logic-based inference mechanisms. Given the standardization brought by the use of *Universal Dependencies*, our techniques are likely to be portable to a large number of languages.

The Prolog-based dialog engine supports spoken interaction with a conversational agent that exposes salient content of the document driven by the user's interest. Its applications range from assistive technologies to visually challenged people, voice interaction with user manuals, teaching from K-12 to graduate level and interactive information retrieval from complex technical or legal documents.

Last but not least, we have used our system's front end to generate the Prolog dataset at http://www.cse.unt.edu/~tarau/datasets/PrologDeepRankDataset.zip, derived from more than 2000 research papers and made it available to other researchers using logic programming based reasoners and content mining tools.

Acknowledgment. We are thankful to the anonymous reviewers of **PADL'2020** for their careful reading and constructive suggestions.

---

[15] https://wiki.dbpedia.org/.

References

1. Lierler, Y., Inclezan, D., Gelfond, M.: Action languages and question answering. In: Gardent, C., Retoré, C. (eds.) IWCS 2017–12th International Conference on Computational Semantics - Short papers, Montpellier, France, 19–22 September 2017. The Association for Computer Linguistics (2017)
2. Inclezan, D., Zhang, Q., Balduccini, M., Israney, A.: An ASP methodology for understanding narratives about stereotypical activities. TPLP **18**(3–4), 535–552 (2018)
3. Mitra, A., Clark, P., Tafjord, O., Baral, C.: Declarative question answering over knowledge bases containing natural language text with answer set programming. In: The Thirty-Third AAAI Conference on Artificial Intelligence, AAAI, pp. 3003–3010. AAAI Press (2019)
4. Inclezan, D.: RestKB: a library of commonsense knowledge about dining at a restaurant. In: Bogaerts, B., et al. (eds.) Proceedings 35th International Conference on Logic Programming (Technical Communications), Las Cruces, NM, USA, 20–25 September 2019. Volume 306 of Electronic Proceedings in Theoretical Computer Science, pp. 126–139. Open Publishing Association (2019)
5. Vaswani, A., et al.: Attention is all you need. CoRR abs/1706.03762 (2017)
6. Devlin, J., Chang, M., Lee, K., Toutanova, K.: BERT: pre-training of deep bidirectional transformers for language understanding. CoRR abs/1810.04805 (2018)
7. Chen, D., Manning, C.: A fast and accurate dependency parser using neural networks. In: Proceedings of the 2014 Conference on Empirical Methods in Natural Language Processing (EMNLP), pp. 740–750. Association for Computational Linguistics (2014)
8. Adolphs, P., Xu, F., Li, H., Uszkoreit, H.: Dependency graphs as a generic interface between parsers and relation extraction rule learning. In: Bach, J., Edelkamp, S. (eds.) KI 2011. LNCS (LNAI), vol. 7006, pp. 50–62. Springer, Heidelberg (2011). https://doi.org/10.1007/978-3-642-24455-1_5
9. Choi, J.D.: Deep dependency graph conversion in English. In: Proceedings of the 15th International Workshop on Treebanks and Linguistic Theories, TLT 2017, Bloomington, IN, pp. 35–62 (2017)
10. Erkan, G., Radev, D.R.: LexRank: graph-based lexical centrality as salience in text summarization. J. Artif. Intell. Res. **22**(1), 457–479 (2004)
11. Mihalcea, R., Tarau, P.: TextRank: bringing order into texts. In: Proceedings of the Conference on Empirical Methods in Natural Language Processing (EMNLP 2004), Barcelona, Spain, July 2004
12. Mihalcea, R., Tarau, P.: An algorithm for language independent single and multiple document summarization. In: Proceedings of the International Joint Conference on Natural Language Processing (IJCNLP), Korea, October 2005
13. Manning, C.D., Surdeanu, M., Bauer, J., Finkel, J., Bethard, S.J., McClosky, D.: The Stanford CoreNLP natural language processing toolkit. In: Association for Computational Linguistics (ACL) System Demonstrations, pp. 55–60 (2014)
14. Fellbaum, C.: WordNet, An Electronic Lexical Database. The MIT Press, Cambridge (1998)
15. Schulte, C.: Programming constraint inference engines. In: Smolka, G. (ed.) CP 1997. LNCS, vol. 1330, pp. 519–533. Springer, Heidelberg (1997). https://doi.org/10.1007/BFb0017464

16. Denecker, M., Kakas, A.: Abduction in logic programming. In: Kakas, A.C., Sadri, F. (eds.) Computational Logic: Logic Programming and Beyond. LNCS (LNAI), vol. 2407, pp. 402–436. Springer, Heidelberg (2002). https://doi.org/10.1007/3-540-45628-7_16

17. Schaub, T., Woltran, S.: Special issue on answer set programming. KI **32**(2–3), 101–103 (2018)

18. Olson, C., Lierler, Y.: Information extraction tool Text2ALM: from narratives to action language system descriptions. In: Bogaerts, B., et al. (eds.) Proceedings 35th International Conference on Logic Programming (Technical Communications), Las Cruces, NM, USA, 20–25 September 2019. Volume 306 of Electronic Proceedings in Theoretical Computer Science, pp. 87–100. Open Publishing Association (2019)

19. Krapivin, M., Autayeu, A., Marchese, M.: Large dataset for keyphrases extraction. Technical report DISI-09-055, DISI, Trento, Italy, May 2008

20. Wielemaker, J., Schrijvers, T., Triska, M., Lager, T.: SWI-Prolog. Theory Pract. Logic. Program. **12**, 67–96 (2012)

21. Haveliwala, T.H.: Topic-sensitive PageRank. In: Proceedings of the 11th International Conference on World Wide Web, WWW 2002, pp. 517–526. ACM, New York (2002)

22. Haveliwala, T., Kamvar, S., Jeh, G.: An analytical comparison of approaches to personalizing PageRank. Technical report 2003–35, Stanford InfoLab, June 2003

23. Tarau, P., Blanco, E.: Dependency-based text graphs for keyphrase and summary extraction with applications to interactive content retrieval. arXiv abs/1909.09742 (2019)

24. de Marneffe, M.C., et al.: Universal Stanford dependencies: a cross-linguistic typology. In: Proceedings of the Ninth International Conference on Language Resources and Evaluation (LREC-2014), Reykjavik, Iceland, pp. 4585–4592. European Languages Resources Association (ELRA), May 2014

25. Choi, J.D., Palmer, M.: Transition-based semantic role labeling using predicate argument clustering. In: Proceedings of the ACL 2011 Workshop on Relational Models of Semantics. RELMS 2011, Stroudsburg, PA, USA, pp. 37–45. Association for Computational Linguistics (2011)

26. Page, L., Brin, S., Motwani, R., Winograd, T.: The PageRank citation ranking: bringing order to the web. Technical report, Stanford Digital Library Technologies Project (1998)

27. Brin, S., Page, L.: The anatomy of a large-scale hypertextual Web search engine. Comput. Netw. ISDN Syst. **30**(1–7), 107–117 (1998). http://citeseer.nj.nec.com/brin98anatomy.html

28. Mihalcea, R.F., Radev, D.R.: Graph-Based Natural Language Processing and Information Retrieval, 1st edn. Cambridge University Press, New York (2011)

29. Nenkova, A., McKeown, K.R.: A survey of text summarization techniques. In: Aggarwal, C., Zhai, C. (eds.) Mining Text Data, pp. 43–76. Springer, Boston (2012). https://doi.org/10.1007/978-1-4614-3223-4_3

30. Allahyari, M., et al.: Text summarization techniques: a brief survey. CoRR abs/1707.02268 (2017)

31. Stevenson, M., Greenwood, M.: Dependency pattern models for information extraction. Res. Lang. Comput. **7**(1), 13–39 (2009)

32. Bunescu, R.C., Mooney, R.J.: A shortest path dependency kernel for relation extraction. In: Proceedings of the Conference on Human Language Technology and Empirical Methods in Natural Language Processing, HLT 2005, Stroudsburg, PA, USA, pp. 724–731. Association for Computational Linguistics (2005)

33. Peng, Y., Gupta, S., Wu, C., Shanker, V.: An extended dependency graph for relation extraction in biomedical texts. In: Proceedings of BioNLP 15, pp. 21–30. Association for Computational Linguistics (2015)
34. Mihalcea, R., Tarau, P., Figa, E.: PageRank on semantic networks, with application to word sense disambiguation. In: Proceedings of the 20st International Conference on Computational Linguistics (COLING 2004), Geneva, Switzerland, August 2004
35. Li, W., Zhao, J.: TextRank algorithm by exploiting wikipedia for short text keywords extraction. In: 2016 3rd International Conference on Information Science and Control Engineering (ICISCE), pp. 683–686 (2016)
36. Mihalcea, R., Csomai, A.: Wikify!: linking documents to encyclopedic knowledge. In: Proceedings of the Sixteenth ACM Conference on Conference on Information and Knowledge Management, CIKM 2007, pp. 233–242. ACM, New York (2007)
37. Bos, J.: Open-domain semantic parsing with boxer. In: Megyesi, B. (ed.) Proceedings of the 20th Nordic Conference of Computational Linguistics, NODALIDA 2015, 1–13 May 2015, pp. 301–304. Institute of the Lithuanian Language, Vilnius, Linköping University Electronic Press/ACL (2015)

Flexible Graph Matching and Graph Edit Distance Using Answer Set Programming

Sheung Chi Chan[1] and James Cheney[1,2]($\boxtimes$)

[1] University of Edinburgh, Edinburgh, UK
jcheney@inf.ed.ac.uk
[2] The Alan Turing Institute, London, UK

Abstract. The *graph isomorphism, subgraph isomorphism*, and *graph edit distance* problems are combinatorial problems with many applications. Heuristic exact and approximate algorithms for each of these problems have been developed for different kinds of graphs: directed, undirected, labeled, etc. However, additional work is often needed to adapt such algorithms to different classes of graphs, for example to accommodate both labels and property annotations on nodes and edges. In this paper, we propose approach based on answer set programming. We show how each of these problems can be defined for a general class of *property graphs* with directed edges, and labels and key-value properties annotating both nodes and edges. We evaluate this approach on a variety of synthetic and realistic graphs, demonstrating that it is feasible as a rapid prototyping approach.

1 Introduction

Graphs are a pervasive and widely applicable data structure in computer science. To name just a few examples, graphs can represent symbolic knowledge structures extracted from Wikipedia [5], provenance records describing how a computer system executed to produce a result [20], or chemical structures in a scientific knowledge base [15]. In many settings, it is of interest to solve *graph matching* problems, for example to determine when two graphs have the same structure, or when one graph appears in another, or to measure how similar two graphs are.

Given two graphs, possibly with labels or other data associated with nodes and edges, the *graph isomorphism* problem (GI) asks whether the two graphs have the same structure, that is, whether there is an invertible mapping from one graph to another that preserves and reflects edges and any other constraints. The *subgraph isomorphism* problem (SUB) asks whether one graph is isomorphic to a subgraph of another. Finally, the *graph edit distance* problem (GED) asks whether one graph can be transformed into another via a sequence of edit steps, such as insertion, deletion, or updates to nodes or edges.

These are well-studied problems. Each is in the class NP, with SUB and GED being NP-complete [12], while the lower bound of the complexity of GI is an open

© Springer Nature Switzerland AG 2020
E. Komendantskaya and Y. A. Liu (Eds.): PADL 2020, LNCS 12007, pp. 20–36, 2020.
https://doi.org/10.1007/978-3-030-39197-3_2

problem [4]. Approximate and exact algorithms for graph edit distance, based on heuristics or on reduction to other NP-complete problems, have been proposed [9,11,17,21]. Moreover, for special cases such as database querying, there are algorithms for subgraph isomorphism that can provide good performance in practice when matching small query subgraphs against graph databases [16].

However, there are circumstances in which none of the available techniques is directly suitable. For example, many of the algorithms considered so far assume graphs of a specific form, for example with unordered edges, or unlabeled nodes and edges. In contrast, many typical applications use graphs with complex structure, such as property graphs: directed multigraphs in which nodes and edges can both be labeled and annotated with sets of key-value pairs (*properties*). Adapting an existing algorithm to deal with each new kind of graph is nontrivial. Furthermore, some applications involve searching for isomorphisms, subgraph isomorphisms, or edit scripts subject to additional constraints [8,22].

In this paper we advocate the use of *answer set programming* (ASP) to specify and solve these problems. Property graphs can be represented uniformly as sets of logic programming facts, and each of the graph matching problems we have mentioned can be specified using ASP in a uniform way. Concretely, we employ the Clingo ASP solver, but our approach relies only on standard ASP features.

For each of the problems we consider, it is clear in principle that it should be possible to encode using ASP, because ASP subsumes the NP-complete SAT problem. Our contribution is to show how to encode each of these problems directly in a way that produces immediately useful results, rather than via encoding as SAT or other problems and decoding the results. For GI and SUB, the encoding is rather direct and the ASP specifications can easily be read as declarative specifications of the respective problems; however, the standard formulation of the graph edit distance problem is not as easy to translate to a logic program because it involves searching for an edit script whose maximum length depends on the input. Instead, we consider an indirect (but still natural) approach which searches for a partial matching between the two graphs that minimizes the edit distance, and derives an edit script (if needed) from this matching. The proof of correctness of this encoding is our main technical contribution.

We provide experimental evidence of the practicality of our declarative approach, drawing on experience with a nontrivial application: generalizing and comparing provenance graphs [8]. In this previous work, we needed to solve two problems: (1) given two graphs with the same structure but possibly different property values (e.g. timestamps), identify the general structure common to all of the graphs, and (2) given a background graph and a slightly larger foreground graph, match the background graph to the foreground graph and "subtract" it, leaving the unmatched part. We showed in [8] that our ASP approach to approximate graph isomorphism and subgraph isomorphism can solve these problems fast enough that they were not the bottleneck in the overall system. In this paper, we conduct further experimental evaluation of our approach to graph isomorphism, subgraph isomorphism, and graph edit distance on synthetic graphs

and real graphs used in a recent Graph Edit Distance Contest (GEDC) [1] and
our recent work [8].

2   Background

Property Graphs. We consider *(directed) multigraphs* $G = (V, E, src, tgt, lab)$
where V and E are disjoint sets of *node identifiers* and *edge identifiers*, respectively, $src, tgt : E \rightarrow V$ are functions identifying the source and target of each
edge, and $lab : V \cup E \rightarrow \Sigma$ is a function assigning each vertex and edge a label
from some set Σ. Note that multigraphs can have multiple edges with the same
source and target. Familiar definitions of ordinary directed or undirected graphs
can be recovered by imposing further constraints, if desired.

A *property graph* is a directed multigraph extended with an additional partial
function $prop : (V \cup E) \times \Gamma \rightharpoonup \Delta$ where Γ is a set of *keys* and Δ is a set of *data
values*. For the purposes of this paper we assume that all identifiers, labels, keys
and values are represented as Prolog atoms.

We consider a partial function with range X to be a total function with range
$X \uplus \{\bot\}$ where $\bot$ is a special token not appearing in X. We consider $X \uplus \{\bot\}$
to be partially ordered by the least partial order satisfying $\bot \sqsubseteq x$ for all $x \in X$.

Isomorphisms. A *homomorphism* from property graph G_1 to G_2 is a function
$h : G_1 \rightarrow G_2$ mapping V_1 to V_2 and E_1 to E_2, such that:

- for all $v \in V_1$, $lab_2(h(v)) = lab_1(v)$ and $prop_2(h(v), k) \sqsubseteq prop_1(v, k)$
- for all $e \in E_1$, $lab_2(h(e)) = lab_1(e)$ and $prop_2(h(e), k) \sqsubseteq prop_1(e, k)$
- for all $e \in E_1$, $src_2(h(e)) = h(src_1(e))$ and $tgt_2(h(e)) = h(tgt_1(e))$

(Essentially, h is a pair of functions $(V_1 \rightarrow V_2) \times (E_1 \rightarrow E_2)$, but we abuse
notation slightly here by writing h for both.) As usual, an isomorphism is an
invertible homomorphism whose inverse is also a homomorphism, and G_1 and
G_2 are isomorphic $(G_1 \cong G_2)$ if an isomorphism between them exists. Note that
the labels of nodes and edges must match exactly, that is, we regard labels as
integral to nodes and edges, while properties must match only if defined in G_1.

Subgraph Isomorphism. A subgraph G' of G is a property graph satisfying:

- $V' \subseteq V$ and $E' \subseteq E$
- $src'(e) = src(e) \in V'$ and $tgt(e) = tgt'(e) \in V'$ for all $e \in E'$
- $lab'(x) = lab(x)$ when $x \in V' \cup E'$
- $prop'(x, k) \sqsubseteq prop(x, k)$ when $x \in V' \cup E'$

In other words, the vertex and edge sets of G' are subsets of those of G that still
form a meaningful graph, the labels are the same as in G', and the properties
defined in G' are the same as in G (but some properties in G may be omitted).

We say that G_1 is *subgraph isomorphic* to G_2 $(G_1 \lesssim G_2)$ if there is a subgraph
of G_2 to which G_1 is isomorphic. Equivalently, $G_1 \lesssim G_2$ holds if there is a
injective homomorphism $h : G_1 \rightarrow G_2$. If such a homomorphism exists, then it
maps G_1 to an isomorphic subgraph of G_2, whereas if $G_1 \cong G'_2 \subseteq G_2$ then the
isomorphism between G_1 and G'_2 extends to an injective homomorphism from
G_1 to G_2.

Table 1. Edit operation semantics

op	V'	E'	src'	tgt'	lbl'	$prop'$
$\mathsf{insV}(n,l)$	$V \uplus \{v\}$	E	src	tgt	$lbl[v := l]$	$prop$
$\mathsf{insE}(e,v,w,l)$	V	$E \uplus \{e\}$	$src[e := v]$	$tgt[e := w]$	$lbl[e := l]$	$prop$
$\mathsf{insP}(x,k,d)$	V	E	src	tgt	lbl	$prop[x,k := d]$
$\mathsf{delV}(v)$	$V - \{v\}$	E	src	tgt	$lbl[v := \bot]$	$prop$
$\mathsf{delE}(e)$	V	$E - \{e\}$	$src[e := \bot]$	$tgt[e := \bot]$	$lbl[e := \bot]$	$prop$
$\mathsf{delP}(x,k)$	V	E	src	tgt	lbl	$prop[x,k := \bot]$
$\mathsf{updP}(x,k,d)$	V	E	src	tgt	lbl	$prop[x,k := d]$

Graph Edit Distance. We consider *edit operations*:

- insertion of a node ($\mathsf{insV}(v,l)$), edge ($\mathsf{insE}(e,v,w,l)$), or property ($\mathsf{insP}(x,k,v,d)$)
- deletion of a node ($\mathsf{delV}(v)$), edge ($\mathsf{delE}(e)$), or property ($\mathsf{delP}(x,k)$)
- in-place update ($\mathsf{updP}(x,k,d)$) of a property value on a given node or edge x with a given key k to value d

The meanings of each of these operations are defined in Table 1, where we write $G = (V, E, src, tgt, lab, prop)$ for the graph before the edit and $G' = (V', E', src', tgt', lab', prop')$ for the updated graph. Each row of the table describes how each part of G' is defined in terms of G. In addition, the edit operations have the following preconditions: Before an insertion, the inserted node, edge, or property must not already exist; before a deletion, a deleted node must not be a source or target of an edge, and a node/edge must not have any properties; before an update, the updated property must already exist on the affected node or edge. If these preconditions are not satisfied, the edit operation is not allowed on G.

We write $op(G)$ for the result of op acting on G. More generally, if ops is a list of operations then we write $ops(G)$ for the result of applying the operations to G. Given graphs G_1, G_2 we define the *graph edit distance* between G_1 and G_2 as $GED(G_1, G_2) = \min\{|ops| \mid ops(G_1) = G_2\}$, that is, the shortest length of an edit script modifying G_1 to G_2.

Computing the graph edit distance between two graphs (even without labels or properties) is an NP-complete problem. Moreover, we consider a particular setting where the edit operations all have equal cost, but in general different weights can be assigned to different edit operations. We can consider a slight generalization as follows: Given a weighting function w mapping edit operations to positive rational numbers, the *weighted graph edit distance* between G_1 and G_2 is $wGED(G_1, G_2) = \min\{\sum_{op \in ops} w(op) \mid ops(G_1) = G_2\}$. The unweighted graph edit distance is a special case so this problem is also NP-complete.

Answer Set Programming. We assume familiarity with general logic programming concepts (e.g. familiarity with Prolog or Datalog). To help make the paper accessible to readers not already familiar with answer set programming, we illustrate some programming techniques that differ from standard logic programming

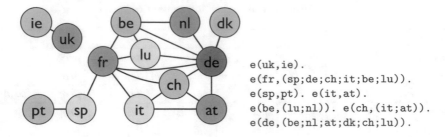

```
e(uk,ie).
e(fr,(sp;de;ch;it;be;lu)).
e(sp,pt). e(it,at).
e(be,(lu;nl)). e(ch,(it;at)).
e(de,(be;nl;at;dk;ch;lu)).
```

Fig. 1. Graph coloring example (Color figure online)

via a short example: coloring the nodes of an undirected graph with the minimum number of colors. Graph 3-coloring is a standard example of ASP, but we will adopt a slightly nonstandard approach to illustrate some key techniques we will rely on later. We will use the concrete syntax of the Clingo ASP solver, which is part of the Potassco framework [13,14]. Examples given here and elsewhere in the paper can be run verbatim using the Clingo interactive online demo[1].

Listing 1.1. Graph 3-coloring

```
1  e(X,Y) :- e(Y,X).
2  n(X) :- e(X,_).
3  color(1..3).
4  {c(X,Y) : color(Y)} = 1 :- n(X).
5  :- e(X,Y), c(X,C), c(Y,D), not C <> D.
```

Listing 1.2. Minimal k-coloring (extending Listing 1.1)

```
1  color(X) :- n(X).
2  cost(C,1) :- c(_,C).
3  #minimize { Cost,C : cost(C,Cost) }.
```

Figure 1 shows an example graph where edge relationships correspond to land borders between some countries. The edges are defined using an association list notation; for example `e(be,(lu;nl))` abbreviates two edges `e(be,lu)` and `e(be,nl)`. Listing 1.1 defines graph 3-coloring declaratively. The first line states that the edge relation is symmetric and the second defines the node relation to consist of all sources (and by symmetry targets) of edges. Line 3 defines a relation `color/1` to hold for values 1, 2, 3. Lines 4–5 define when a graph is 3-colorable, by defining when a relation `c/2` is a valid 3-coloring. Line 4 says that `c/2` represents a (total) function from nodes to colors, i.e. for every node there is exactly one associated color. Line 5 says that for each edge, the associated colors of the source and target must be different. Here, we are using the `not` operator solely to illustrate its use, but we could have done without it, writing `C = D` instead.

---

[1] https://potassco.org/clingo/run/.

Listing 1.1 is a complete program that can be used with Fig. 1 to determine that the example graph is not 3-colorable. What if we want to find the least k such that a graph is k-colorable? We cannot leave the number of colors undefined, since ASP requires a finite search space, but we could manually change the '3' on line 5 to various values of k, starting with the maximum $k = |V|$ and decreasing until the minimum possible k is found.

Instead, using *minimization constraints*, we can modify the 3-coloring program above to instead compute a minimal k-coloring (that is, find a coloring minimizing the number of colors) purely declaratively by adding the clauses shown in Listing 1.2. Line 1 defines the set of colors simply to be the set of node identifiers (plus the three colors we already had, but this is harmless). Line 2 associates a cost of 1 with each used color. Finally, line 3 imposes a minimization constraint: to minimize the sum of the costs of the colors. Thus, using a single Clingo specification we can automatically find the minimum number of colors needed for this (or any) undirected graph. The 4-coloring shown in Fig. 1 was found this way.

3   Specifying Graph Matching and Edit Distance

In this section we give ASP specifications defining each problem. We first consider how to represent graphs as flat collections of facts, suitable for use in a logic programming setting. We choose one among several reasonable representations: given $G = (V, E, src, tgt, lab, prop)$ and given three predicate names $\mathrm{n}, \mathrm{e}, \mathrm{p}$ we define the following relations:

$$Rel_G(\mathrm{n}, \mathrm{e}, \mathrm{p}) = \{\mathrm{n}(v, lab(v)) \mid v \in V\}$$
$$\cup \{\mathrm{e}(e, src(e), tgt(e), lab(e)) \mid c \in E\}$$
$$\cup \{\mathrm{p}(x, k, d) \mid x \in V \cup E, prop(x, k) = d \neq \bot\}$$

Clearly, we can recover the original graph from this representation.

In the following problem specifications, we always consider two graphs, say G_1 and G_2, and to avoid confusion between them we use two sets of relation names to encode them, thus $Rel_{G_1}(\mathrm{n}_1, \mathrm{e}_1, \mathrm{p}_1) \cup Rel_{G_2}(\mathrm{n}_2, \mathrm{e}_2, \mathrm{p}_2)$ represents two graphs. We also assume without loss of generality that the sets of vertex and edge identifiers of the two graphs are all disjoint, i.e. $(V_1 \cup E_1) \cap (V_2 \cup E_2) = \emptyset$, to avoid any possibility of confusion among them.

We now show how to specify homomorphisms and isomorphisms among graphs. The Clingo code in Listing 1.3 defines when a graph homomorphism exists from G_1 to G_2. We refer to this program extended with suitable representations of G_1 and G_2 as $Hom_h(G_1, G_2)$. The binary relation h, representing the homomorphism, is specified using two constraints. The first says that h maps nodes of G_1 to nodes of G_2 with the same label, while the second additionally specifies that h maps edges of G_1 to those of G_2 preserving source, target, and label. Notice in particular that the cardinality constraint ensures that h represents a total function with range $V_1 \cup E_1$, so in any model satisfying the first clause, every node in G_1 is matched to one in G_2, which means that the body of the second clause is satisfiable for each edge. The third clause simply constrains h so that any properties of nodes or edges in G_1 must be present on the matching node or edge in G_2.

Listing 1.3. Graph homomorphism

```
1  {h(X,Y) : n2(Y,L)} = 1 :- n1(X,L).
2  {h(X,Y) : e2(Y,S2,T2,L), h(S1,S2), h(T1,T2)} = 1 :- e1(X,S1,T1,L).
3  :- p1(X,K,D), h(X,Y), not p2(Y,K,D).
```

Listing 1.4. Graph isomorphism (extending Listing 1.3)

```
1  {h(X,Y) : n1(X,L)} = 1 :- n2(Y,L).
2  {h(X,Y) : e1(X,S1,T1,L), h(S1,S2), h(T1,T2)} = 1 :- e2(Y,S2,T2,L).
3  :- p2(Y,K,D), h(X,Y), not p1(X,K,D).
```

Listing 1.5. Subgraph isomorphism (extending Listing 1.3)

```
1  {h(X,Y) : n1(X,L)} <= 1 :- n2(Y,L).
2  {h(X,Y) : e1(X,S1,T1,L), h(S1,S2), h(T1,T2)} <= 1 :- e2(Y,S2,T2,L).
```

Next to define when h is a graph *isomorphism*, we add the symmetric clauses shown in Listing 1.4. We write $Iso_h(G_1, G_2)$ for the combination of Listings 1.3 and 1.4. Since the two listings together imply that h represents a homomorphism in the forward direction and simultaneously represents a homomorphism from G_2 to G_1 in the backward direction, these four clauses suffice to specify that h is an isomorphism.

To specify subgraph isomorphism, we simply require that h is an injective homomorphism from G_1 to G_2, as shown in Listing 1.5. We refer to the specification in Listing 1.5 as $Sub_h(G_1, G_2)$. The two additional constraints specify that the inverse of h is a *partial* homomorphism. This is equivalent to h being an injective homomorphism.

Finally we consider the specification of the graph edit distance problem. On the surface, this seems challenging, since the graph edit distance is defined as the length of a minimal edit script mapping one graph to another, and there are infinitely many possible edit scripts. However, there is clearly always an upper bound d on the edit distance: consider an edit script that just deletes G_1 and inserts G_2, and take d to be the length of this script. So, given two graphs and this upper bound d we could proceed by specifying a search space over edit scripts of bounded length, defining the meaning of each edit operator, and seeking to minimize the number of steps necessary to get from G_1 to G_2. However, this encoding seems rather heavyweight, and requires preprocessing to determine d.

Instead, we follow a different strategy, analogous to the approach adopted for graph coloring earlier. The strategy is based on the observation that the graph edit distance is closely related to the *maximum subgraph problem* [6], that is, given two graphs G_1, G_2, find the largest graph that is subgraph isomorphic to both. If we identify such a graph then (as we shall show) we can read off an edit script that maps G_1 to G_2, which first deletes unmatched structure from G_1, then updates properties in-place, and finally inserts new structure needed in G_2. Furthermore, to identify the maximum common subgraph, we do not need to construct a new graph separate from G_1 and G_2; instead, we can think of the maximum common subgraph as an isomorphic pair of subgraphs of G_1 and G_2. So in other words, we will search for a partial isomorphism h between G_1 and G_2, use it as a basis for extracting an edit script, and minimize its cost.

Listing 1.6. Graph edit distance

```
1  {h(X,Y) : n2(Y,L)} <= 1 :- n1(X,L).
2  {h(X,Y) : n1(X,L)} <= 1 :- n2(Y,L).
3  {h(X,Y) : e2(Y,S2,T2,L), h(S1,S2), h(T1,T2)} <= 1 :- e1(X,S1,T1,L).
4  {h(X,Y) : e1(X,S1,T1,L), h(S1,S2), h(T1,T2)} <= 1 :- e2(Y,S2,T2,L).
5
6  delete_node(X) :- n1(X,_), not h(X,_).
7  insert_node(Y,L) :- n2(Y,L), not h(_,Y).
8
9  delete_edge(X) :- e1(X,_,_,_), not h(X,_).
10 insert_edge(Y,S,T,L) :- e2(Y,S,T,L), not h(_,Y).
11
12 update_prop(X,K,V1,V2) :- p1(X,K,V1), h(X,Y), p2(Y,K,V2), V1 <> V2.
13 delete_prop(X,K) :- p1(X,K,_), h(X,Y), not p2(Y,K,_).
14 delete_prop(X,K) :- p1(X,K,_), delete_node(X).
15 delete_prop(X,K) :- p1(X,K,_), delete_edge(X).
16 insert_prop(Y,K,V) :- p2(Y,K,V), h(X,Y), not p1(X,K,_).
17 insert_prop(Y,K,V) :- p2(Y,K,V), insert_node(Y,_).
18 insert_prop(Y,K,V) :- p2(Y,K,V), insert_edge(Y,_,_,_).
19
20 node_cost(Y,1) :- insert_node(Y,_).
21 node_cost(X,1) :- delete_node(X).
22
23 edge_cost(Y,1) :- insert_edge(Y,_,_,_).
24 edge_cost(X,1) :- delete_edge(X).
25
26 prop_cost(X,K,1) :- update_prop(X,K,V1,V2).
27 prop_cost(X,K,1) :- delete_prop(X,K).
28 prop_cost(Y,K,1) :- insert_prop(Y,K,V).
29
30 #minimize { NC,X : node_cost(X,NC);
31             EC,X : edge_cost(X,EC);
32             LC,X,K : prop_cost(X,K,LC)}.
```

Listing 1.6 accomplishes this. The first four lines specify that h must be a partial isomorphism, by dropping the requirement that h must match all nodes/edges on one side with those of another, and dropping the hard constraint that properties must match. Lines 6–7 define when a node must be deleted or inserted. Nodes that are in G_1 and not matched in G_2 must be deleted, and conversely those that are in G_2 and not matched in G_1 must be inserted. Lines 9–10 similarly specify when edges must be inserted or deleted. Lines 12–18 define when a property is updated in-place, deleted, or inserted. If a property key is present on an object in G_1 and on the matching object in G_2 but with a different value, then the key's value needs to be updated. If it is present in G_1 but not present on the matching object in G_1 then it is deleted. Likewise, if it is present in G_1 but the associated object is deleted then the property also must be deleted. Dually, properties are inserted if they are present in G_2 but not in G_1, either because the matching object does not have that property or because there is no matching object because the property is on an inserted object. Lines 20–28 specify the costs associated with each of the edit operations. We assign each operation a cost of 1. It would also be possible to assign different (integer) costs to different kinds of updates, or even to specify different costs depending on labels, keys, or values.

4   Correctness

We first state the intended correctness properties for the homomorphism, isomorphism, and subgraph isomorphism problems:

Theorem 1. *1. There exists a homomorphism $h : G_1 \to G_2$ if and only if $Hom_h(G_1, G_2)$ is satisfiable.*
2. There exists an isomorphism $h : G_1 \to G_2$ if and only if $Iso_h(G_1, G_2)$ is satisfiable.
3. $h : G_1 \to G_2$ witnesses a subgraph isomorphism if and only if $Sub_h(G_1, G_2)$ is satisfiable.

Proof. See Appendix A of the extended version [7]. □

Next we turn to graph edit distance. To assist with the reasoning, we define the following canonical form:

Definition 1 (Edit script canonical form). *An edit script is in* canonical form *if it is of the form $del_p; del_e; del_v; upd_p; ins_v; ins_e; ins_p$, where:*

- *del_p, del_e and del_v are sequences of property deletions, edge deletions, and node deletions respectively;*
- *upd_p is a sequence of property updates;*
- *ins_v, ins_e, and ins_p are sequences of node insertions, edge insertions, and property insertions, respectively.*

Edit scripts obtained from $GED_h(G_1, G_2)$ are in this form. Moreover, any valid edit script can be converted to a canonical one by applying a set of rewrite rules, as shown in Fig. 2. We first consider *marked* versions op^* of each edit operation, for example writing $\mathsf{delP}^*(x, k)$ for the marked version of delP. A marked operation op^* has the same effect as op when applied to a graphs; the mark is only to indicate which operation is actively being rewritten. The idea here is that if we

$$\mathsf{delE}^*(e); \mathsf{delP}(x,k) \longrightarrow \mathsf{delP}(x,k); \mathsf{delE}^*(e)$$

$$\mathsf{delV}^*(v); \mathsf{delP}(x,k) \longrightarrow \mathsf{delP}(x,k); \mathsf{delV}^*(v)$$

$$\mathsf{delV}^*(v); \mathsf{delE}(e) \longrightarrow \mathsf{delE}(e); \mathsf{delV}^*(v)$$

$$\mathsf{updP}^*(x,k,d); \mathsf{delP}(y,k') \longrightarrow \begin{cases} \mathsf{delP}(y,k') & \text{if } x=y, k=k' \\ \mathsf{delP}(y,k'); \mathsf{updP}^*(x,k,d) & \text{otherwise} \end{cases}$$

$$\mathsf{updP}^*(x,k,d); \mathsf{delE}(e) \longrightarrow \mathsf{delE}(e); \mathsf{updP}^*(x,k,d)$$

$$\mathsf{updP}^*(x,k,d); \mathsf{delV}(v) \longrightarrow \mathsf{delV}(v); \mathsf{updP}^*(x,k,d)$$

$$\mathsf{insV}^*(v,l); \mathsf{delP}(x,k) \longrightarrow \mathsf{delP}(x,k); \mathsf{insV}^*(v,l)$$

$$\mathsf{insV}^*(v,l); \mathsf{delE}(e) \longrightarrow \mathsf{delE}(e); \mathsf{insV}^*(v)$$

$$\mathsf{insV}^*(v,l); \mathsf{delV}(v') \longrightarrow \begin{cases} \epsilon & \text{if } v=v' \\ \mathsf{delV}(v'); \mathsf{insV}^*(v,l) & \text{otherwise} \end{cases}$$

$$\mathsf{insV}^*(v,l); \mathsf{updP}(x,k,d) \longrightarrow \mathsf{updP}(x,k,d); \mathsf{insV}^*(v,l)$$

$$\mathsf{insE}^*(e,v,w,l); \mathsf{delP}(x,k) \longrightarrow \mathsf{delP}(x,k); \mathsf{insE}^*(e,v,w,l)$$

$$\mathsf{insE}^*(e,v,w,l); \mathsf{delE}(e') \longrightarrow \begin{cases} \epsilon & \text{if } e=e' \\ \mathsf{delE}(e'); \mathsf{insE}^*(e,v,w,l) & \text{otherwise} \end{cases}$$

$$\mathsf{insE}^*(e,v,w,l); \mathsf{delV}(v') \longrightarrow \mathsf{delV}(v'); \mathsf{insE}^*(e,v,w,l)$$

$$\mathsf{insE}^*(e,v,w,l); \mathsf{updP}(x,k,d) \longrightarrow \mathsf{updP}(x,k,d); \mathsf{insE}^*(e,v,w,l)$$

$$\mathsf{insE}^*(e,v,w,l); \mathsf{insV}(v',l) \longrightarrow \mathsf{insV}(v',l); \mathsf{insE}^*(e,v,w,l)$$

$$\mathsf{insP}^*(x,k,d); \mathsf{delP}(y,k') \longrightarrow \begin{cases} \epsilon & \text{if } x=y, k=k' \\ \mathsf{delP}(y,k'); \mathsf{insP}^*(x,k,d) & \text{otherwise} \end{cases}$$

$$\mathsf{insP}^*(x,k,d); \mathsf{delE}(e) \longrightarrow \mathsf{delE}(e); \mathsf{insP}^*(x,k,d)$$

$$\mathsf{insP}^*(x,k,d); \mathsf{delV}(v) \longrightarrow \mathsf{delV}(v); \mathsf{insP}^*(x,k,d)$$

$$\mathsf{insP}^*(x,k,d); \mathsf{updP}(y,k',d') \longrightarrow \begin{cases} \mathsf{insP}^*(x,y,d') & \text{if } x=y, k=k' \\ \mathsf{updP}(y,k',d'); \mathsf{insP}^*(x,k,d) & \text{otherwise} \end{cases}$$

$$\mathsf{insP}^*(x,k,d); \mathsf{insV}(v,l) \longrightarrow \mathsf{insV}(v',l); \mathsf{insP}^*(x,k,d)$$

$$\mathsf{insP}^*(x,k,d); \mathsf{insE}(e,v,w,l) \longrightarrow \mathsf{insE}(e,v,w,l); \mathsf{insP}^*(x,k,d)$$

$$op^*; ops \longrightarrow op; ops \qquad \text{if no earlier rule applies}$$

Fig. 2. Edit script rewrite rules

have a canonical edit script ops and wish to add a new edit operation, we use the rewrite rules to canonicalize $op^*; ops$. The rules are applied in order and at each step, the first matching rule is applied. Note that there is a catch-all rule $op^*; ops \longrightarrow op; ops$, which only applies if none of the other rules do. Essentially, the rewrite rules consider all of the possible pairs of adjacent operations that can appear in a non-canonical form, with the first element marked. In each case, they show how to simplify the edit script by either moving the marked operation closer to the end, or removing the mark. Removal can happen as a result of either cancellation of the marked operation by another operation (e.g. a delete undoing an insert), or by removing the mark once it has reached an appropriate place for it in the canonical form.

Lemma 1. *If ops is an edit script mapping G_1 to G_2, then there is a canonical edit script ops' mapping G_1 to G_2 such that $|ops'| \leq |ops|$.*

Proof. See Appendix A of the extended version [7]. □

Theorem 2. *The specification $GED_h(G_1, G_2)$ always has a solution, and the edit script described by the insertion, deletion and update predicates is a valid, canonical script mapping G_1 to G_2. Moreover, the cost of the optimal solution to $GED_h(G_1, G_2)$ equals $GED(G_1, G_2)$.*

Proof. For the first part, we observe that the empty relation $h = \emptyset$ always solves $GED_h(G_1, G_2)$ if we ignore the minimization constraint. Therefore, the cost of this solution is an upper bound. Moreover, if we apply the edit operations described by the insert, delete and update relations in the order required by the canonical form, then each edit operation is valid, all structure present in G_1 and not G_2 is removed, all properties whose values differ in G_1 and G_2 are updated, and all structure present in G_2 and not G_1 is inserted. Therefore, the corresponding edit script maps G_1 to G_2.

To show that the minimum cost obtained from solving the $GED_h(G_1, G_2)$ specification coincides with $GED(G_1, G_2)$, one direction is easy: for any h (including the one corresponding to a minimum cost solution) the collection of edit operations resulting from $GED_h(G_1, G_2)$ is a valid edit script so its length d must be greater than or equal to the minimum over all valid scripts. To show the reverse direction, we use Lemma 1. Given a minimum-length edit script that is not in canonical form, we can rewrite it to one that is canonical, with equal cost (since the original script was already minimum-length). □

5   Discussion

We have argued that using ASP offers considerable flexibility. To illustrate this claim, we consider three modifications to our approach.

Weighted Graph Edit Distance. If the operations have different (integer) weights, implemented using a suitable modification to the cost predicates in some specification $wGED_h(G_1, G_2)$, then the same argument as above suffices to show that a minimum-weight canonical script always exists to be found by the ASP specification. The key point is that weights are defined on individual edit operations, and the rewrite rules only permute or delete operations, so preserve or decrease weight.

Relabeling. We have treated labels as hard constraints: it is not possible to change the label of a node in G_1 to a different label in G_2, short of deleting the node and inserting a new one with a different label. On the other hand, properties are soft constraints in the sense that we may delete or update a property value without also being obliged to delete and re-create the underlying node or edge structure. It is natural to consider an in-place relabeling operation as well. Such behavior can be encoded on top of the already-developed framework by using a single "blank" label for nodes and edges and introducing an unused property key called "label" instead; now this can be updated in-place like other properties. Alternatively, we can accommodate this behavior more directly as shown in Listing 1.7. The first four lines relax the constraint that node and edge labels have to be preserved by h. The next two lines define the `relabel_node` and `relabel_edge` predicates to detect when two matched nodes or edges have different labels. Finally, the `node_cost` and `edge_cost` predicates are extended to charge a cost of 1 per relabeling.

Listing 1.7. Graph edit distance with relabeling (modifies Listing 1.6)

```
1  {h(X,Y) : n2(Y,_)} <= 1 :- n1(X,_).
2  {h(X,Y) : n1(X,_)} <= 1 :- n2(Y,_).
3  {h(X,Y) : e2(Y,S2,T2,_), h(S1,S2), h(T1,T2)} <= 1 :- e1(X,S1,T1,_).
4  {h(X,Y) : e1(X,S1,T1,_), h(S1,S2), h(T1,T2)} <= 1 :- e2(Y,S2,T2,_).
5  ...
6  relabel_node(X,L2) :- n1(X,L1),h(X,Y), n2(Y,L2), L1 <> L2.
7  relabel_edge(X,L2) :- e1(X,_,_,L1),h(X,Y),e2(Y,_,_,L2), L1 <> L2.
8  ...
9  node_cost(X,1) :- relabel_node(X,_).
10 edge_cost(X,1) :- relabel_edge(X,_).
```

Ad Hoc Constraints. The use of ASP opens up many other possibilities for controlling or constraining the various isomorphism or edit distance problems. One example which we found useful in previous work [8] was to modify the definitions of isomorphism or subgraph isomorphism to treat properties as soft constraints and minimize the number of mismatched properties.

Another potentially interesting class of constraints is to allow "access control" constraints on the possible edit scripts, for example specifying that certain nodes or edges in one graph cannot not be modified and so must be matched with equivalent constructs in the other graph. This is similar to the approximate constrained subgraph matching problem [22].

6   Evaluation

Graph matching and edit distance are widely studied problems and a thorough comparison of our approach with state-of-the-art algorithms is beyond the scope of this paper. However, we do not claim that our approach is faster, only that it is easy to implement and modify, rendering it suitable for rapid prototyping situations. Nevertheless, in this section we summarize a preliminary evaluation that supports a claim that our approach is fast enough to be useful for rapid prototyping. Our experiments were run on an 2.6 GHz Intel Core i7 MacBook Pro machine with 8 GB RAM and using Clingo v5.2.0.

First, we consider the various problems on synthetic graphs, such as k-cycles and k-chains (linear sequences of k edges), with only one possible node and edge label and no properties. These problems are not representative of typical real problems, but illustrate some general trends. We considered each of the problems: (HOM), (ISO) $G_1 \cong G_2$, (SUB) $S_n \lesssim C_n$, and (GED) $GED(G_1, G_2)$. We first considered comparisons where G_1 and G_2 are k-cycles or k-chains, for $k \in \{10, 20, \ldots, 100\}$. We found the running times for each of these problems

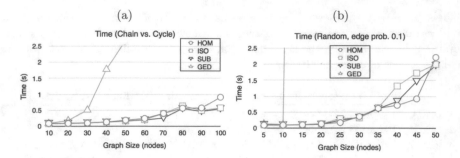

Fig. 3. Synthetic results: (a) chains and cycles (b) randomly generated graphs

to be relatively stable independent of whether the comparison was between two
k-chains, a k-chain with a k-cycle, or two k-cycles, so we have averaged across all
four scenarios. We also considered randomly generated graphs with k nodes and
each edge generated with probability 0.1, with $k \in \{5, 10, \ldots, 50\}$. We attempted
each problem with a running time limit of 30 seconds; the results are shown in
Fig. 3 results. Unsurprisingly, the HOM instances are solved fastest, and GED
slowest.

Second, we consider some real graphs from the Mutagenesis dataset (MUTA),
a standard dataset used for evaluating graph edit distance algorithms [15], for
example in a recent graph edit distance competition (GEDC) [1]. In the contest,
eight algorithms were run on different problems for up to 30 s, and compared
in terms of time, accuracy (for approximate algorithms), and success rate (for
exact algorithms). We modified the GED specification to allow node and edge
relabeling and use the same weight function as in the second (and more challenging) configuration used in the contest, for which even the best algorithm
(called F2) was not able to deal with graphs of size larger than 30. We consider three datasets MUTA-10, MUTA-20 and MUTA-30 each consisting of ten
chemical structure graphs of size 10, 20 or 30 respectively. We also consider a
dataset MUTA-MIXED which consists of ten graphs of varying sizes. We considered all unordered pairs of the graphs in each subset and attempted to find the
GED with a timeout of 30 s. Table 2 shows the results compared with the four
exact algorithms reported in [1]. The first two algorithms, F2 and F24threads,
are implementations of a binary linear programming encoding of graph edit distance [17], the first being the plain single-threaded algorithm, and the second
running with four threads. The other two, DF and PDFS, are sequential and
parallel implementations of a depth-first, branch-and-bound algorithm [2,3].

Table 2 illustrates that our approach is competitive with DF and slightly
worse than PDFS, but does not match the performance of the two F2 algorithms.
These results should be taken with a grain of salt, since we have not replicated
the GEDC results on our (slightly faster) hardware. Memory did not appear to
be a bottleneck for our approach.

We have implemented and used variations of the isomorphism and subgraph
isomorphism specifications for property graphs in a provenance graph analysis
system called ProvMark [8]. In this earlier work, we found that for graphs of

Table 2. Success rate (optimal solution found in under 30 s) on Mutagenesis dataset

	MUTA-10	MUTA-20	MUTA-30	MUTA-MIXED
F24threads [1,17][†]	100%	98%	23%	44%
F2 [1,17][†]	100%	94%	15%	41%
PDFS [1,3][†]	100%	26%	11%	10%
Our approach	100%	26%	10%	4%
DF [1,2][†]	100%	14%	10%	10%

[†]Experiments from [1] run on a 4-core 2.0 GHz AMD Opteron 8350 with 16 GB RAM.

Table 3. Performance improvement vs. ProvMark [8]

Experiment	Size	Old time (s)	New time (s)	Speedup
creat-bg-gen	1006	0.060	0.034	1.9×
creat-fg-gen	1060	0.070	0.037	1.9×
creat-comp	1033	0.053	0.026	2.1×
execve-bg-gen	1006	0.061	0.036	1.7×
execve-fg-gen	1340	0.114	0.051	2.2×
execve-comp	1173	0.083	0.042	1.9×

up to around 100 nodes and edges, and a few hundred properties, these problems are usually solvable within a few seconds. However, these problems may not be representative of other scenarios.

The specifications we used to define approximate subgraph isomorphism problems in ProvMark are similar to those presented here, but we subsequently experimented with several different approaches with different performance. Here, we compare the performance of ProvMark on subgraph isomorphism problems over two representative example graphs considered in our previous experiments: the graph generalization and comparison problems resulting from benchmarking the **creat** and **execve** system calls using the CamFlow provenance recording system [20]. See [8] for further details and the Clingo code of the previous approaches.

Table 3 shows the running time of the old version and new version of approximate subgraph isomorphism. The code for both specifications is in Appendix C of the extended version [7]. The problem sizes (that is, the number of nodes, edges, and properties of the two graphs) is shown under "Size". The "Old Time" column corresponds to the time obtained using the old approach and "New Time" shows the time obtained using the code in Listing 1.5 modified to allow approximate property matching. The "Speedup" column shows the ratio between the old and new time. In most cases, the speedup is around a factor of two. As future work, we plan to use graph edit distance with the results of the ProvMark system, for example for clustering or regression testing across runs.

7   Related Work

The lower bound of the complexity of graph isomorphism is a well-known open problem [4], but subgraph isomorphism and graph edit distance are NP-complete [12]. A number of practical algorithms for graph isomorphism have been studied, however, including NAUTY [18], which has also been integrated with Prolog [10]. However, most such algorithms consider graphs with vertex labels but not edge labels or properties, so are not directly applicable to property graph isomorphism. Subgraph isomorphism has been studied extensively over the past years, one survey [19] summarizes the state-of-art algorithms for solving partial or simplified version of the problem. Subgraph isomorphism is also studied for graph databases, where the query subgraph is usually small but the other graph may be very large. Lee et al. [16] evaluated five such algorithms on query graphs of up to 24 edges and databases of up to tens of thousands of nodes and edges. Approximate subgraph matching with constraints has also been studied, particularly in biomedical settings [22], and it would be interesting to investigate whether our approach is competitive with their CSP-based algorithm. Graph edit distance has also been studied extensively [11], with much attention on approximate algorithms that can provide results quickly [21].

While several approaches to graph matching and edit distance have been based on expressing these problems as constraint satisfaction problems, satisfiability, or linear programming problems, to the best of our knowledge there is no previous work based on answer set programming. Moreover, our approach easily accommodates richer graph structure such as hard or soft label constraints, properties, and multiple edges between pairs of nodes, whereas the algorithms we have seen generally consider ordinary graphs (without properties and with at most one edge between two nodes).

8   Conclusions

The graph edit distance problem is a widely studied problem that has many applications. Exact solutions to it, and to related problems such as graph isomorphism and subgraph isomorphism, are challenging to compute efficiently due to their NP-completeness or unresolved complexity (in the case of graph isomorphism). There are a number of proposed algorithms in the literature, with one of the most effective based on a reduction to binary linear programming [17]. In this paper, we investigated an alternative approach using answer set programming (ASP), specifically the Clingo solver. This approach may not be competitive with the best known techniques in terms of performance, but has the potential advantage that it is straightforward to modify the problem specification to accommodate different kinds of graphs, cost metrics or other variations, or to accommodate ad hoc constraints that can also be expressed using ASP. Our approach has already proved useful for a real application [8], and our experimental evaluation suggests that it is also competitive with two out of four exact algorithms from a graph edit distance competition.

Our work may be valuable to others interested in rapid prototyping of graph matching or edit distance problems using declarative programming. Additional work could be done to facilitate this, for example using Clingo's Python wrapper library. Graph matching and edit distance problems may also be an interesting class of challenge problems for developers of ASP solvers.

Acknowledgments. Effort sponsored by the Air Force Office of Scientific Research, Air Force Material Command, USAF, under grant number FA8655-13-1-3006. The U.S. Government and University of Edinburgh are authorised to reproduce and distribute reprints for their purposes notwithstanding any copyright notation thereon. Cheney was also supported by ERC Consolidator Grant Skye (grant number 682315). This material is based upon work supported by the Defense Advanced Research Projects Agency (DARPA) under contract FA8650-15-C-7557.

References

1. Abu-Aisheh, Z., et al.: Graph edit distance contest: results and future challenges. Pattern Recogn. Lett. **100**, 96–103 (2017)
2. Abu-Aisheh, Z., Raveaux, R., Ramel, J.-Y., Martineau, P.: An exact graph edit distance algorithm for solving pattern recognition problems. In: Proceedings of the International Conference on Pattern Recognition Applications and Methods (ICPRAM 2015), pp. 271–278 (2015)
3. Abu-Aisheh, Z., Raveaux, R., Ramel, J.-Y., Martineau, P.: A parallel graph edit distance algorithm. Expert Syst. Appl. **94**, 41–57 (2018)
4. Arvind, V., Torán, J.: Isomorphism testing: perspectives and open problems. Bull. EATCS **86**, 66–84 (2005)
5. Auer, S., Bizer, C., Kobilarov, G., Lehmann, J., Cyganiak, R., Ives, Z.: DBpedia: a nucleus for a web of open data. In: Aberer, K., et al. (eds.) ASWC/ISWC -2007. LNCS, vol. 4825, pp. 722–735. Springer, Heidelberg (2007). https://doi.org/10.1007/978-3-540-76298-0_52
6. Bunke, H.: On a relation between graph edit distance and maximum common subgraph. Pattern Recogn. Lett. **18**(8), 689–694 (1997)
7. Chan, S.C., Cheney, J.: Flexible graph matching and graph edit distance using answer set programming (extended version). CoRR, abs/1911.11584 (2019)
8. Chan, S.C., et al.: ProvMark: a provenance expressiveness benchmarking system. In: Proceedings of the 20th International Middleware Conference (Middleware 2019), pp. 268–279. ACM (2019)
9. Chen, X., Huo, H., Huan, J., Vitter, J.S.: An efficient algorithm for graph edit distance computation. Knowl.-Based Syst. **163**, 762–775 (2019)
10. Frank, M., Codish, M.: Logic programming with graph automorphism: integrating nauty with prolog (tool description). TPLP **16**(5–6), 688–702 (2016)
11. Gao, X., Xiao, B., Tao, D., Li, X.: A survey of graph edit distance. Pattern Anal. Appl. **13**(1), 113–129 (2010)
12. Garey, M.R., Johnson, D.S.: Computers and Intractability: A Guide to the Theory of NP-Completeness. W. H. Freeman, New York (1979)
13. Gebser, M., et al.: The potsdam answer set solving collection 5.0. KI-Künstliche Intelligenz **32**(2–3), 181–182 (2018)
14. Gebser, M., Kaufmann, B., Kaminski, R., Ostrowski, M., Schaub, T., Schneider, M.T.: Potassco: the Potsdam answer set solving collection. AI Commun. **24**(2), 107–124 (2011)

15. Kazius, J., McGuire, R., Bursi, R.: Derivation and validation of toxicophores for mutagenicity prediction. J. Med. Chem. **48**(1), 312–320 (2005)
16. Lee, J., Han, W.-S., Kasperovics, R., Lee, J.-H.: An in-depth comparison of subgraph isomorphism algorithms in graph databases. PVLDB **6**(2), 133–144 (2012)
17. Lerouge, J., Abu-Aisheh, Z., Raveaux, R., Héroux, P., Adam, S.: New binary linear programming formulation to compute the graph edit distance. Pattern Recogn. **72**, 254–265 (2017)
18. McKay, B.D.: Practical graph isomorphism. Congressus Numerantium **30**, 45–87 (1981)
19. McKay, B.D., Piperno, A.: Practical graph isomorphism, II. J. Symb. Comput. **60**, 94–112 (2014)
20. Pasquier, T., et al.: Practical whole-system provenance capture. In: Proceedings of the 2017 Symposium on Cloud Computing (SoCC 2017), pp. 405–418 (2017)
21. Riesen, K.: Structural Pattern Recognition with Graph Edit Distance - Approximation Algorithms and Applications. Springer, Cham (2015). https://doi.org/10.1007/978-3-319-27252-8
22. Zampelli, S., Deville, Y., Dupont, P.: Approximate constrained subgraph matching. In: Proceedings of the 11th International Conference on Principles and Practice of Constraint Programming (CP 2005), pp. 832–836 (2005)

On Repairing Web Services Workflows

Thanh H. Nguyen[✉] , Enrico Pontelli , and Tran Cao Son

New Mexico State University, Las Cruces, NM 88003, USA
{tnguyen,epontell,tson}@cs.nmsu.edu

Abstract. When a composite web service—i.e., a composition of individual web services—is executed and fails, it is desirable to reuse as much as possible the results that have been obtained thus far. For example, a travel agent, after receiving an order to arrange for a trip from *LA* to *NY* from a customer, would typically identify the flights and the hotels, obtain the confirmation from the customer, and place the reservations using the credit card information provided by the user; if something is wrong (e.g., at the last step, the credit card information was wrong), the travel agent would prefer to place the reservations using another means (e.g., a different card) instead of starting from the beginning.

This paper introduces an approach for dealing with service failures in the context of workflow execution. The paper defines the notion of a web service composition (WSC) problem and the notion of a *solution workflow* for a WSC problem. The paper describes two approaches to repair a partially executed workflow, with the goal of effectively reusing parts of the workflow that have been successfully executed. The usefulness of these approaches are demonstrated in an implementation using Answer Set Programming (ASP) in the well-known *shopping domain*.

Keywords: Repair · Reuse · Workflow · Web Services Composition

1 Introduction

The Semantics Web has been long considered as a killer application of the Internet that will, according to [1], *"unleash a revolution of new possibilities"* of the Web [1]. One of the key features of the Semantics Web is that it provides an environment suitable for intelligent agents to automatically: *(i)* discover and compose web services to create personalized services or workflows (i.e., *Web Services Composition (WSC)*); *(ii)* execute these personalized services whenever their users request; *(iii)* monitor such executions; and *(iv)* deal with failures of the services. These features are often provided by a WSC framework with two phases: one is responsible for the composition of web services and the other for the execution and monitoring the composition of web services.

Our interest, in this paper, is on the second phase of a WSC framework, *dealing with failures during the execution of a workflow*. This is because web services are inherently dynamic and cannot be expected to be stable all the time—developers often modify them, introduce faults, and modify APIs in unexpected manners. There are many different situations that can cause failures of web services [2,9]—ranging from *physical failures*, e.g., due to network failures, to *development failures*, e.g., due to incorrect APIs

© Springer Nature Switzerland AG 2020
E. Komendantskaya and Y. A. Liu (Eds.): PADL 2020, LNCS 12007, pp. 37–53, 2020.
https://doi.org/10.1007/978-3-030-39197-3_3

and incorrect logic, to *interaction faults*, e.g., due to incorrect parameter exchanges and misunderstood behavior. This paper focuses on the question of how to deal with physical failures.

There is a growing literature that addresses the problem of *recovery* when the execution of a web service fails. Several research contributions explore the problem of services monitoring, often based on *checkpointing* and oriented towards orchestration and choreography [13]. Proposed recovery methodologies include execution rollback to previous checkpoints and the use of redundancy to assist with server failures (e.g., [5, 14, 16]). Alternative approaches have explored the use of replacement of failed services in an attempt to repair a workflow (e.g., [4, 15]). The idea of replacement has been expanded in [11], by allowing both rollback steps (with re-execution of failed services) as well as substitution of sequences of services with new workflows. A variety of studies have also proposed Several web service architectures that provide monitoring, fault detection, and exception event handlers have been described (e.g., [2, 3, 12]). Most of these approaches rely on static recovery techniques or relatively simple repetitions of the composition process. In [10], the authors propose a method based on partial-order planning that makes use of feedbacks from the plan execution to improve new plan search and to repair failed services. The method is illustrated using a shopping example. Unfortunately, the system available at http://sws.mcm.unisg.ch:8080/axis/services/MegashopService?wsdl is no longer active.

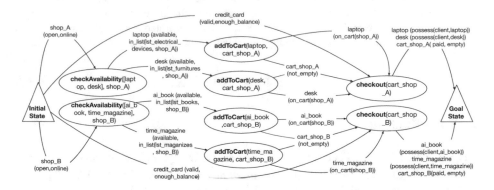

Fig. 1. Shopping for some items from different web-sites (Web Shopping Domain)

In this paper, we investigate the problem of repairing a web services workflow whose execution failed. We develop a general framework for repairing web services workflows, that aims at *reusing as much as possible* the results obtained by an incomplete execution of the workflow. The framework could potentially be used in any WSC realization. We illustrate the framework by examples from the shopping domain.

2   Web Shopping Domain

Throughout the paper, we will illustrate our definitions using elements of the *Web shopping domain* as described in [10]. It consists of an ontology describing different classes of e-commerce shops (e.g., `electronic`, `furniture`, etc.), items sold in these shops (e.g., `laptops`, `books`, `desks`, etc.), containers (e.g., `shop_cart`), payment methods (e.g., `credit card payment`), and their subclasses (e.g., `shop_type_A` is a subclass of `shops`, `cart_shop_A` is a subclass of `shop_cart`, `ai_book` is a subclass of `books`, etc.). In addition, each type of shop provides a diversity of services and operations. They are listed below.

- *checkAvailability*: checks for the availability of a set of items. This service takes as input a list of items and returns the list of items and their metadata that are available in the shop. This service is available at all the shops.
- *addToCart*: places an item into a shopping cart. This service takes two inputs: a shopping cart and an item in the shop; the service produces an output which is the cart containing the added item. This service is provided in shops of type *A* and *B*.
- *removeFromCart*: removes an item from a shopping cart. It is the reverse of *addToCart* and is available at the shops of type *A* and *B*.
- *checkout*: purchases the items currently in the shopping cart; the service is available at shops of type *A* and *B*. It requires a valid credit card as an input. The output is that this cart is paid and the items belong to the client.
- *getItemsList*: returns the list of items that are in the shop's catalog. The input of this service is a shop and the output is the list of items in the shop's categories. This service is provided by shops of type *A* and *B*.
- *buytItem*: purchases a single item in shop. This service takes an item in the shop and a valid credit card as inputs. This service belongs to shops of type *A* and *C*.
- *getList*: works only for shops of type *C* and retrieves a list of all available items in the shop.

In shops of type *B*, every item needs to be placed into a shopping cart before it can be purchased (by the service *checkout*). In shops of type *C*, a selected item can be purchased directly by the service *buyItem*. Both purchasing methods (shopping cart or direct) can be used in shops of type *A*.

Figure 1 shows an example of a workflow over a WSC problem in the *web shopping domain*, aimed at purchasing some items (a `laptop`, an `ai_book`, a `time_magazine` and a `desk`) from different online stores with `credit_card` information that has been submitted by users. The initial state supplies a `credit_card` (and its information) to the services `checkout` or `buyItem`. The *Web Shopping Ontology* provides the information and status of the shops (`shop_A`, `shop_B` etc.) in the initial state, which are used in service `checkAvailability` to verify the availability of the requested item in shops as well as to retrieve the metadata of the requested items. Let us assume that, in this example, `credit_card` is `valid` and has `enough_balance` to use; these shops are `online` and `open`. In the goal state, `possess(client,X)` denotes that item *X* is owned by the *client*.

3   The Web Service Composition Problem

In order to formalize the notion of repair, we need a precise definition of the WSC problem and its solutions. The well-known abstract view of a WSC problem as a planning problem is easy to understand but assumes groundedness (i.e., actions are propositional terms)—which is not the case in our context, as parameters of a web service are often specified by *types* and will be instantiated only when the service is executed. We therefore start by defining the notion of a WSC problem.

An *abstract* resource is specified by its *type*, typically described as a class in an ontology. A *concrete* resource is specified by its *type* and *concrete data*, which is an instance of the resource type. A *named abstract/concrete resource* is a resource associated with a unique identifier. Let us denote with $\mathscr{T}$ the set of resource types. We use the notations (n,t,nil) and (n,t,d), where n is the name of the resource, $t \in \mathscr{T}$ is a resource type and d is an instance of t, to describe a *named abstract* and *named concrete* resource, respectively; *nil* represents an unknown value.

A Web service receives a set of named resources and produces a set of named resources. For example, the getItemsList service receives a shop object (e.g., shop_A of the type shops) and produces a list of all available items that are in the shop's catalogs (e.g., list_catalog_A of the type list). At the *specification level*, a Web service over a set of abstract resource types $\mathscr{T}$ is a pair $(a,e(a))$, where a is the service name and $e(a)$ is a tuple of pairs of *named abstract resources*, i.e., each element in $e(a)$ is of the form (in,out) where in,out denote sets of named resources. Each element in $e(a)$ is called a *precondition-effect* pair for a. For example, $e(\text{addToCart}) = (in_1, out_1)$ where $in_1 = \{(\text{cart\_id}, \text{shop\_cart}, \text{nil}), (\text{it\_id}, \text{item}, \text{nil})\}$ and $out_1 = \{(\text{cart\_id}, \text{shop\_cart}, \text{nil}), (\text{it\_id}, \text{item}, \text{nil})\}$.

The execution of a service a will take concrete data conforming to the specification in *in* and output concrete data of the type specified by *out*. For example, in Fig. 1, an instance of the addToCart service receives a shop cart object of the type cart_shop_A, a subclass of the type shop_cart, and an object of the type laptop, a subclass of the type item, as inputs, and produces as output a shopping cart containing the item.

Definition 1. *A Web service composition (WSC) problem $\mathscr{P}$ is a tuple $(\mathscr{T}, A, S_0, S_g)$ where*

- *$\mathscr{T}$ is a set of abstract resource types;*
- *A is a set of web services over $\mathscr{T}$;*
- *S_0 and S_g are two sets of concrete resources.*

Let $\mathscr{P} = (\mathscr{T}, A, S_0, S_g)$ be a web service composition problem. A *state* s of $\mathscr{P}$ is a set of concrete resources over $\mathscr{T}$. Let x be a set of abstract resources. We say that a set x_c of concrete resources is an instance of x if there exists a bijection b from x to x_c such that $b((n,t,nil)) = (n,t,d)$ for each $(n,t,nil) \in x$. Given a state s and a set of abstract resources x, we denote:

$$s|_x = \{(n,t,d) \mid (n,t,d) \in s, (n,t,nil) \in x\}.$$

We say that s contains an instance of x iff $s|_x$ is an instance of x. Given a state s and a service $a \in A$, the execution of a in s results in one of the three situations: **(i)** There exists a precondition-effect pair (i,o) of a such that $s|_i$ is an instance of i. In this case, we say that (i,o) is an active precondition-effect of a in s and the execution of a will produce an instance, denoted by $res(a,s)$, of o; **(ii)** There exists no precondition-effect pair (i,o) of a such that $s|_i$ is an instance of i. In this case, the execution of a will produce $\emptyset$, which will also be denoted by $res(a,s)$; or **(iii)** the execution of a fails, which will be denoted by $\bot$. In the following, a service $a \in A$ is *executable* in a state s if the cases **(i)** or **(ii)** occur. The WSC problem related to the example in Fig. 1 can be specified by $\mathscr{P}_s = (\mathscr{T}_s, A_s, S_0, S_g)$ where:

- $\mathscr{T}_s$ consists of the types (classes) in the ontology of the Web Shopping Domain;
- A_s consists of the services described in the previous section;
- $S_0 = \{$credit_card(valid, enough_balance), shop_A(open, online), ...$\}$
- $S_g = \{$possess(client, laptop), possess(client, desk), possess (client, ai_book), possess(client, time_magazine)$\}$.

Definition 2. *A workflow over a WSC problem* $\mathscr{P} = (\mathscr{T}, A, S_0, S_g)$ *is a tuple* $G = (V, E, v_0, v_g)$ *where* (V, E) *is an acyclic directed graph with the set of nodes* V *and the set of labeled edges* E, $v_0, v_g \in V$ *are referred to as the* initial *and* goal *state of* G, *respectively, and*

- *each* $v \in V \setminus \{v_0, v_g\}$ *is associated to an action* $a \in A$, *denoted by* $act(v)$;
- *each* $(u,v) \in E$ *is labeled with a set of abstract resources, denoted by* $l_E(u,v)$; *and*
- $\{x \mid (x, v_0) \in E\} = \emptyset$ *and* $\{x \mid (v_g, x) \in E\} = \emptyset$.

A workflow over a WSC problem in the shopping domain is given Fig. 1. The two triangles represent the initial and goal state (v_0, v_g) respectively. Ellipses represent nodes of the graph, each node is associated to a service. Ingoing and outgoing links represent preconditions and effects of the service. For example, the top-left node is associated to checkAvailability, which requires a shop (in this case, shop_A from the initial state) and a set of items (that the client wishes to buy).

Given a workflow G over a problem $\mathscr{P}$, the execution of G starts from its initial state by sending concrete resources to its neighbors in accordance to the specification on the edges. Whenever all concrete resources from the predecessors of a node v are delivered to v, the service attached to v, $act(v)$, will be executed. If the execution is successful, i e., it produces the proper concrete resources to be sent to the neighbors, then the execution continues; otherwise the execution of the workflow fails. The process continues until every service in the workflow is executed. The execution is said to be successful if the concrete resources specified at the goal state of G are produced. Formally, this process can be defined via a state function as follows.

Definition 3. *Let* $G = (V, E, v_0, v_g)$ *be a workflow over* $\mathscr{P} = (\mathscr{T}, A, S_0, S_g)$. *The state function of* G, *denoted by* st, *is a function that maps each node of* G *into a state of* $\mathscr{P}$ *or nil and is defined as follows.*

- $st(v_0) = S_0$;
- *for each* $v \in V \setminus \{v_0\}$
    (a) *if there exists some* $u \in V$ *such that* $(u,v) \in E$ *and* $st(u) = nil$ *then* $st(v) = nil$;
    (b) *otherwise, let* $in(v) = \bigcup_{(u,v) \in E} st(u)|_{l_E(u,v)}$,
        (b.1) *if* $v = v_g$ *then* $st(v) = in(v)$;
        (b.2) *if* $v \neq v_g$ *and* $in(v) \cup res(act(v), in(v))$ *is not an instance of* $l_E(v,z)$ *for some* $(v,z) \in E$ *then* $st(v) = nil$;

(b.3) if $v \neq v_g$ and Case (b.2) does not occur then $st(v) = in(v) \cup res(act(v), in(v))$.

We say that the execution of G succeeds if $st(v) \neq nil$ for every $v \in V$. Otherwise, the execution of G fails. G is a solution of $\mathscr{P}$ if the execution of G succeeds and $S_g \subseteq st(v_g)$. Otherwise, G is not a solution of $\mathscr{P}$.

In (Case b) of Definition 3, $in(v)$ is the set of concrete resources received by node v. $st(v)$ denotes the set of concrete resources which includes $in(v)$ and the result of the execution of $act(v)$ in $in(v)$. The situation $st(v) = nil$ indicates that the execution of the workflow at node v fails. Such situation can occur in different ways: **(i)** the execution of one of the predecessor of v failed (Case a); **(ii)** the execution of $act(v)$ does not result in proper concrete resources for the continuation of the execution of the workflow (Case b.2).

Observe that Definition 3 only considers G to be a solution of $\mathscr{P}$ if all services associated to G are executed successfully. This implies that G does not contain any redundant nodes, producing concrete resources not needed by any of its successors. This might sound too strong but it is reasonable for two reasons. First, the generation of G—similar to the generation of a plan—does not usually generate redundant nodes. Second, the definition could easily be relaxed to accommodate workflows with redundant nodes.

Observe also that Definition 3 assumes that communication between services is perfect and all services are executed. During the execution of a workflow, failures can happen when a service becomes unavailable. This could also be classified as a service failure. The execution monitoring server is responsible for dealing with this type of failures, as discussed in the next section.

4   Repair

Let $\mathscr{P} = (\mathscr{T}, A, S_0, S_g)$ be a WSC problem. Assume that $G = (V, E, v_0, v_g)$ is a workflow over $\mathscr{P}$. Furthermore, assume that G is a solution of $\mathscr{P}$ under the normal condition (e.g., communication between services is perfect, no machine failures, etc.), i.e., if the execution of G is successful then G will be a solution of $\mathscr{P}$. We are interested in situations where the execution of G is not successful due to the unavailability of a service attached to some node in G. In such a case, recovery measures are needed in order to achieve the goal of $\mathscr{P}$. For example, if the execution of G fails at node v, which is associated to the service $act(v)$, then a simple repair could consist of replacing $act(v)$ with another service $a \in A$ that takes the concrete resources at v and produces the concrete resources needed for the continuation of the execution of G. It is easy to see that this may not be always possible, due to the fact that no such service may exist. We call the process of identifying a new workflow G' that is a solution of $\mathscr{P}$, under the condition that the execution of G fails, as the *repair process*.

4.1   Formalization

Let $\mathscr{P} = (\mathscr{T}, A, S_0, S_g)$ be a WSC problem and $G = (V, E, v_0, v_g)$ be a workflow over $\mathscr{P}$. Let us assume that st is the state function of G.

Definition 4. *Let G be a workflow over $\mathscr{P}$, we define:*

$$A^{st}_{failed} = \{act(v) \mid st(v) = nil, st(u) \neq nil \text{ for all } u \text{ such that } (u,v) \in E\}.$$

We are interested in identifying another workflow G' which achieves the same goal and such that G' *reuses as much as possible the services in G that have been successfully executed*. It is easy to see that G' must not consider the services that are not available. Intuitively, a service $act(v)$ associated to a node v fails with respect to st if it does not allow the execution of the workflow to continue.

By G_{st} we denote the subgraph (V_{st}, E_{st}) of (V, E) such that $V_{st} = \{v \mid v \in V, st(v) \neq nil\}$ and $E_{st} = \{(v,u) \mid (v,u) \in E, v,u \in V_{st}\}$. For each $(u,v) \in E_{st}$, $l_{E_{st}}(u,v) = l_E(u,v)$. Thus, (V_{st}, E_{st}) is the graph containing all nodes whose services have been successfully executed. We explore two approaches for the repair process.

Planning from Failed State. The first alternative is to consider a new WSC problem whose initial state corresponds to the set of available concrete resources in G_{st}.

Let $V^{st}_0 = \bigcup_{v \in V_{st}} st(v)$. Intuitively, $V_0(st)$ denotes the set of concrete resources that are available. Let $\mathscr{P}' = (\mathscr{T}, A \setminus A^{st}_{failed}, V^{st}_0, S_g)$. We can achieve the goal of $\mathscr{P}$ by identifying a new workflow $G' = (V', E', v'_0, v'_g)$ over $\mathscr{P}'$. To evaluate how much G' reuses the executed services in G, we define the notion of a *reusable resource* as follows. Given a node v in a graph G, let us denote with $pre_G(v)$ the set of all predecessors of v in G—i.e., $u \in pre_G(v)$ iff there exists a non-empty path in G from u to v.

Definition 5. *Let $\mathscr{P}' = (\mathscr{T}, A \setminus A^{st}_{failed}, V^{st}_0, S_g)$ and $G' = (V', E', v'_0, v'_g)$ be a workflow over $\mathscr{P}'$ that is a solution of $\mathscr{P}'$. A concrete resource $(n,t,d) \in V^{st}_0 \setminus st(v_0)$ is said to be reused by G' if:*

– *for every $u \subset pre_{G'}(v)$, $(n,t,d) \subset st(u)$ and $(n,t,d) \notin res(act(u), in(u))$; and*
– *$(n,t,d) \in in(v)$ and, if (i,o) is the active precondition-effect of $act(v)$ in $in(v)$, then $(n,t,nil) \in i$.*

Intuitively, Definition 5 says that the concrete resource is reused if it is generated by G_{st} and is needed in G'. The above definition allows us to define the score of reusable resources as follows.

Definition 6. *Let G' be a solution of $\mathscr{P}'$. The amount of reusable resources of G' is denoted by $reused(G') = |\{(n,t,d) \mid (n,t,d) \in V^{st}_0 \setminus st(v_0), (n,t,d) \text{ is reused by } G'\}|$.*

We say that G' reuses more than G'', denoted by $G'' \prec_r G'$, if $reused(G') \geq reused(G'')$. It is easy to see that $\prec_r$ creates a transitive, reflexive, and antisymmetric relation among solutions of $\mathscr{P}'$. The identification of the workflow that reuses as much as possible of G is then equivalent to determining the solutions of $\mathscr{P}'$ which are maximal elements of $\prec_r$. The Implementation section will discuss how to compute such solutions.

Replanning with Successful Services. Replanning from the failed state might be use-ful. However, this will mean that we have to ignore the workflow G completely. In many situations, it is better to keep G as the original workflow might have components that have been included as desirable by the user. This idea also appears in the discussion of designing a workflow when users' preferences are taken into consideration [7]. For this reason, we develop an alternative approach to reuse the workflow G. This approach aims at keeping the services that have been executed successfully in the new workflow.

Let $G' = (V', E', v'_0, v'_g)$ be another solution of $\mathscr{P}$. We define a relation $\mapsto$ between G and G', as the minimal relation satisfying the following properties:

- $v_0 \mapsto v'_0$
- if $(x, y) \in E_{st}$, $(x', y') \in E'$, $x \mapsto x'$ and $act(y) = act(y')$ then $y \mapsto y'$

We next define the function $\pi : V' \longrightarrow \{0, 1\}$ as follows.

$$\pi(y') = \begin{cases} 1 & \text{if } \exists y \in V_{st}, y \mapsto y' \\ 0 & \text{otherwise} \end{cases} \tag{1}$$

Note that the second case in the definition of π occurs if either $y' = v'_0$ or if there is no node in G_{st} which is related to y'. Finally, we define a function: $score(G, G') = sum_{\{x' \in V'\}} \pi(x')$.

Definition 7. *A workflow G' is said to* re-use executed services and their relations as much as possible with current workflow G *if* $score(G, G')$ *is maximal.*

In Fig. 2, the blue arrow lines illustrate the relations $\mapsto$ between nodes in G and possible associated nodes in G' (e.g., *init* node in $G \mapsto$ *init* node in G', service node a in $G \mapsto$ service a in G', etc.); and G_{st} (grey area) is the part of G that was executed successfully.

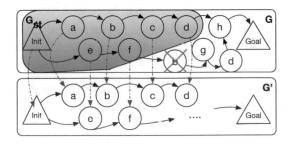

Fig. 2. Relation between G and G'

4.2 Implementation

In order to experiment with the notions of recovery discussed in the previous section, we obtained the source code from the authors of the code in the Phylotastic project as described in [8]. We implement the two notions of recovery on top of their implementation. The system described in the Phylotastic project has been developed using Answer Set Programming (ASP) and includes the *execution monitoring* module that captures the state of execution of a workflow. The implementation described in this paper will focus on the repairing phase. For reference, we denote with $\Pi(\mathscr{P})$ the planning module in the Phylotastic project and include the basic rules of the system below.

From Ontology to ASP Encoding: The ontology encoding the types, resources, services, etc. of the Web Shopping Domain is translated into an ASP program in $\Pi(\mathscr{P})$. This task is accomplished using a *translation program*. For example, a service in the class pur_ol_op takes item and credit_card as inputs and produces outputs item—has been purchased (possess(client, item)) and a receipt—will be sent to client by email (have(receipt, sentByEmail)). Operation buyItem is an instance of this class which purchases the available item if the provided credit_card is valid and enough_balance. The ASP encoding of this operation and its resources is the following:

Listing 1.1. ASP encoding for buyItem operation

```
1   class(purchase_op).  class(pur_onl_op).
2   subclass(pur_onl_op,purchase_op).
3   operation(buyItem).  type(buyItem,pur_onl_op).
4   class(credit_card).  class(receipt).
5   class(payment_method).  class(item).
6   subclass(credit_card,payment_method).
7   has_input(pur_onl_op,item_1,item).
8   has_input(pur_onl_op,card_1,credit_card).
9   has_output(pur_onl_op,item_1,item).
10  has_output(pur_onl_op,receipt_1,receipt).
11  input_spec(buyItem,item,item_1,have(item,available)).
12  input_spec(buyItem,credit_card,card_1,
13      have(credit_card,valid)).
14  input_spec(buyItem,credit_card,card_1,
15      have(credit_card,enough_balance)).
16  output_spec(buyItem,item,item_1,possess(client,item)).
17  output_spec(buyItem,receipt,receipt_1,
18      have(receipt,sentByEmail)).
```

The predicate names are self explanatory.

Web Services Planning Engine: The planning engine of $\Pi(\mathscr{P})$ is similar to any planning engine implemented using ASP. It consists of different types of rules, divided into groups as follows.

– *Initial state:* The rule translates information given in S_0 to indicate that the data is available at time step 0. For example, credit_card(valid, enough_balance) is translated to

Listing 1.2. Initial State

```
1  init(credit_card,have(credit_card,valid)).
2  init(credit_card,have(credit_card,enough_balance)).
3  exists(X,F,0) :- init(X,F).
```

- *Planning:* In this listing, T denotes a step in the workflow; D_I/D_O the input and output type of a service, respectively; and $occ(A,T)$ says that A occurs at step T. Lines 1–2 enforce the precondition of a service. Lines 3–6 define g_m which indicates that an input I (type D_I) of A is provided by an output O (type D_O) at time $T_1 \leq T$. Line 7 defines $match/4$, which says that the input I of A is available at step T. Lines 8–10 generate action occurrences and make sure only actions whose preconditions are satisfied can be executed. Lines 11–15 define $map/8$ which maps between outputs produced at one step to inputs at later steps.

Listing 1.3. Planning Engine

```
1   {executable(A,T)} :- operation(A).
2   :- executable(A,T), input_spec(A,I,N,D),not match(A,I,D,T).
3   p_m(A,I,D_I,T,O,D_O,T_1):- operation(A),T_1≤T,
4       input_spec(A,I,N_I,D_I), exists(O,D_O,T_1),
5       subclass(O,I), subclass(D_O,D_I).
6   1{g_m(A,I,D_I,T,O,D_O,T_1):p_m(A,I,D_I,T,O,D_O,T_1)}1 :- step(T_1).
7   match(A,I,D_I,T) :- g_m(A,I,D_I,T,_,_,_).
8   1{occ(A,T) : operation(A)}1.
9   :- occ(A,T), not executable(A,T).
10  exists(O,D_O,T+1) :- occ(A,T), output_spec(A,O,N_O,D_O).
11  map(A,I,D_I,T,B,O,D_O,T_1):- occ(A,T),T>=T_1,
12      occ(B,T_1-1),g_m(A,I,D_I,T,O,D_O,T_1),
13      input_spec(A,I,N_I,D_I), output_spec(B,O,N_O,D_O).
14  map(A,I,D_I,T,initG,O,D_O,0):- occ(A,T),
15      g_m(A,I,D_I,T,O,D_O,0), input_spec(A,I,N_I,D_I).
```

The program $\Pi(\mathscr{P})$ will also contain a generic rule of the form ":- not goal(n)" where $goal(n)$ indicates that the goal is satisfied at step n. For a constant n, $\Pi(\mathscr{P},n)$ denotes the program $\Pi(\mathscr{P})$ with steps taken values in $\{1,\ldots,n\}$ with the goal checking rule at n. Answer sets of $\Pi(\mathscr{P},n)$ represent workflows solving $\mathscr{P}$. The current execution and monitoring system of the Phylotastic project is responsible for the execution of workflows generated by $\Pi(\mathscr{P},n)$. It *stops* whenever a failure occurs. $\Pi(\mathscr{P},n)$ is enhanced as follows.

Repairing Method 1: Planning from Failed State. We encode the available resources at the failed state by ASP atoms of the form $res\_gen/4$. We alter the execution and monitoring system to record this information. To plan from the failed state, we only need to add the available resources to the initial state, remove the failed services by encoding them as $failed(op,\_)$ to prevent Π to consider these services in the planning phase. Let $F(\mathscr{P})$ denote the set of facts of the form $res\_gen/4$ or $failed/2$ that is supplied by the execution monitoring system when a failure occurs.

To compute the amount of reused resources, we add the rules[1] in Listing 1.4 to $\Pi(\mathscr{P})$. In Listing 1.4, the first rule (Lines 1–2) records the successful execution of operation X at step T and defines *res_prod*, the resource R named N has been produced by an operation X at step T. The lines 3–5 define the predicate *res_reuse*, which says that the resource R named N of the type D_R and data Data$_R$ is reused. Line 6 counts the number of reused resources. Line 7 enables the identification of answer sets with maximal number of reused resources and Line 8 prevents reuse of failed services.

Listing 1.4. Planning From Failed State (Π_{pff})

```
1  res_prod(R,N,D_R):- res_gen(R,N,D_R,Data_R),
2      output_spec(X,R,N,D_R), occ(X,T).
3  res_reuse(R,N,D_R,Data_R) :- occ(X,T),
4      res_gen(R,N,D_R,Data_R), not res_prod(R,N,D_R),
5      map(X,I,D_I,T,initG,R,D_R,0).
6  reused(V) :- V = #count{R,N,D_R,Data_R : res_reuse(R,N,D_R,Data_R
       )}.
7  #maximize{V : reused(V)}.
8  :- failed(F,T), is_used_op(F).
```

Let $\Pi_1^f(n) = \Pi(\mathscr{P},n) \cup \Pi_{pff} \cup F(\mathscr{P})$. We can show the following:

Proposition 1. *If A is an answer set of $\Pi_1^f(n)$ then A encodes a workflow solution of $\mathscr{P}$ that does not include any failed service and reuses the maximal number of resources specified in $F(\mathscr{P})$.*

Proof. The fact that A satisfies $\Pi(\mathscr{P},n)$ indicates that A encodes a workflow solution of $\mathscr{P}$. The rules on Lines 6–8 (Listing 1.4) ensure the other properties of the solution. □

Repairing Method 2: Replanning with Successful Services. Let G_{st} be the workflow whose execution fails. We assume that G_{st} and the services that have been executed successfully are encoded by a program $F(G_{st})$, which consists of facts of the form *old_occ_exe*/2 or *old_map_exe*$(S,I,D_I,T_1,S_0,O,D_O,T_0)$. We add to $\Pi(\mathscr{P},n)$ a new set of rules Π_{rss} (Listing 1.5) and $F(G_{st})$ and generate new solution G' for $\mathscr{P}$ such that $score(G_{st},G')$ is maximal. In addition, $F(G_{st})$ also records failed services.

The program Π_{rss} (Listing 1.5) implements the function $\mapsto$. The first rule (Line 1) says that we will map the initial state of G_{st} to the initial state of G'. Other rules defined φ (Lines 2–6, 7–11) extend the $\mapsto$ relation whenever possible. In these rules, s_equal(Y,Y') represents the fact that two services Y and Y' are equivalent in terms of functionality. The rules defining π (Lines 12–14) compute the value of π as defined in Eq. 1. Π_{rss} computes the number of reused services, instructs the solver to find answer sets containing the maximal number of reused services (Lines 15–16), and makes sure that the generated workflow G' does not include failed services (Line 17–18).

---

[1] The rules have been simplified somewhat for readability.

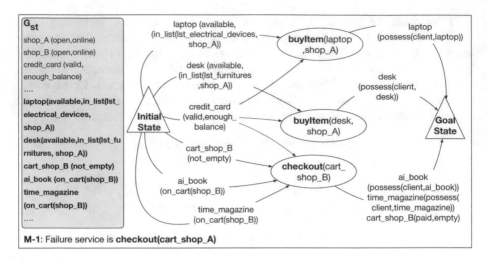

Fig. 3. Recovery workflow (Web Shopping Domain): Replanning from Failed State

Listing 1.5. Replanning with Successful Services (Π_{rss})

```
1   φ(initG,0,initG',0).
2   φ(Y,T₁,Y',T₃) :- φ(initG,0,initG',0),
3       old_occ_exe(Y,T₁), occ(Y',T₃),
4       old_map_exe(Y,I,DF_I,T₁,initG,O,DF_O,0),
5       map(Y',I,DF_I,T₃,initG',O,DF_O,0),
6       s_equal(Y,Y').
7   φ(Y,T₁,Y',T₃) :- φ(X,T₂,X',T₄),
8       old_occ_exe(Y,T₁), occ(Y',T₃),
9       old_map_exe(Y,I,DF_I,T₁,X,O,DF_O,T₂+1),
10      map(Y',I,DF_I,T₃,X',O,DF_O,T₄+1),
11      T₁>=T₂+1,T₃>=T₄+1,s_equal(Y,Y').
12  π(initG',0).
13  π(Y',0) :- occ(Y',T₃), not φ(_,_,Y',T₃).
14  π(Y',1) :- occ(Y',T₃), φ(_,_,Y',T₃).
15  score(V_φ) :- V_φ = #sum{V_Y',Y' : π(Y', V_Y')}.
16  #maximize{V_φ : score(V_φ)}.
17  :- failed(F,T_F), occ(F,T), not succ(F,T).
18  succ(F,T) :- failed(F,T_F), occ(Y,T), Y = F, φ(F,_,Y,T).
```

Proposition 2. *If A is an answer set of $\Pi_2^f(n) = \Pi(\mathscr{P},n) \cup \Pi_{rss} \cup F(G_{st})$ then A encodes a workflow solution of $\mathscr{P}$ that does not include any failed service and reuses the maximal number of services specified in $F(G_{st})$.*

Proof. Similar to Proposition 1.   □

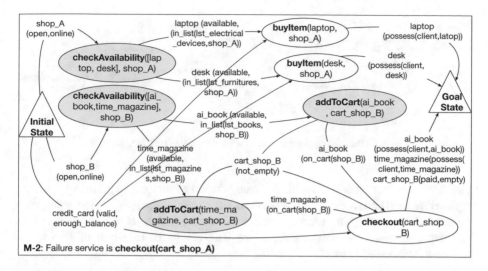

Fig. 4. Recovery workflow (Web Shopping): Replanning with Successful Services (Color figure online)

4.3 Experimental Evaluation

Web Shopping Domain. We experimented the approaches with the problem described in the second section[2]. A failure of service (checkout(cart_shop_A)) is injected during the execution of the workflow generated in Fig. 1. Figure 3 shows a new workflow generated by $\Pi_1^f(3)$ that uses the planning from the failed state method (0.5 s). Figure 4 shows a new workflow generated by $\Pi_2^f(7)$ that uses the replanning with successful services method (2 s). Observe that the repaired workflow on the left, generated by $\Pi_1^f(3)$, utilizes the available resources and is simpler comparing to the original one. On the other hand, the workflow on the right, generated by $\Pi_2^f(7)$, contains new services that replace the failed service and is able to reuse the majority of the executed services.

In Fig. 3, the new initial state includes all *concrete resources* which have been produced successfully before failure point when *executing* the original workflow. For example, ai_book(on_cart(shop_B)) is the concrete resource produced by service addToCard when executing the original workflow. Program $\Pi_1^f(3)$ generated a new workflow from new initial state to original goal state and reused concrete resource ai_book(on_cart(shop_B)). In Fig. 4, the gray background eclipse nodes and their links simulate whole or a part of executed structure G_{st} while repairing services are represented by blue text nodes.

Phylotastic Domain. We did further experimental evaluation to evaluate the two repairing methods with problems in the *Phylotastic* domain as well. The detail information about *Phylotastic* domain is described in [8]. Basically, the *Phylotastic Ontology* is

---

[2] We used a computer running Ubuntu 16.4 LTS, 8GB DDR3, 2.5 GHz Intel-Core i5, and ASP solver clingo.

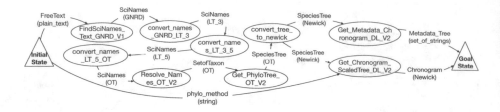

Fig. 5. Generating a chronogram and its metadata from free plain text

a services repository that deals with the manipulation of services (e.g., names, species, phyloreferences) and representations of evolutionary knowledge (e.g., taxonomies, phylogenies). There are some primary classes of services such as `names_operation`, `tree_operation`, `taxon_operation`, etc. The results of repairing in *Phylotastic* domain are discussed below.

– **Use case 1: From Free Plain Text to a Chronogram and its Metadata.** We experimented with a WSC problem in the *Phylotastic* domain, aimed at creating a `chronogram`, a scaled species phylogeny with branch lengths, in `newick` format, along with its metadata, from a plain text document. The initial state supplies a `FreeText` (more precisely, an object of the type `FreeText`) to the service `FindSciNames_Text_GRND_V1` (type of `names_extraction_text`) and a string (`phylo_method`) to the service `Get_Chronogram_ScaledTree_DL_V2` (type of `tree_transformation`), which also needs a `speciesTree` in `newick` format to produce the `chronogram`, etc. A workflow solving for this problem is given in Fig. 5. In this experiment, we consider two scenarios: (**S1**) The service `convert_tree_to_newick` fails; and (**S2**) the service `Get_Chronogram_ScaledTree_DL_V2` fails. The workflows generated using the two methods are depicted in Fig. 6. The two workflows on the left are generated from the failed state. Available resources are

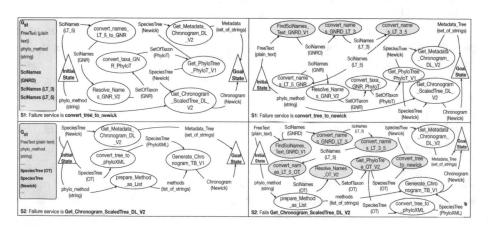

Fig. 6. Repaired workflows: *Phylotastic* generating a chronogram and its metadata (Color figure online)

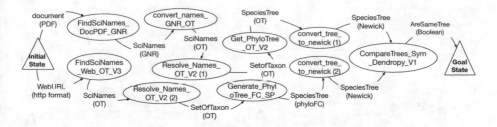

Fig. 7. Compare species trees from different sources

listed in the gray box. The reused resources are highlighted in Blue. In both scenarios, the new workflow differs significant from the original one (e.g., new services are used). The two workflows on the right are generated by replanning using successful services. The new services that need to be inserted are highlighted in Blue. As it can be seen, almost a half of all executed services are reused in (**S1**) and only a few are added in (**S2**).

- **Use case 2: Compare Species Trees from Different Sources.** In this use case, an user provides inputs data including a document (PDF format), and a Web address (http_URL format). Each document contains information about a phylogeny tree. The requirement is to examine whether or not the two phylogeny trees generated from these inputs sources (document and Web-page content) have the same phylogeny structure (Fig. 7). There are two concrete services that are used more than one time in the workflow: Resolve_Names_OT_V2 and convert_tree_to_newick. They are drawn with a number next to it (1 and 2) in Figs. 7 and 8 in order to identify which service will be executed before another in the execution ordering[3]. For example, Resolve_Names_OT_V2(1) and Resolve_Names_OT_V2(2) describe the same service and Resolve_Names_OT_V2(1) is executed before Resolve_Names_OT_V2(2). Again, we inject two different service failures in two scenarios: (**S1**) The failure is at the very end of the process (CompareTrees_Sym_Dendropy_V1); and (**S2**) The failure is at convert_tree_to_newick(2) (meaning that the first execution of the service convert_tree_to_newick succeed while the second execution fails). Figure 8 depicts the four recovery workflows for use case 2. The left two are workflows generated from the failed state while the right ones are generated by replanning with using successful services.

Comparison Between Two Methods. We close this section with a brief discussion on the advantages and disadvantages of the two methods for repairing failed workflows. Clearly, both aim at *reusing as much as possible the results obtained from the incomplete execution of the workflow* but with a slight different focus. Method 2 (*Replanning with Successful Services*) attempts to take advantage of the information in the original workflow and Method 1 (*Planning from Failed State*) ignores this information. This leads to the following main differences:

---

[3] The ordering is done so we can experiment with the failure of the services. It is also possible for the order to be reverse.

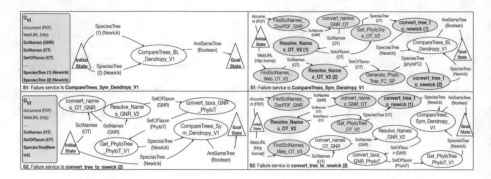

Fig. 8. Repaired workflows: *Phylotastic* compare species trees from different sources

- **Planning from Failed State.** In this method, the replanning process often starts from a state that is richer in resources than the initial state of the original problem. This is due to the fact that the execution of a service does not remove the outputs of services that have been successfully executed earlier. Given that the original workflow is minimal under certain metric (e.g., shortest plan) then the new initial state is closer to the goal than the original one. Therefore, Method 1 could be faster than Method 2—it can be observed in the experiment.

- **Replanning with Successful Services.** The replanning in this method is more complex than Method 1. It involves the generation of a new workflow (G') and then a *subgraph isomorphism* between the new workflow and the partial executed workflow (G' and G_{st}). In our implementation, this is done in a single ASP program. This is the added overhead and is the main reason for Method 2 to take longer to find a new plan as in the experiments. On the other hand, as suggested in [7], maintaining the skeleton of the original workflow is a desirable feature of the replanning process.

5   Conclusion, Discussion, and Future Work

We formally defined the notion of a WSC problem that enables the introduction of two methods for repairing a workflow whose execution fails when a services fails. The most interesting feature of the two new methods lies in the precise definition of the rather relative statement of *reusing as much as possible what has been executed*. In one method, the focus is on the available resources that have been produced by the executed services and a new workflow is generated from the failed state. In another method, the focus is on reusing the original workflow in generating the new one. We experimentally evaluate the proposed methods in the shopping domain by integrating them into an existing WSC framework. (Available online at: http://workflow.phylotastic.org)

We note that the WSC problem defined in this paper inherits several characteristics of a WSC problem defined in the literature (e.g., as in [6]), which views the WSC problem as a planning problem and its solution is generally a graph (a workflow) and not a sequential plan. On the other hand, due to fact that web services need resources to start their execution but do not usually *remove* them, the replanning problem with respect to a WSC problem is different from replanning in general. Our first method of replanning relies on this property of WSC problems. Last but not least, we are not aware of any comparable WSC system that we could use in our experiments. The several WSC systems reviewed in the introduction are no longer functional or inaccessible. Our intermediate goal is to identify potential applications that could benefit by the proposed methods and allows us to experiment and validate the scalability of the proposed system.

References

1. Berners-Lee, T., Hendler, J., Lassila, O.: The semantics web. Sci. Am. **284**(5), 34–43 (2001)
2. Chan, K.S.M., Bishop, J., Steyn, J., Baresi, L., Guinea, S.: A fault taxonomy for web service composition. In: Di Nitto, E., Ripeanu, M. (eds.) ICSOC 2007. LNCS, vol. 4907, pp. 363–375. Springer, Heidelberg (2009). https://doi.org/10.1007/978-3-540-93851-4_36
3. Chen, H.P., Zhang, C.: A queueing-theory-based fault detection mechanism for SOA-based applications. In: The 9th IEEE International Conference on E-Commerce Technology and the 4th IEEE International Conference on Enterprise Computing, E-Commerce and E-Services (CEC-EEE 2007), pp. 157–166 (2007)
4. Erradi, A., Maheshwari, P., Tosic, V.: Recovery policies for enhancing web services reliability. In: 2006 IEEE International Conference on Web Services (ICWS 2006), pp. 189–196 (2006)
5. Mansour, H.E., Dillon, T.S.: Dependability and rollback recovery for composite web services. IEEE Trans. Serv. Comput. **4**, 328–339 (2011)
6. McIlraith, S., Son, T., Zeng, H.: Semantic Web services. IEEE Intell. Syst. **16**(2), 46–53 (2001). (Special Issue on the Semantic Web)
7. Nguyen, T., Pontelli, E., Son, T.: Phylotastic: an experiment in creating, manipulating, and evolving phylogenetic biology workflows using logic programming. Theory Pract. Logic Program. **18**(3–4), 656–672 (2018)
8. Nguyen, T.H., Son, T.C., Pontelli, E.: Automatic web services composition for phylotastic. In: Calimeri, F., Hamlen, K., Leone, N. (eds.) PADL 2018. LNCS, vol. 10702, pp. 186–202. Springer, Cham (2018). https://doi.org/10.1007/978-3-319-73305-0_13
9. Nwana, H.: Software agents: an overview. Knowl. Eng. Rev. **11**(3), 205–244 (1996)
10. Peer, J.: A POP-based replanning agent for automatic web service composition. In: Gómez-Pérez, A., Euzenat, J. (eds.) ESWC 2005. LNCS, vol. 3532, pp. 47–61. Springer, Heidelberg (2005). https://doi.org/10.1007/11431053_4
11. Saboohi, H., Amini, A., Abolhassani, H.: Failure recovery of composite semantic web services using subgraph replacement. In: 2008 International Conference on Computer and Communication Engineering, pp. 489–493 (2008)
12. Vaculín, R., Wiesner, K., Sycara, K.P.: Exception handling and recovery of semantic web services. In: Fourth International Conference on Networking and Services (ICNS 2008), pp. 217–222 (2008)
13. Vargas-Santiago, M., Hernández, S.E.P., Rosales, L.A.M., Kacem, H.H.: Survey on web services fault tolerance approaches based on checkpointing mechanisms. JSW **12**, 507–525 (2017)
14. Yin, J., Chen, H., Deng, S., Wu, Z., Pu, C.: A dependable ESB framework for service integration. IEEE Internet Comput. **13**, 26–34 (2009)
15. Yin, K., Zhou, B., Zhang, S., Xu, B., Chen, Y.: Qos-aware services replacement of web service composition. In: 2009 International Conference on Information Technology and Computer Science vol. 2, pp. 271–274 (2009)
16. Zhao, W.: Design and implementation of a Byzantine fault tolerance framework for web services. J. Syst. Softw. **82**, 1004–1015 (2009)

Answer Set Programming Systems

AQuA: ASP-Based Visual Question Answering

Kinjal Basu[✉][ID], Farhad Shakerin[ID], and Gopal Gupta[ID]

The University of Texas at Dallas, Richardson, USA
{Kinjal.Basu,Farhad.Shakerin,gupta}@utdallas.edu

Abstract. AQuA (ASP-based Question Answering) is an Answer Set Programming (ASP) based visual question answering framework that truly "understands" an input picture and answers natural language questions about that picture. The knowledge contained in the picture is extracted using YOLO, a neural network-based object detection technique, and represented as an answer set program. Natural language processing is performed on the question to transform it into an ASP query. Semantic relations are extracted in the process for deeper understanding and to answer more complex questions. The resulting knowledge-base—with additional commonsense knowledge imported—can be used to perform reasoning using an ASP system, allowing it to answer questions about the picture, just like a human. This framework achieves 93.7% accuracy on CLEVR dataset, which exceeds human baseline performance. What is significant is that AQuA translates a question into an ASP query without requiring any training. Our framework for Visual Question Answering is quite general and closely simulates the way humans operate. In contrast to existing purely machine learning-based methods, our framework provides an explanation for the answer it computes, while maintaining high accuracy.

Keywords: Answer set programming · Visual question answering · Commonsense reasoning · Natural language understanding

1 Introduction

Answering questions about a given picture, or Visual Question Answering (VQA), is a long-standing goal of Artificial Intelligence research. To answer questions about a picture, humans generally first recognize the objects in the picture, then they reason with the questions asked using their commonsense knowledge. To be effective, we believe a VQA system should work in a similar way. Thus, to perceive a picture, ideally, a system should have intuitive abilities like object and attribute recognition and understanding of spatial-relationships. To answer questions, it must use reasoning. Natural language questions are complex and ambiguous by nature, and also require commonsense knowledge for their interpretation. Most importantly, reasoning skills such as counting, inference, comparison, etc., are needed to answer these questions.

© Springer Nature Switzerland AG 2020
E. Komendantskaya and Y. A. Liu (Eds.): PADL 2020, LNCS 12007, pp. 57–72, 2020.
https://doi.org/10.1007/978-3-030-39197-3_4

To build VQA systems, researchers have created several datasets such as [3,12,13,22,25,33]. However, according to Johnson et al. [9] approaches based on neural network-based models tend to "cheat" while answering the questions by exploiting the correlations between word occurrences instead of truly understanding the content. CLEVR [9] is a recent VQA dataset of 100k rendered images along with complex and challenging questions over them. The images depict simple 3D shapes which makes recognition task easy, however, to answer the questions, a system should be able to perform logical reasoning over object attributes and their relationships.

The experiments conducted by *Johnson et. al.* in [9] suggest that approaches based on end-to-end training of neural network models perform poorly on CLEVR, no matter how sophisticated the architecture is. The state-of-the-art neural-based VQA systems incorporate convolutional layers, recurrent/LSTM models, and attention networks. Also, some models translate questions into intermediate functional units that are either programmed or are trainable neural modules.

Surveys of state-of-the-art neural-based VQA systems can be found elsewhere [27,30]. The main point to note is that none of these systems follow the methodology that humans use: recognize images via pattern recognition while answer questions through reasoning. In this paper we propose the AQuA framework that attempts to emulate a human for VQA. We strongly believe that AQuA's method is the most effective approach for VQA and does not suffer from the flaws (discussed later) found in all purely neural network-based approaches. What is more, AQuA can provide full justification for the answers it computes, something that is not possible for neural network-based methods because of their "black box" nature.

AQuA replicates a human's VQA behavior by incorporating commonsense knowledge and using ASP for reasoning. VQA in the AQuA framework employs the following sources of knowledge: (i) knowledge about objects extracted using the YOLO algorithm [21], (ii) semantic relations extracted from the question, (iii) query generated from the question, and (iv) commonsense knowledge. AQuA runs on the query-driven, scalable s(ASP) [15] answer set programming system that can provide a proof tree as a justification for the query being processed.

AQuA processes and reasons over raw textual questions and does not need any annotation or generation of function units such as what is employed by several approaches proposed for the CLEVR dataset [10,29,32]. Also, instead of predicting an answer, AQuA augments the parsed question with commonsense knowledge to truly understand it and to compute the correct answer (e.g., it understands that *block* means *cube*, or *shiny object* means *metal object*).

This paper makes the following novel contributions: (i) presents a fully explainable framework to handle VQA that outperforms existing neural-based systems in terms of accuracy and explainability, (ii) demonstrates that a general (i.e., not domain specific), scalable VQA system can be built without training, (iii) understands textual knowledge with the help of commonsense knowledge, and (iv) provides a method that guarantees a correct answer as long as the objects in the picture are recognized correctly and syntactic & semantic processing of the question yields a correct query.

2 Background

Answer Set Programming (ASP): An answer set program is a collection of rules of the form -

$$l_0 \leftarrow l_1, \ldots, l_m, \, not \, l_{m+1}, \ldots, \, not \, l_n.$$

Classical logic denotes each l_i is a literal [4]. In an ASP rule, the left hand side is called the *head* and the right-hand side is the *body*. Constraints are ASP rules without *head*, whereas facts are without *body*. The variables start with an uppercase letter, while the predicates and the constants begin with a lowercase. We will follow this convention throughout the paper. The semantics of ASP is based on the stable model semantics of logic programming [5]. ASP supports *negation as failure* [4], allowing it to elegantly model common sense reasoning, default rules with exceptions, etc., and serves as the secret sauce for AQuA's sophistication.

s(ASP) System: s(ASP) [15] is a query-driven, goal-directed implementation of ASP. This is indispensable for automating commonsense reasoning, as traditional grounding and SAT-solver based implementations of ASP are not scalable. There are three major advantages of using s(ASP): 1. s(ASP) does not ground the program, which makes AQuA framework fast and scalable, 2. it only explores the parts of the knowledge base that are needed to answer a query, and 3. it provides justification tree for an answer.

YOLO Object Detection Model: Redmon et. al. [20,21] proposed a convolutional neural network architecture to detect multiple objects from different categories in a given image and to simultaneously draw bounding boxes around them. The novelty of this method lies in the fact that it combines the classification and regression tasks together by only using the extracted features from deep convolutional layers in a single step which makes real-time predictions possible.

The AQuA framework utilizes YOLO to extract characteristics of interest in the form of logical predicates from images. These predicates are then used by ASP engine to perform all sorts of reasoning on different relations between objects. In CLEVR domain these characteristics are shape, size, material, color, and spatial relationships between objects such as front, left, right, etc. Figure 3 shows an example of the predicates found by YOLO that are used by the s(ASP) engine to answer questions.

Stanford CoreNLP Tools: Stanford CoreNLP [14] is a set of tools for natural language processing. AQuA only uses *Parts-of-Speech (POS) tagger* and *Dependency Parser* from this set. Based on the context, POS tagger generates the necessary parts of speech such as noun, verb, adjective, etc., for each question. It identifies the question type (e.g., what, where, how) and disambiguated words (e.g., *block* as a *verb* vs. *block* as a *noun*). On the other hand, dependency graph provides the grammatical relations between words in the sentence. Dependency relations follow enhanced universal dependency annotation [24]. Figure 1 shows an example of POS tagging and dependency graph of a question.

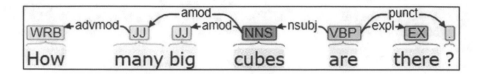

Fig. 1. Example of POS tagging and dependency graph

3   Technical Approach

In this section, we propose AQuA, a framework to perform visual question answering following a process used by us humans. AQuA represents knowledge using ASP paradigm and it is made up of five modules that perform the following tasks: (i) object detection and feature extraction using the YOLO algorithm [21], (ii) preprocessing of the natural language question, (iii) semantic relation extraction from the question, (iv) Query generation based on semantic analysis, and (v) commonsense knowledge representation. AQuA runs on the query-driven, scalable s(ASP) [15] answer set programming system that can provide a proof tree as a justification for a query being processed.

Figure 2 shows AQuA's architecture. The five modules are labeled, respectively, YOLO, Preprocessor, Semantic Relation Extractor (SRE), Query Generator, and Commonsense Knowledge.

3.1   Preprocessor

This module extracts information from the question by using Stanford CoreNLP parts-of-speech (POS) tagger and dependency graph generator. The lemma and the POS are fetched for every word along with the dependency graph of the sentence. Using this information, AQuA translates a question to a sequence of predicates that would encode the natural language question as an ASP query. Also, this information is used to infer the question type: *how_many*, *what_number*, *is_there*, etc., using which the answer types (such as *boolean*, *numeric*, *value*, etc.) are determined. The output of the Preprocessing module will be consumed by the Query Generator and the Semantic Relation Extraction (SRE) modules.

AQuA transforms natural language questions to a logical representation before feeding it to the ASP engine. This logical representation module is inspired by Neo-Davidsonian formalism [2], where every event is recognized with a unique identifier. Similarly, AQuA maintains an identifier for each word (a simple position index in the question). It identifies each object, even if there are two objects

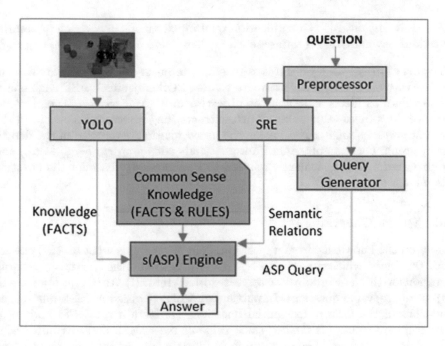

Fig. 2. System architecture

with the same name (e.g., *"How many matte blocks are behind the red block?"*, here question refers to two different blocks: the *queried object* and the *referenced object*).

3.2 SRE: Semantic Relations Extractor

Semantic relation labeling is the process of assigning relationship labels to two different phrases in a sentence based on the context. To extract semantic relations from the passage, we have created default logic rules with exceptions [26]. These rules utilize the POS and the dependency graph of the sentence from the Preprocessing step. To understand the CLEVR dataset questions, AQuA requires two types of semantic relations (i.e., *quantification* and *property*) to be extracted (if they exists) from the questions.

Quantification: In the AQuA framework, all the existential questions are considered as a special type of numeric comparison questions. Considering all the filters given in the question for the queried object, the ASP engine counts the number of queried object from the picture and compares the object count with the number given in the question. The compared number from the question is captured using *quantification* semantic relation in the form of *quantification(number, object)*. For example, *quantification(1, cube_4)* semantic relation (the suffix *4* is the identifier of the word *cube*) is extracted from the question

"*Are there any cubes?*". Quantification relation also helps in covering existential questions beyond CLEVR dataset such as "*Are there greater than five objects?*"

Property: In the CLEVR dataset questions, objects (POS: noun) are accompanied with none/one/many attribute values (POS: adjective). ASP engine uses these values as filters to search the object(s) in a given picture. Therefore, to capture this object-value pairs, AQuA extracts the *property* relationship in the form of *property(value, object)* using the *amod* relations expressed in the dependency graph. For example, AQuA automatically adds *property(big_4, ball_6)* and *property(red_5, ball_6)* semantic relation to the knowledge base for the question "*Is there a big red ball?*"

3.3   Query Generator

Based on the knowledge from a question, AQuA generates a list of ASP clauses with the query, which runs on the s(ASP) engine to find the answer. In general, questions with one-word answer are categorized into: (i) yes/no questions, and (ii) attribute/value questions. In particular, CLEVR question bank has yes/no questions in the form of existential questions (*Is there a red ball?*) and those that compare values (*Is the ball same color as the cube?*), and attribute/value questions in the form of counting objects (*How many red balls are there?*) and querying object attributes (*What is the color of the shiny cylinder?*). To handle each type of question, AQuA generates a set of ASP clauses. For example, the following set of clauses are generated to tackle the yes/no question: "*Is there a big ball?*"

(1) query(Q, A) :- question(Q), answer(Q, A).
(2) answer('is there a big ball ?', yes) :- find_ans ('is there a big ball ?').
(3) answer('is there a big ball ?', no) :- *not* find_ans('is there a big ball ?').
(4) find_ans(Q) :- question(Q), find_all_filters(ball, 5, L),
                    list_object(L, Ids), list_length(Ids, C),
                    quantification(N, ball_5), gte (C, N) .
(5) question('is there a big ball ?').

In the code above, clause (1) captures the answer of the question (Q) in the variable A. Clause (2) says that if *find_ans* predicate succeeds, return *yes* to the answer variable A from clause (1). Whereas, if *find_ans* fails, clause (3) produces *no* as an answer to the clause (1)'s answer variable A. If all the sub-goals from the body of the clause (4) succeed then *find_ans* becomes *true*, *false* otherwise. Lastly, fact (5) represents the natural language question.

Similar to the yes/no question, the following set of clauses are generated for the attribute/value question: "*What color is the cube ?*"

---

(1) query(Q, A) :- question(Q), answer(Q, A).

(2) answer('what color is the cube ?', A) :-
　　　　　　　　find_ans('what color is the cube ?', A).

(3) find_ans(Q, A) :- question(Q), find_all_filters(cube, 5, L),
　　　　　　　　list_object(L, Ids), get_att_val(Ids, color, A) .

(4) question('what color is the cube ?').

Here, clauses (1) and (4) are identical to clauses (1) and (5) for the yes/no question discussed above. Clause (2) stores the answer in variable A and passes it to clause (1). Clause (3) captures the answer in the head variable A that is defined in the body.

3.4   Commonsense Knowledge

Similar to a human, AQuA requires commonsense knowledge to correctly compute answers to questions. For the CLEVR dataset questions, AQuA needs to have commonsense knowledge about properties (e.g., color, size, material), directions (e.g., left, front), and shapes (e.g., cube, sphere). AQuA will not be able to understand question phrases such as '... *red metal cube* ...', unless it knows *red* is a color, *metal* is a material, and *cube* is a shape. In some cases, AQuA requires deeper knowledge to understand the questions. For example, phrase like '... *shiny object* ...' requires two step inferences: (i) *shiny* refers to *metal*, and, (ii) *metal* is a *material*. Commonsense knowledge can be categorized in two different parts based on the type: (i) commonsense facts, which are grounded and always true. (ii) commonsense rules, which are required for reasoning tasks (i.e., counting, spatial reasoning, etc.).

Commonsense Facts: For CLEVR, commonsense facts are of two types: (i) attribute values (e.g., *red* is a *color*, *cube* is a *shape*), and, (ii) similar values (e.g., *block* and *cube*). Thus, these facts are represented using two types of relational predicates:

is_property(V, A): This relationship stores the attribute value pair, V and A. For example, *red* is a *color* will be represented as *is_property(red, color)*.

is_similar(X1, X2): This relationship stores two similar words, $X1$ and $X2$, one of which can be used in place of the other without changing the meaning. For example, *big* is similar to *large* is represented as *is_similar(big, large)*.

We humans incrementally augment/refine our commonsense knowledge from information we encounter in everyday life. Thus, we add/remove facts as our knowledge evolves. If we want to add another shape (such as *pyramid*), we only need to add another *is_property* relation. The system will automatically incorporate this knowledge and be able to handle questions involving *pyramids*.

Commonsense Rules: Commonsense rules deal with all the reasoning tasks that AQuA needs to handle. Depending on the CLEVER dataset question, AQuA executes several sub-tasks (e.g., list-length, list-union, numeric-comparison such as greater-than-equal, less-than) underneath the primary reasoning tasks (e.g., sorting a list of object from left to right based on its spatial position) required to answer a question. Following is an example of a set of rules required to filter a list of objects that match a specific attribute-value pair. The code is straightforward as it recursively traverses the list.

```
(1) filter(_, _, [], []).
(2) filter(Att, Val, [Id | T1], [Id | T2]) :- property(Id, Att, Val),
                                  filter(Att, Val, T1, T2).
(3) filter(Att, Val, [Id | T1], T2) :- not property(Id, Att, Val),
                                  filter(Att, Val, T1, T2).
```

3.5 ASP Engine

ASP engine is the brain of our system. All the knowledge (image representation, commonsense knowledge, semantic relations) and the query in ASP syntax are executed using the query-driven s(ASP) system. Depending on the query it only explores part of the knowledge which is needed to compute the answer. Also, s(ASP) does not do unnecessary grounding which saves lots of memory. Due to this benefit, we are able to test all the questions in the same iteration without facing any memory overflow issues.

An AQuA query in s(ASP) is always of the form *"?- query (Q, A)"* where Q represents the question and A the computed answer.

4   Experiments and Results

AQuA is a novel, general framework for visual QA. Questions are answered in this framework through the use of commonsense reasoning rather than with machine learning. If the questions are correctly parsed and correctly converted into a query, the answer computed by AQuA is always correct. Unlike other neural-based systems, AQuA does not need training over questions. Thus, the question bank provided in the dataset for testing is of no use to AQuA. Instead, the validation QA set is directly used to compute an answer and compare it to the actual answer given in the validation QA dataset to generate the results.

We tested our AQuA framework on the CLEVR dataset. The validation set for CLEVR contains 149,991 questions and 15,000 images. We simplified the testing process slightly by limiting the question length to 15 words. We built this system for natural language questions answering over the CLEVR image set using the AQuA framework without focusing on any particular question type. As mentioned earlier, we also did not use the functional programs/units given for each question in the validation set since AQuA performs its own parsing and semantic analysis. We ran AQuA on 45,157 questions that fit the selection criteria imposed (e.g., questions with 15 words or less) to generate ASP queries. An accuracy of **93.7%** was achieved with 42,314 correct answers. This performance is beyond the average human accuracy [9].

Table 1. Performance results

Question type		Accuracy (%)	
Exist		**96**	
Count		**91.7**	
Compare value	Shape	87.42	**92.89**
	Color	94.32	
	Size	92.17	
	Material	96.14	
Compare integer	Less than	97.7	**98.05**
	Greater than	98.6	
	Equal	NA*	
Query attribute	Shape	94.01	**94.39**
	Color	94.87	
	Size	93.82	
	Material	94.75	

* Equality questions are minuscule in number so
currently ignored.

We have extensively studied the 2,843 questions that produced erroneous results. 2,092 questions out of 2,843 do not match the correct answer and other 751 questions throw ASP exceptions. Our manual analysis showed that mismatch happens mostly because of errors caused by the YOLO module: failing to detect a partially visible object, wrongly detecting a shadow as an object, wrongly detecting two overlapping objects as one, etc. Eliminating these errors through manual intervention resulted in another 2,626 questions out of the 2,843 questions being answered correctly. Only 217 incorrectly answered questions remained. Further analysis indicated that these could be attributed to wrong parsing or oversimplified spatial reasoning. As an example of parsing error, *block* sometime is parsed as a *verb* instead of a *noun*. With respect to oversimplification of spatial reasoning, note that objects in CLEVR have 3D shapes, but we only considered X and Y coordinates to calculate relative positioning of referenced objects (e.g., for *behind the block* concept). In the future, we can eliminate such errors by using more sophisticated spatial reasoning.

Even with these errors, our results are very promising as AQuA outperforms many state-of-the-art ML based methods on the CLEVR dataset illustrating the advantage of our approach that uses both machine learning and reasoning. Quantitative results for each question type are summarized in Table 1.

5   Example

To illustrate the AQuA framework further, we next discuss a full-fledged VQA example showing the data-flow and intermediate outputs from each step.

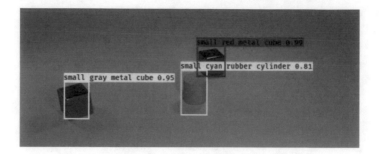

Fig. 3. Object detection using YOLO.

Image: Figure 3 shows an image from the validation set. Objects in the image are detected and labeled with its attribute. The decimal number at the end of each label shows the correctness probability of that object using the YOLO model.

Object representation: All the detected objects from the Fig. 3 are converted to ASP facts. Every object has a unique id number. Five attributes are detected for each object: *shape, color, material, size, and coordinates.*

object(1, cylinder, cyan, rubber, small, 246, 185).
object(2, cube, red, metal, small, 270, 130).
object(3, cube, gray, metal, small, 79, 191).

Question: Now, from the question set we have the following question for the image shown in Fig. 3.

'Is there a matte thing in front of the metallic thing behind the gray cube?'

Parsed Output: The question is parsed using the Stanford CoreNLP parser to get the *lemma, POS, and dependency graph.* Figure 4 shows the parser's output.

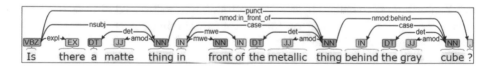

Fig. 4. POS tagging and dependency graph.

Semantic Relations: The following semantic relations are next extracted by applying default ASP rules. The word index is given for each word followed by a '_' (underscore). The lemma *'thing'* occurs twice in the question each occurrence representing a different object. Thus, the two occurrences are given distinct identifiers.

```
quantification(1, thing_5).
property(matte_4, thing_5).
property(metallic_10, thing_11).
property(gray_14, cube_15).
```

Commonsense Knowledge: The following figure shows the necessary commonsense knowledge needed to understand this question.

```
is_property(cube, shape).
is_property(cylinder, shape).
is_property(metal, material).
is_property(rubber, material).
is_property(small, size).
is_property(red, color).
is_property(cyan, color).
is_property(gray, color).
is_similar(matte, rubber).
```

Query: This question involves transitive referential reasoning: (i) *matte thing in front of the metallic thing*, and (ii) *metallic thing behind the gray cube*. Our framework can handle any level of transitivity. The query generated for this question is shown below. For these type of questions, a human will always start reasoning from the final referenced object. Similarly, our automatically generated query will perform spatial reasoning starting out from the *cube*. After resolving all the reference relations, it checks whether the desired object exists or not.

```
find_ans(Q) :- question(Q), get_all_id(L1), find_all_filters(cube, 15, L2),
               filter_all(L2, L1, [H0|T0]), get_behind_list(H0, L3),
               find_all_filters(thing, 11, L4), filter_all(L4, L3, [H1|T1]),
               get_front_list(H1, L5), find_all_filters(thing, 5, L6),
               filter_all(L6, L5, Ids), list_length(Ids, C),
               quantification(N, thing_5), gte(C, N).
```

Answer: The given answer matches with actual answer, which is *yes*.

Justification: As stated earlier, because of its query driven nature, s(ASP) will automatically generate a justification for any answer it computes [15]. A justification essentially is an explanation of how the answer is computed. Unfortunately, details are omitted due to lack of space.

6   Discussion

Our goal is to create a VQA framework that can answer questions based on logical reasoning, in a manner similar to how humans answer questions. Humans use pattern recognition for understanding pictures (akin to using neural networks to detect and localize objects in a picture) and commonsense reasoning for answering question about them. We believe that this is the most effective way for VQA. Our experiments demonstrate that if knowledge from the picture is represented correctly, and the question is parsed/processed properly, the AQuA framework will not fail in obtaining the correct answer. Our goal is to reach 100% accuracy (simulate an unerring human). The object detection model we use has around **5.3%** error rate. Upgrading to state-of-the-art neural-based object detection models [8,32] can increase our accuracy to nearly 100%. Similarly, if the error rate for Stanford CoreNLP tools is reduced, we can reach even higher accuracy.

AQuA has many other advantages as well, which other machine learning-based methods do not. As explained earlier, the AQuA framework provides explanation for a computed answer. Explainability is an important consideration for any intelligent system. The AQuA framework is also *interpretable*. Unlike neural network based methods, our AQuA framework is completely transparent. This means that the system can be well understood, debugged and improved. The AQuA framework is quite general, i.e., it can be applied to any type of VQA with reasonable effort. Thus, our framework can be used for any other visual question answering domain with minimal changes, unlike current machine learning approaches. A particular machine learning model can only work well in a specific narrowed down domain like CLEVR. But, that model cannot be used in any other similar domain without training it again with new data or without transferring the learning from another model. In contrast, the AQuA framework based on commonsense reasoning can be applied to other domains without much change.

Also, our approach is incremental in nature. AQuA can be easily expanded with more question types which will lead to greater accuracy. On the contrary, expanding the capabilities of a machine learning system often requires hyperparameter tuning, which often results in reduced accuracy.

Table 2. Question type wise summarized result from various state-of-the-art neural-network based model for CLEVR

Method	Count	Exist	Compare number	Compare attribute	Query attribute	Overall
Humans [10]	86.7	96.6	86.4	96.0	95.0	92.6
CNN+LSTM+SAN [10]	59.7	77.9	75.1	70.8	80.9	73.2
N2NMN [7]	68.5	85.7	84.9	88.7	90.0	83.7
Dependency Tree [1]	81.4	94.2	81.6	97.1	90.5	89.3
CNN+LSTM+RN [23]	90.1	97.8	93.6	97.1	97.9	95.5
IEP [10]	92.7	97.1	98.7	98.9	98.1	96.9
CNN+GRU+FiLM [19]	94.5	99.2	93.8	99.0	99.2	97.6
DDRprog [29]	96.5	98.8	98.4	99.0	99.1	98.3
MAC [8]	97.1	99.5	99.1	99.5	99.5	98.9
TbD+reg+hres [16]	97.6	99.2	99.4	99.6	99.5	99.1
NS-VQA [32]	99.7	99.9	99.9	99.8	99.8	99.8

7   Contribution and Related Works

The main contribution of this paper is an effective, efficient, and robust framework to handle any type of visual question answering. This framework is interpretable, expandable, scalable and explainable.

Significant research has been done on VQA, however, most of the recent work has been based on using neural network technology. For example, Stacked Attention Networks (CNN + LSTM + SA) [31], Relation Networks (CNN + LSTM + RN) [23], and Feature-wise Linear Modulation (CNN + GRU + FiLM) [19] combine the CNN-extracted image features with LSTM-extracted question features and pass them through multi-layer perceptron network. N2NMN [7], Dependency Tree [1] and TbD+reg+hres [16] assemble a graph of trained neural modules on the fly, each responsible for performing a single unit of computation to answer a question. IEP [10], DDRprog [29] and NS-VQA [32] construct intermediate functional units that unlike N2NMN are handcrafted programs. The latter incorporates segmentation techniques to achieve more accurate vision results. MAC [8] proposes differentiable reasoning units of recurrent neural network that would decompose the reasoning task to multiple small steps. A common issue in all these systems is that they heavily rely on supervised training which is computationally expensive and requires huge amount of annotated data. Moreover, the black-box nature of neural networks does not allow any justification as to why a model arrives at a certain answer. With the exception of TbD+reg+hres, which provides partial transparency via visualization of attention regions, other proposals are not explainable. In addition, a mechanism to incorporate commonsense knowledge is completely absent from all neural-based proposals.

Unlike AQuA, in many practical question-answering situations, it is impossible to understand the semantics of the question without making background assumptions from a commonsense knowledge base. Bypassing the natural language processing part, neural-based models are trained on domain-specific questions to map a question to a sequence of functional units. Thus, these models are not generalized enough to be trivially applied to other domains. Furthermore, they even fail to answer questions from the same domain in case of natural language sophistication (e.g., syntactic variation, co-referenced words)

Table 2 shows the summarized result for various state of the art neural network models for CLEVR dataset. First, neural-based methods for VQA have several deficiencies: they require training even for the natural language part (questions), models are inscrutable blackboxes, impossible to debug, etc. Use of training not only involves expensive computation, it requires laborious annotation of the data for questions. In contrast, the AQuA framework emulates methods employed by humans and answers questions through commonsense reasoning while providing explanation for the answer. Second, many of the methods such as NS-VQA [32] have more than 99% accuracy, however, these results are misleading as these methods are not general. They construct intermediate functional units that are handcrafted programs. In contrast, no such handcrafting is needed in AQuA. Commonsense knowledge is accumulated and can be transferred from one domain to another. Third, neural-based systems are not composable in the sense that if we introduce a new shape in the CLEVR dataset (e.g., a pyramid), then they will have to be retrained from scratch. In contrast, in AQuA all we have to do is to add small amount of new knowledge (e.g., a pyramid is also a shape) for the system to answer questions about the new object added.

8   Future Work

One obvious future work will be to be able to handle a broader class of questions, i.e., be able to parse them and turn them into ASP queries that are correctly answered. Also, as discussed earlier, we can use better, state-of-the-art neural network models for object detection that will almost remove every error from the picture processing end.

All the natural language or visual question answering systems suffer from NLP errors such as parsing issues (wrong parsing). We have used Stanford CoreNLP parser, which shows many wrong POS tagging and dependency graph errors. Researchers have created many other state-of-the-art parsers like Spacy [6], dependency parsing from AllenNLP [11], etc. In the future, we can have a voting mechanism between different parsers thereby increasing our accuracy.

For CLEVR dataset, only a limited amount of commonsense knowledge is needed: only few commonsense facts (about *color, shape, material, size*, and *similarities*) and commonsense reasoning rules (about *counting, comparing, sorting*, and *spatial relationships*) are needed. Reasoning rules are general and can be used for other datasets. However, commonsense facts are very specific to this dataset. Currently, we are manually putting the commonsense facts in ASP format. As future work, we plan to automate the commonsense facts generation process: based on the context, AQuA will fetch the knowledge from online sources such as WordNet [17], ConceptNet [28], etc., and will represent it in ASP format [18]. This will make the system more robust and flexible. Adding more commonsense knowledge and improving the ability to handle a broader class of questions is akin to a human acquiring more knowledge and learning to answer more complex questions. In this regard our approach is identical to how humans do VQA and, indeed, we are exploring practical and more advanced applications of the AQuA framework.

9   Conclusion

We presented an ASP-based VQA framework called AQuA and applied it to the CLEVR dataset with excellent results. AQuA automatically transforms visual knowledge to logical facts using the YOLO model. We also showed how AQuA automatically crafts the ASP query from a natural language question. We used the query driven s(ASP) engine to perform commonsense reasoning to obtain the answer. Our approach always finds the correct answer, if adequate knowledge is present and the natural language analysis works correctly. The AQuA framework not only gives promising results on the CLEVR dataset, it also enjoys other benefits such as explainability, generalizability, and interpretability.

Acknowledgement. We are indebted to Dhruva Pendharkar for his early work on natural language question answering. Thanks also to Sarat Varanasi for discussion and help. Authors gratefully acknowledge support from NSF grants IIS 1910131 and IIS 1718945.

References

1. Cao, Q., Liang, X., Li, B., Li, G., Lin, L.: Visual question reasoning on general dependency tree. In: Proceedings of the IEEE Conference on Computer Vision and Pattern Recognition, pp. 7249–7257 (2018)
2. Davidson, D.: Inquiries into Truth and Interpretation: Philosophical Essays, vol. 2. Oxford University Press, Oxford (2001)
3. Gao, H., Mao, J., Zhou, J., Huang, Z., Wang, L., Xu, W.: Are you talking to a machine? Dataset and methods for multilingual image question. In: NIPS 2015, pp. 2296–2304 (2015)
4. Gelfond, M., Kahl, Y.: Knowledge Representation, Reasoning, and the Design of Intelligent Agents: The Answer-Set Programming Approach. Cambridge University Press, Cambridge (2014)
5. Gelfond, M., Lifschitz, V.: The stable model semantics for logic programming. In: ICLP/SLP, vol. 88, pp. 1070–1080 (1988)
6. Honnibal, M., Montani, I.: spaCy 2: natural language understanding with bloom embeddings, convolutional neural networks and incremental parsing. **7** (2017, to appear)
7. Hu, R., Andreas, J., Rohrbach, M., Darrell, T., Saenko, K.: Learning to reason: end-to-end module networks for visual question answering. In: Proceedings of the IEEE International Conference on Computer Vision, pp. 804–813 (2017)
8. Hudson, D.A., Manning, C.D.: Compositional attention networks for machine reasoning. arXiv preprint arXiv:1803.03067 (2018)
9. Johnson, J., Hariharan, B., van der Maaten, L., Fei-Fei, L., Lawrence Zitnick, C., Girshick, R.: CLEVR: a diagnostic dataset for compositional language and elementary visual reasoning. In: IEEE CVPR 2017, pp. 2901–2910 (2017)
10. Johnson, J., et al.: Inferring and executing programs for visual reasoning. In: Proceedings of the IEEE International Conference on Computer Vision, pp. 2989–2998 (2017)
11. Joshi, V., Peters, M., Hopkins, M.: Extending a parser to distant domains using a few dozen partially annotated examples. arXiv preprint arXiv:1805.06556 (2018)
12. Krishna, R., et al.: Visual genome: connecting language and vision using crowd-sourced dense image annotations. Int. J. Comput. Vision **123**(1), 32–73 (2017)
13. Malinowski, M., Fritz, M.: A multi-world approach to question answering about real-world scenes based on uncertain input. In: NIPS 2014, pp. 1682–1690 (2014)
14. Manning, C.D., Surdeanu, M., Bauer, J., Finkel, J., Bethard, S.J., McClosky, D.: The Stanford CoreNLP natural language processing toolkit. In: ACL System Demonstrations, pp. 55–60 (2014)
15. Marple, K., Salazar, E., Gupta, G.: Computing stable models of normal logic programs without grounding. arXiv:1709.00501 (2017)
16. Mascharka, D., Tran, P., Soklaski, R., Majumdar, A.: Transparency by design: closing the gap between performance and interpretability in visual reasoning. In: Proceedings of the IEEE Conference on Computer Vision and Pattern Recognition, pp. 4942–4950 (2018)

17. Miller, G.A.: WordNet: a lexical database for english. Commun. ACM **38**(11), 39–41 (1995). https://doi.org/10.1145/219717.219748
18. Pendharkar, D., Gupta, G.: An ASP based approach to answering questions for natural language text. In: Alferes, J.J., Johansson, M. (eds.) PADL 2019. LNCS, vol. 11372, pp. 46–63. Springer, Cham (2019). https://doi.org/10.1007/978-3-030-05998-9_4
19. Perez, E., et al.: FiLM: visual reasoning with a general conditioning layer. In: AAAI (2018)
20. Redmon, J., Divvala, S.K., Girshick, R.B., Farhadi, A.: You only look once: unified, real-time object detection. In: CVPR, pp. 779–788. IEEE Computer Society (2016)
21. Redmon, J., Farhadi, A.: YOLOv3: an incremental improvement. arXiv preprint arXiv:1804.02767 (2018)
22. Ren, M., Kiros, R., Zemel, R.: Exploring models and data for image question answering. In: NIPS 2015, pp. 2953–2961 (2015)
23. Santor, A., et al.: A simple neural network module for relational reasoning. In: NIPS 2017, pp. 4967–4976 (2017)
24. Schuster, S., Manning, C.D.: Enhanced English universal dependencies: an improved representation for natural language understanding tasks. In: LRED 2016, pp. 2371–2378 (2016)
25. Shah, S., Mishra, A., Yadati, N., Talukdar, P.P.: KVQA: knowledge-aware visual question answering. In: AAAI (2019)
26. Shakerin, F., Salazar, E., Gupta, G.: A new algorithm to automate inductive learning of default theories. TPLP **17**(5–6), 1010–1026 (2017)
27. Shrestha, R., Kafle, K., Kanan, C.: Answer them all! Toward universal visual question answering models. In: Proceedings of the IEEE Conference on Computer Vision and Pattern Recognition, pp. 10472–10481 (2019)
28. Speer, R., Chin, J., Havasi, C.: ConceptNet 5.5: an open multilingual graph of general knowledge. In: Proceedings AAAI, pp. 4444–4451 (2017)
29. Suarez, J., Johnson, J., Li, F.F.: DDRprog: a CLEVR differentiable dynamic reasoning programmer. arXiv preprint arXiv:1803.11361 (2018)
30. Wu, Q., Teney, D., Wang, P., Shen, C., Dick, A., van den Hengel, A.: Visual question answering: a survey of methods and datasets. Comput. Vis. Image Underst. **163**, 21–40 (2017)
31. Yang, Z., He, X., Gao, J., Deng, L., Smola, A.J.: Stacked attention networks for image question answering. CVPR, pp. 21–29 (2015)
32. Yi, K., et al.: Neural-symbolic VQA: disentangling reasoning from vision and language understanding. In: NIPS 2018, pp. 1031–1042 (2018)
33. Yu, L., Park, E., Berg, A.C., Berg, T.L.: Visual madlibs: fill in the blank image generation and question answering. arXiv preprint arXiv:1506.00278 (2015)

Diagnosing Data Pipeline Failures Using Action Languages: A Progress Report

Alex Brik[1]([✉])[ID] and Jeffrey Xu[2][ID]

[1] Google Inc., Mountain View, USA
abrik@google.com
[2] University of California Los Angeles, Los Angeles, USA

Abstract. In this paper we describe our work towards automating diagnosing failures of data processing pipelines at Google Inc. using action language Hybrid $\mathcal{ALE}$. We describe Diagnostic Modeling Library - a component providing a novel abstraction layer on top of Hybrid $\mathcal{ALE}$, describe the requirements and give an overview of our system, which has been deployed on a limited number of data processing pipelines.

Data processing pipelines (pipelines, for short) are software systems that process collections of data and produce either transformed data, aggregated data or some other output. Industrial pipelines can consist of hundreds of jobs, with outputs of some jobs consumed as inputs by others within the pipeline. In addition, pipelines themselves can have input dependencies on other pipelines. When working well, this architecture allows efficient and effective processing of large amounts of data. When a malfunction occurs, it can stop data processing tasks, causing a set of cascading failures. The failures can cause an alert being dispatched to on-call engineers (on-calls, for short).

For the on-calls, an alert is a diagnostic challenge, as it can point to one of the later, rather than an earlier among the cascading failures. The earlier failures have to be found before the underlying problem can be resolved. Moreover, multiple possible causes of failure may have to be investigated. Automating the diagnosing process can decrease the time required to fix failures, and thus, improve the fault tolerance of the system and increase on-calls productivity.

Action languages [5] allow to formalize reasoning about effects of actions in dynamic domains. Constructing a mathematical model of an agent and its environment based on the theory of action languages has been studied and has applications to planning and diagnostic problems, see [3] for an overview. In [1] an action language Hybrid $\mathcal{ALE}$ was introduced in order to facilitate the development of diagnostic programs for the industrial pipelines. Hybrid $\mathcal{ALE}$ provides a mechanism for accessing outside data sources with user-provided algorithms. This feature of Hybrid $\mathcal{ALE}$ allows Hybrid $\mathcal{ALE}$ programs to gather information about pipelines from the outside sources in order to provide an accurate diagnosis. Unlike most other action languages that translate to ASP [4], Hybrid $\mathcal{ALE}$ translates to Hybrid ASP (H-ASP) [2] - an extension of ASP that allows ASP-like rules to interact with outside sources.

© Springer Nature Switzerland AG 2020
E. Komendantskaya and Y. A. Liu (Eds.): PADL 2020, LNCS 12007, pp. 73–81, 2020.
https://doi.org/10.1007/978-3-030-39197-3_5

In this paper we describe our work at Google Inc. on automating diagnosing of pipeline failures using Hybrid $\mathcal{ALE}$. Our diagnostic system is deployed on a limited number of pipelines. We start by specifying the requirements and by motivating the use of an action language based approach in general and Hybrid $\mathcal{ALE}$ in particular. We then review Hybrid $\mathcal{ALE}$, and introduce Diagnostic Modeling Library - a component providing an abstraction layer on top of Hybrid $\mathcal{ALE}$. The use of Diagnostic Modeling Library simplifies model creation. We then discuss generating explanations and suggestions and give an overview of our system.

1 Requirements

Once on-calls receives a notification of a pipeline's failure, they typically have to perform the following tasks:

1. Determine the (most likely) causes of failure.
2. Obtain a detailed description of the failure, including possibly error messages produced by the failed job and other relevant information.
3. Understand why the failure has occurred.
4. Determine how to repair the failure.
5. Proceed with the repair.

Determining the causes of failure is only the first step in the repair process. An ideal system for helping on-calls would automate steps 1–5. In our work we focus on automating steps 1–4.

On-calls often operate at the description level of individual jobs, jobs' inputs and outputs. This is the lowest description level where failure and success can be quickly and effectively determined. This fact determines the types of models we focus on. Such a model can be represented as an acyclic digraph (dependency graph), where vertices are jobs and an edge from A to B represents the fact that some of the outputs of A are inputs of B. For such a model, the process of diagnosing the source of failure consists of starting with vertices without in-edges, and performing a breadth-first search to determine the earliest set of vertices whose corresponding jobs have failed.

We now formulate the following engineering requirements for our system:

1. Provide a mechanism facilitating efficient creation of diagnostic models capable of the following: identifying pipeline jobs, describing dependencies between jobs, describing jobs' termination status.
2. Provide a mechanism for determining termination status of individual jobs (based on the external data sources)
3. Provide a mechanism for describing multiple possible diagnoses
4. Provide a mechanism for explaining the diagnoses in a user understandable form (possibly by gathering information from external data sources)
5. Provide a mechanism for generating suggestions for repairing the failures (possibly by gathering information from external data sources)

These requirements don't necessitate an action language based approach. We could create a library for describing dependency graphs that would model the pipelines. We could then provide mechanisms for association callbacks with graph vertices to determine the termination status of the corresponding jobs based on the external data sources. Our library would use the dependency graph to identify sources of failure. We could provide additional mechanisms for associating callbacks to generate explanations and suggestions. In the cases when uncertainty exists, multiple trajectories would be examined.

There are two main reasons for choosing an action language based approach:

1. Availability of necessary functionality.
   (a) Answer set semantics provides a convenient mechanism for reasoning about multiple trajectories.
   (b) Action languages provide an elegant formalism for describing actions and their consequences, thus facilitating model creation.
2. Extensibility.
   (a) Typically, requirements of the software systems change over time. Because of that, a diagnostic system has to be easily extensible. Using formal languages as the basis for creating diagnostic models facilitates extensibility vs. an ad-hoc system.

Hybrid $\mathcal{ALE}$ provides an additional convenience: a principled way to combine arbitrary algorithms with the ASP-like rules, and a principled way to pass arbitrary data between such algorithms.

2   Hybrid $\mathcal{ALE}$

We now review action language Hybrid $\mathcal{ALE}$. A key concept related to action languages is that of a *transition diagram*, which is a labeled directed graph, where vertices are states of a dynamic domain, and edge labels are subsets of actions. An edge indicates that the simultaneous execution of the actions in the label of an edge can transform a source state into a destination state. The transformation is not necessarily deterministic, and for a given source state there can be multiple edges having different destination states, labeled with the same set of actions. In Hybrid $\mathcal{ALE}$, one considers *hybrid transition diagrams*, which are directed graphs with two types of vertices: action states and domain states. A *domain state* is a pair $(A, \mathbf{p})$ where A is a set of propositional atoms and $\mathbf{p}$ is a vector of sequences of 0s and 1s. We can think of A as a set of Boolean properties of a system, and $\mathbf{p}$ as a description of the parameters used by external computations called *domain parameters* and time. We let $\mathbf{q}|_{domain}$ denote a vector of domain parameters only. An *action state* is a tuple $(A, \mathbf{p}, a)$ where A and $\mathbf{p}$ are as in the domain state, and a is a set of actions. An out edge from a domain state must have an action state as its destination. An out edge from an action state must have a domain state as its destination. Moreover, if $(A, \mathbf{p})$ is a domain state that has an out-edge to an action state $(B, \mathbf{r}, a)$, then $A = B$ and $\mathbf{p}|_{domain} = \mathbf{r}|_{domain}$. We note that there is a simple bijection between the set of transition diagrams and the set of hybrid transition diagrams.

In Hybrid $\mathcal{ALE}$, there are two types of atoms: *fluents* and *actions*. There are two types of parameters: *domain parameters* and *time*. The fluents are partitioned into *inertial* and *default*. A *domain literal* l is a fluent atom p or its negation $\neg p$. The domain parameters are partitioned into *inertial* and *default*.

A *domain algorithm* is a Boolean algorithm P such that for all generalized positions $\mathbf{q}$ and $\mathbf{r}$, if $\mathbf{q}|_{domain} = \mathbf{r}|_{domain}$, then $P(\mathbf{q}) = P(\mathbf{r})$. An *action algorithm* is an advancing algorithm A such that for all $\mathbf{q}$ and for all $\mathbf{r} \in A(\mathbf{q})$, $time(\mathbf{r}) = time(\mathbf{q}) + 1$. For an action algorithm A, the signature of A, $sig(A)$, is the vector of parameter indices $i_1, ..., i_k$ of domain parameters fixed by A.

Hybrid $\mathcal{ALE}$ allows the following types of statements.

1. **Default declaration for fluents:** *default fluent l*
2. **Default declaration for parameters:** *default parameter i with value w*
3. **Causal laws:** *a causes $\langle l, L \rangle$ with A if $p_0, ..., p_m : P$,*
4. **State constraints:** *$\langle l, L \rangle$ if $p_0, ..., p_m : P$,*
5. **Noconcurrency condition**: *impossible $a_0, ..., a_k$ if $p_0, ..., p_m : P$,*
6. **Allow condition:** *allow a if $p_0, ..., p_m : P$,*
7. **Trigger condition:** *trigger a if $p_0, ..., p_m : P$,*
8. **Inhibition condition:** *inhibit a if $p_0, ..., p_m : P$*

where l is a domain literal, i is a parameter index, w is a parameter value, a is an action, A is an action algorithm, $i_0, ..., i_k$ are parameter indices, L and P are domain algorithms, $p_0, ..., p_m$ are domain literals, and $a_0, ..., a_k$ are actions $k \geq 0$ and $m \geq -1$. If L or P are omitted then the algorithm T is substituted.

A *default declaration for fluents* declares a default fluent and specifies its default value. If l is a positive literal, then the default value is *true*, and if l is a negative fluent then the default value is *false*. A *default declaration for parameters* declares that i is a default parameter and that w is its default value. A *causal law* specifies that if $p_0, ..., p_m$ hold and P is true when a occurs, then l holds and L is true after the occurrence of a. In addition, after a occurs, the values of the parameters $sig(A)$ are specified by the output of the action algorithm A. A *state constraint* specifies that whenever $p_0, ..., p_m$ hold and P is true, l also holds and L is true. A *noconcurrency condition* specifies that whenever $p_0, ..., p_m$ hold and P is true, $a_0, ..., a_k$ cannot occur concurrently pairwise. An *allow condition* specifies that whenever $p_0, ..., p_m$ hold and P is true, an action a can occur (although not necessarily so). A *trigger condition* specifies that whenever $p_0, ..., p_m$ hold and P is true, an action a necessarily occurs (unless inhibited). An *inhibition condition* specifies that whenever $p_0, ..., p_m$ hold and P is true, action a cannot occur. A *system description* SD is a set of Hybrid $\mathcal{ALE}$ statements.

We omit the definition of semantics of Hybrid $\mathcal{ALE}$ for brevity. Interested readers are encouraged to consult [1].

3   Diagnostic Modeling Library

While creating diagnostic models using Hybrid $\mathcal{ALE}$ we have noticed repeated modeling patterns. In addition, requiring engineers to learn Hybrid $\mathcal{ALE}$ restricts the adoption of our diagnostic system. The Diagnostic Modeling Library encapsulates several modeling patterns expressed in Hybrid $\mathcal{ALE}$, and provides a convenient interface requiring a minimal understanding of action languages that focuses on a job as a basic modeling unit.

job := DeclareJob(job_name, job_prereqs): declares a job *job_name*. *job_prereqs* specifies job's dependencies. The function specifies a single action *do(job_name)*, which is triggered if the prerequisites *job_prereqs* are satisfied. In order to add failure modes, *AllowFailure* or *TriggerFailure* functions need to be used in addition to *DeclareJob*. It's Hybrid $\mathcal{ALE}$ translation is:

> *default fluent finished_default(job_name)*
> *do(job_name) causes finished_default(job_name)*
> *finished(job_name) if finished_default(job_name)*
> *trigger do(job_name) if job_prereqs, -finished(job_name)*
> *succeeded(job_name) if finished_default(job_name), -failed(job_name)*

job.AllowFailure(failure_type, failure_prereqs, FailureCheck, Failure-Callback): specifies that a failure of type *failure_type* for the job can occur if *failure_prereqs* are satisfied and *FailureCheck* domain algorithm returns true. If the failure occurs, then the parameters in the consequent state are partly determined by *FailureCallback* action algorithm. The Hybrid $\mathcal{ALE}$ translation is:

> *allow failure_type(job.job_name) if job.job_prereqs, failure_prereqs,*
>   *-finished(job.job_name): FailureCheck*
> *failure type(job job_name) causes failure(job.job_namc) with FailureCallback*

job.TriggerFailure(failure_type, failure_prereqs, FailureCheck, Failure-Callback): specifies that a failure of type *failure_type* for the job is triggered if *failure_prereqs* are satisfied and *FailureCheck* domain algorithm returns true. If the failure occurs, then the parameters in the consequent state are partly determined by *FailureCallback* action algorithm. The Hybrid $\mathcal{ALE}$ translation is:

> *trigger failure_type(job.job_name) if job.job_prereqs, failure_prereqs,*
>   *-finished(job.job_name): FailureCheck*
> *failure_type(job.job_name) causes failure(job.job_name) with FailureCallback*

job.ValidateSuccess(invalidation_prereqs, InvalidationAlg): allows to invalidate a trajectory in case of job's success. In particular, if the job succeeds and *invalidation_prereqs* are satisfied and *InvalidationAlg* - a domain algorithm returns true, the trajectory becomes invalid. The Hybrid $\mathcal{ALE}$ translation is:

FALSE if finished_default(job.job_name), succeeded(job.job_name),
  invalidation_prereqs: InvalidationAlg

Here *FALSE* is a special fluent that results in the trajectory becoming invalid.

job.ValidateFailure(invalidation_prereqs, InvalidationAlg): allows to invalidate a trajectory in case of job's failure. In particular, if the job fails and *invalidation_prereqs* are satisfied and *InvalidationAlg* - a domain algorithm returns true, the trajectory becomes invalid. The Hybrid $\mathcal{ALE}$ translation is:

FALSE if finished_default(job.job_name), failed(job.job_name),
  invalidation_prereqs: InvalidationAlg

This is an incomplete interface. Nevertheless, the five functions above are the most commonly used.

As an example the library usage, let's suppose that our pipeline consists of three jobs: A, B and C. Job B is dependent on job A, and job C is dependent on job B. Suppose that it is possible to determine whether job A has failed by using *AFailureCheck* algorithm, and it is possible to determine whether job C failed by using *CFailureCheck* algorithm. It is not possible to determine whether job B failed by any readily available algorithm. Nevertheless, we know that if job C succeeds, then job B must have succeeded. We can capture this information in the following model, with lines started with '#' indicating comments, and symbol '_' indicating an empty argument:

```
# Declare job A with no prerequisites
jobA := DeclareJob(A, _)
# Specify that AFailureCheck identifies A's failure
jobA.TriggerFailure(failure, _, AFailureCheck, _)
# Declare job B dependent on job A
jobB := DeclareJob(B, finished(A))
# Specify that job B can fail
jobB.AllowFailure(failure, _, _, _)
# Declare job C dependent on job B
jobC := DeclareJob(C, finished(B))
# Specify that CFailureCheck identifies C's failure
jobC.TriggerFailure(failure, _, CFailureCheck, _)
# Specify that job C's success invalidates job B's failure
jobC.ValidateSuccess(failed(B), _)
```

4 Generating Explanations and Suggestions

Repairing the failures of pipelines can be facilitated if the diagnostic software provides explanations or other relevant information about the source of the failure, and if the diagnostic software provides the suggestions for repairing.

Both the explanations and the suggestions can be specific to a trajectory and to a failure. We did not attempt to solve the problem of automatic generation of explanation and suggestions based on the formal model of a diagnosed system. Nevertheless, we have made some initial steps in providing useful additional information about the failures and possible ways to repair them to on-calls.

Our approach uses a combination user-generated information and information from outside sources about the failure. Often, engineers familiar with a pipeline can provide a short list of failure descriptions and another list with suggestions for repairing. These can be integrated with the diagnostic model with the help of lookup tables. In the tables, both explanations and suggestions are keyed by an action representing a failure or by a specific fluent generated during a failure. Messages in the tables can be automatically customized based on the date or other parameters specific to the particular diagnosing evaluation, thus making them more helpful to on-calls.

Additional information about the failures can be retrieved from the outside data sources using action algorithms. In the modeling diagnostic library, both *AllowFailure* and *TriggerFailure* functions can be evoked with *FailureCallback* action algorithm. *FailureCallback* algorithm can retrieve information, such as error messages generated by the failed job and use it to generate an explanation recorded in *explanation(job_name)* parameter in the consequent state. When a diagnosis is reported, the value of *explanation(job_name)* parameter is reported as well. A similar mechanism can also be used to generate suggestions based on the information from outside sources. Such an explanation or a suggestion is reported together with an associated action or a fluent, thus providing a more meaningful description of the failure.

5   Job Termination Status and Automatic Model Generation

Data processing pipelines at Google are typically run using Borg system [6]. This provides several advantages. First, data processing pipelines are described using BCL configuration files [6]. A BCL description of a pipeline contains a description of all the jobs in the pipeline as well as the dependencies. Second, in many cases, it is possible to determine whether a particular job run failed or succeeded using the Borg monitoring system, and in some cases to retrieve error messages generated by the failed jobs as well as other relevant information.

We have used these features of the Borg system for the following:

1. To facilitate automatic creation of basic diagnostic models using the Model Diagnostic Library
2. To automatically determine job's run's termination status as well to automatically generate failure explanations by retrieving error messages generated during job's run
3. When the automatically generated model is insufficient, it can serve as a skeleton for a more detailed manually enhanced model.

This architecture is illustrated in Fig. 1. Pipeline configuration is used by model generator to create a model. The automatically created model contains

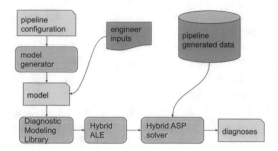

Fig. 1. Diagnostic system architecture.

callbacks that access data relevant for determining jobs' termination status. The model can then be refined with the help of the engineers familiar with the pipeline. The model is expressed using diagnostic library. Diagnostic library translates the model into a Hybrid $\mathcal{ALE}$ description, and Hybrid $\mathcal{ALE}$ description is further translated into Hybrid ASP. Hybrid ASP solver then uses the model to generate diagnoses, and possibly explanations and suggestions.

6   Conclusion

In this paper we discussed our work on a system deployed on a limited number of pipelines at Google Inc. for automating diagnosing of pipeline failures using action language Hybrid $\mathcal{ALE}$. We specified the requirements that guided our work, and motivated the use of Hybrid $\mathcal{ALE}$. To simplify model creation we introduced Diagnostic Modeling Library - a component providing an abstraction layer on top of Hybrid $\mathcal{ALE}$. We discussed initial progress in extending the functionality of a diagnostic system to include explanation and suggestion generation - the functionality that makes a diagnostic system more useful for on-calls. We reviewed the architecture of our system: from automatic model generation, and manual model refinement to generating diagnosis based on the model and external data. Our approach is generally applicable and is not Google-specific.

References

1. Bomanson, J., Brik, A.: Diagnosing data pipeline failures using action languages. In: Balduccini, M., Lierler, Y., Woltran, S. (eds.) LPNMR 2019. LNCS, vol. 11481, pp. 181–194. Springer, Cham (2019). https://doi.org/10.1007/978-3-030-20528-7_14
2. Brik, A., Remmel, J.B.: Hybrid ASP. In: Gallagher, J.P., Gelfond, M. (eds.) ICLP (Technical Communications). LIPIcs, vol. 11, pp. 40–50. Schloss Dagstuhl - Leibniz-Zentrum fuer Informatik (2011)
3. Gelfond, M., Kahl, Y.: Knowledge Representation, Reasoning, and the Design of Intelligent Agents: The Answer-Set Programming Approach. Cambridge University Press, Cambridge (2014)

4. Gelfond, M., Lifschitz, V.: The stable model semantics for logic programming. In: ICLP/SLP, pp. 1070–1080 (1988)
5. Gelfond, M., Lifschitz, V.: Action languages. Electron. Trans. Artif. Intell. **2**, 193–210 (1998)
6. Verma, A., Pedrosa, L., Korupolu, M., Oppenheimer, D., Tune, E., Wilkes, J.: Large-scale cluster management at Google with Borg. In: Proceedings of the European Conference on Computer Systems (EuroSys). ACM, Bordeaux (2015)

VRASP: A Virtual Reality Environment for Learning Answer Set Programming

Vinh T. Nguyen[1(✉)], Yuanlin Zhang[1], Kwanghee Jung[1], Wanli Xing[2], and Tommy Dang[1]

[1] Texas Tech University, Lubbock, TX 79409, USA
{vinh.nguyen,y.zhang,kwanghee.jung,tommy.dang}@ttu.edu
[2] University of Florida, Gainesville, FL 32611, USA
wanli.xing@coe.ufl.edu

Abstract. Answer Set Programming (ASP) is a dominant programming paradigm in Knowledge Representation. It is used to build intelligent agents – knowledge-intensive software systems capable of exhibiting intelligent behaviors. It is found that ASP can also be used to teach computer science in middle and high schools. However, the current ASP systems do not provide direct support for a programmer to produce an intelligent agent that a general user can directly interact with, which may greatly compromise the potential attraction of ASP to the secondary school students. In this paper, we propose a Virtual Reality (VR) programming environment called *VRASP* that allows a student to produce an avatar (agent) in a virtual world that is able to answer questions in spoken natural language from a general user. The VR application is accessible from anywhere so that the students' friends can interact with the agent. As a result, it gives the students a feeling of achievement and thus encourages them to solve problems using ASP. *VRASP* was evaluated with 10 users. Results of these studies show that students are able to communicate with the environment intuitively with an accuracy of 78%.

Keywords: ASP solver · Virtual Agent · Virtual Reality · SPARC programming

1 Introduction

Answer Set Programming (ASP) is a promising language paradigm for teaching Computing and for the integration of teaching Computing and STEM (i.e., science, technology, engineering, and mathematics) in K-12 (for kindergarten to 12th grade). ASP is a language for developing intelligent agents – knowledge-intensive software systems capable of exhibiting intelligent behaviors, and allows students to write the mathematical model underlying those agents. With a well-developed theory, efficient reasoning systems (which are usually called ASP *solvers*) and representation methodology, ASP has found numerous applications [2]. It is also found that ASP can be used to teach computing and its

© Springer Nature Switzerland AG 2020
E. Komendantskaya and Y. A. Liu (Eds.): PADL 2020, LNCS 12007, pp. 82–91, 2020.
https://doi.org/10.1007/978-3-030-39197-3_6

integration with other subjects in middle and high schools [16,17]. However, the-state-of-the-art ASP programming environments stop at the mathematical models, i.e., ASP programs, queries and getting answer sets. As a result, the K-12 ASP students can only show their friends or parents a mathematical model, instead of a direct interactive intelligent agent. In this regard, it is difficult for their friends or parents to quickly appreciate their programs. Therefore, the student's motivation might not be as high as ASP allows. Many studies in the literature have shown that students' performance in terms of computational thinking, problem-solving, productivity and creativity will be improved in accordance with the increasing motivation [12]. This motivation can be affected by student's friends, peers or parents. For example, a previous research conducted by Resnic and colleagues [12] described a case study where a 13-year-old girl developed a series of how to programming projects when she was motivated by her followers by using Scratch - a visual programming environment that allows children (primarily ages 8 to 16) to learn computer programming. Her astonishing productivity thus did influence, inspire, and propagate to other young students in the long run. Yet, to achieve this result, an easy to use supporting environment plays a critical role for helping students to transcribe an idea to a production work. To motivate K-12 students to learn Computing through ASP and address the issue mentioned before, we design and implement a prototype of a web-based programming environment *VRASP*. Using *VRASP*, the student is able to create an intelligent agent inside a virtual reality (VR) environment. Specifically, the students can use an editor in *VRASP* to develop an ASP program for the agent using the ASP syntax, customize the default VR environment, and "run" the VR environment. Once they are happy with the agent and its environment, they can publish the artifact through a URL link. A general user with this link can interact with the agent, through the VR environment, by asking questions in spoken English. Our main motivation in this study was to leverage the advantages of VR technology with an affordable Head Mounted Display headset (i.e., Google Cardboard). We expect the development of this new artifact will help motivate students' interests in learning Computing through ASP and help them to obtain a feeling of accomplishment through the sharing of their products with their friends or parents without any knowledge in Computing. We carried out a very preliminary evaluation of this web-based programming environment using 10 real users.

The remainder of the paper is organized as follows: Sect. 2 summarizes similar work. Section 3 addresses theoretical foundations underlying *VRASP* and the system design and simulation process. The evaluation design and results are reported in Sect. 4 and we conclude our paper with future work in Sect. 5.

2   Related Work

The use of VR has proven to be an effective means in education in many studies [3]. They showed increase in both students' motivation and test scores. Existing studies pose several challenges for adapting VR technology widely in K-12 sector such as: (1) the lack of HMD devices to suite the needs of students, (2) the complexity of creating virtual world, which requires a dedicated 3D software, making it difficult for children to learn and share their work. Thus, to fill this gap there is a need to have a friendly programming environment that enables users to create, manipulate and share their work with ease, especially in the context of learning declarative programming. Recently, web-based VR has emerged as a new trend to bring VR experience to a larger audience [10,13]. Kao and Harrell [4] presented a research on the impact of the avatar types on student performance and engagement. Alice [1] is a visual programming language with an integrated development environment (IDE). It allows the programmers to use drag-and-drop to create computer animations using 3D models. Studies show that Alice helps to improve both retention rate and students' learning outcomes. Recently, Vosinakis et al. [15] proposed a programming environment – MeLoISE – for students to learn PROLOG, a classical Logic Programming language. In this environment, the students can create scenarios in a 3D virtual world. For every scenario created, the programming environment automatically generates a PROLOG program to represent the scenario. The students can edit the program, ask queries to this program and see the answers in window.

3   The *VRASP* Design

Our web-based system is an extension of *onlineSPARC* [7]. onlineSPARC provides an online programming environment for SPARC, a recent ASP variant with type. However, onlineSPARC does not provide a materialized agent that a general user can interact with. Our proposed application is positioned as a supplemental learning/teaching material rather than replacing it. We assume that students have basic knowledge of ASP program before using the VR application.

Theoretical Foundations: The design of *VRASP* is influenced by three areas of theoretical frameworks. The first one is learning by design [5]. Designing an intelligent agent to solve daily life or STEM problems is at the core of the Logic Programming based approach to learning Computing and STEM [16]. *VRASP* is designed to directly support this approach, by materializing an intelligent agent into an avatar in a virtual reality. Therefore, instead of using traditional way to ask students to choose from a list of avatars, we require students to design the avatars and related rules by himself to promote their learning of practical skills (e.g., computational thinking design, visual design, and art). Second, our research also broadly resides in embodied cognition [6] where students are embodied as an avatar to interaction with the virtual environment. Such embodiment has been shown to improve students' learning in various settings and contexts [11]. Third, we also trace back our design to classical multimedia learning theories [8]. In addition to the dynamic visual presentation of the avatar and its VR environment to the student, we also implement the audio interaction between the student and VRASP.

The Intelligent Agent Design: The design of the materialized intelligent agent is as follows: (a) The agent is an avatar inside a virtual reality environment, and in spoken English, a general user can ask questions to the agent which will answer in turn.

Fig. 1. The *VRASP* learning interface. (1) ASP editor, (2) sharing with a URL, (3) sharing with a QR code, (4) VR editor, and (5) changing between VR and 3D mode

The default VR programming environment is a virtual room shown in Fig. 1 where the intelligent agent is the avatar. Users can navigate the room and interact with the agent using natural spoken English. The navigation is performed by using keyboard arrow buttons on a traditional computer or by hand moving actions on devices with a touch screen. When a user moves to a location close enough to the agent, the agent will say some random welcome sentences that are pre-defined by users to indicate that it is aware of the user and is ready to answer questions. When a user moves far away from the agent, his/her speech will not be able to raise the attention of the agent.

The *VRASP* Interface Design: The *VRASP* has two components:

– Programming component: an editor for students to create and edit an ASP program, and an interface for editing the agent avatar and its VR environment.

– Avatar and VR environment enacting component: once a student completes the ASP program and the design of the VR environment, *VRASP* is able to create the environment and the agent so that an end user can interact with them. The resulting VR environment is shareable to anyone through an URL link or a QR code.

The *VRASP* programming environment is shown in Fig. 1. The programming component is achieved through the two buttons (1) (for editing the ASP program) and (4) (for editing the visual aspect of the VR environment) in Fig. 1. The ASP editor (see Fig. 2a) allows students to create the ASP program.

Figure 2b illustrates the VR editor where students can leverage their creative design to add new 3D objects to the scene, modify objects' appearance (e.g., texture, color), and position them in the scene.

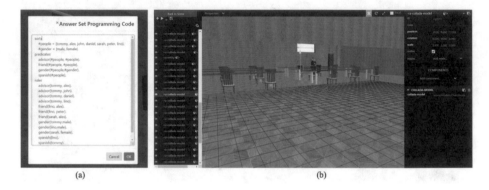

(a)   (b)

Fig. 2. (a) The ASP editor for students to edit their SPARC programs, (b) the VR editor which allows users to customize the virtual 3D environment such as adding model, change position, location, and scale of a 3D object

Once students end the edits and save the results, *VRASP* enacts the intelligent agent and its VR environment for students to test them. When the students are satisfied with their agent and VR environment, they can share it by clicking button (2) to get an URL for it or button (3) a QR code. A user simply uses their mobile device to scan the QR code, and the browser will automatically navigate to the URL of the intelligent agent. With a modern cell phone and an affordable headset (e.g., Google Cardboard), users are able to experience the Virtual Reality by enabling the VR mode as in button (5) of Fig. 1.

The Design for Implementing *VRASP*: To implement *VRASP* (see demo at [9]) programming environment, the following modules were developed: (1) the main control algorithm - the user interface of *VRASP* (Fig. 1) can be thought of as a menu system, the main control algorithm is straightforward. For example, when the ASP editor is clicked, the editing interface (Fig. 2a) will show up and once the editing is finished, the system will show the main user interface. (2) edit ASP program and VR environment - the ASP editor we use is a HTML text editor and (3) enact the avatar and its VR environment. The avatar behavior can be carried out by the following steps:

– Get the question input as a voice and translate the speech into text t. We use the Web Speech API to achieve this translation. The speech recognition service will check the speech input against a list of grammar. When a word or phrase is successfully recognised, it is returned as a result as a text string.
– The question in text will be translated into an ASP query q. Details can be found in the following section.
– The SPARC solver will be called with the ASP program for the agent and the query q. The SPARC solver will return the answer(s) to q.
– The answer(s) will be translated into text which in turn is translated into audio via *Speech Synthesis*. Generally speaking, the synthesized speech is created by concatenating pieces of recorded speech that are stored in a database.

Translate Questions in Text to ASP Queries: We will use a very rudimentary method for our prototype implementation of *VRASP*. The translation is based on a *dictionary* that consists of pairs (S, Q) where S is a string representing an "abstract" question and Q is the ASP query for S. The "abstract" questions represent the substantives of the variations of a question in text. For example, consider the relation of $friend(X, Y)$. We will answer only two type of questions: yes/no-questions and what question. In the yes/no questions, we extract the objects and the relations among them from the question text. For what-questions, we also need to extract the variables. These questions are in a rather regular text format. But the form of the questions from different people may still vary. Consider the program in Fig. 2a, we can have questions such as "Is Alex a friend of Lino?" or "Who are the friends of Alex?" The substance in the first question is Alex, friend and Lino. So, the "abstract" question for the first one is "alex, friend, lino". The query for this question is $friend(alex, lino)$.

So, a dictionary example could be

```
("alex friend lino": friend(alex, lino)).
("lino friend alex": friend(lino, alex)).
("Who friend alex": friend(X, alex)).
```

To build the dictionary, we extract all relations (i.e., predicates) from the ASP program. For each relation we figure out the abstract questions for yes/no and what questions on this relation and the queries for such questions. For any question in text, we will compare it with each abstract question in the dictionary using *cosine similarity* (a measure of similarity between two non-zero vectors with a score from 0 to 1). For comparison, each string has to be translated into a component vector - a vector of string. For example, the component vector A of *"alex friend lino"* is [-al,ale, lex, ex_, x_f, _fr, fri, rie, ien, end, nd_, d_l, lin, ino, no-].

Let the cv be the function mapping a string to its component vector. The cosine similarity between two strings defined as follows:

$$Score(A, B) = \frac{cv(A).cv(B)}{||cv(A)||\,||cv(B)||} \tag{1}$$

where A and B are two strings. $\alpha.\beta$ is the dot product of vectors α and β, and $||\alpha||$ is the norm/magnitude of vector α. Our pattern matching based algorithm to convert text to ASP query has a limitation in dealing with negations in a sentence. For example, if one asks "Isn't Alex a friend of Lino?", it will syntactically match "Is Alex a friend of Lino?", which is the complete opposite; in the future, we will work on solving this issue.

To translate a question in text to a query, we compare it with the "abstract" questions in the dictionary and find the one with the highest cosine similarity or randomly select the one with the same ranked score. Then we use the query, for this "abstract" question, as the translation of the question given in text.

4   Evaluation

4.1   Evaluation Design

Users in our study can be defined as the end users who experience the product (i.e., family members, friends, etc.) and communicate with the system via a natural spoken language. Thus, the system's ability to create an uninterrupted communication channel plays an important role in contributing to the completeness of the application. To measure how likely the proposed system can meet the desired goal. In this experiment, we seek to answer the research questions, namely (1) to what extent the application can response accurately to the questions posed by users? The term *accuracy* is defined as whether a speech is mapped correctly to its query. (2) Which part of the proposed application needs to improve?

We recruited 10 volunteers, including seven males and three females from the Computer Science Department to participate in this study. Eight of them are PhD students and the other two are pursuing master degree. All participants were introduced the purpose of the study, the type of information collected, the application design and how it works. Each user will be given approximated 30 min in the study. There are two phases in our study design, the first phase involves training stage where users get to know the system by editing simple SPARC program. When users finished the training process, they moved to the second phase. In this stage, participants were given a set of questions proposed by the evaluator to communicate with the system. The proposed questions were based on the SPARC program shown in Fig. 2a.

4.2   Result

Table 1 shows the results of the speech-to-query transcribing accuracy. It can be seen that the Web Speech API can recognize a majority of different voices, except for the first, third and fourth questions. Overall, the API can correctly recognize 78/100 speeches (accounted for 78%). After analyzing the transcript (speech to text) for each user, we found that the API misinterprets the word *"whom"* with *"home"* and *"lino"* with *"selena"* or *"lee no"*.

Table 1. Accuracy results in testing phase ($\sqrt{}$ is for the correct answers, *empty* is for incorrect answers)

Users	Q1	Q2	Q3	Q4	Q5	Q6	Q7	Q8	Q9	Q10
User 1		√			√	√	√	√	√	√
User 2		√	√		√	√	√	√	√	√
User 3		√		√	√	√	√	√	√	√
User 4		√				√	√	√	√	√
User 5		√	√	√	√	√	√	√	√	√
User 6		√			√	√	√	√	√	√
User 7	√	√	√	√	√	√	√	√	√	√
User 8		√		√			√		√	√
User 9		√	√	√	√	√	√	√	√	√
User 10		√			√	√	√	√	√	√
Total √ answer	1	10	4	5	8	9	10	9	10	10

User's Feedback: To further improve and iterative refine the proposed application, we asked users for feedback on the application design in terms of the visual layout design, interactivity, and ease of use. Responses from users suggest that the study should revise and rephrase the questions and choose words in such a way that the Web Speech API would be able to recognize the speech easier.

5 Conclusion and Future Work

In this paper, we introduced *VRASP*, a programming environment that allows students of ASP to build intelligent agents as avatars in a VR environment, capable of answering questions from general users using spoken English. The programming environment is expected to offer students a more concrete feeling of an intelligent agent and a feeling of achievement by building and sharing an intelligent agent capable of interacting with the general audience. We would argue that by sharing the programming environment with their peers, students' motivation would be increased and thus the learning performance would be amplified.

In future work, we will apply more sophisticated methods including machine learning and natural language processing techniques to improve speech recognition accuracy and the formulation of queries from the text. We note the work on the translation of text to formal languages, e.g., [14] providing a NL2KR platform for this purpose. However, these systems usually need training. Our translation method is simple and no training is needed, but translation accuracy might not be the as competitive as the existing work. In the future, we will develop more robust and easy to use translation algorithms based on the existing work.

Acknowledgement. We thank the anonymous reviewers for their comments which improve this paper significantly. Zhang is partially supported by NSF grant DRL-1901704.

References

1. Cooper, S., Dann, W., Pausch, R.: Alice: a 3-D tool for introductory programming concepts. J. Comput. Sci. Coll **15**, 107–116 (2000)
2. Erdem, E., Gelfond, M., Leone, N.: Applications of answer set programming. AI Mag. **37**(3), 53–68 (2016)
3. Freina, L., Ott, M.: A literature review on immersive virtual reality in education: state of the art and perspectives. In: The International Scientific Conference eLearning and Software for Education, vol. 1, p. 133. "Carol I" National Defence University (2015)
4. Kao, D., Harrell, D.F.: Toward avatar models to enhance performance and engagement in educational games. In: 2015 IEEE Conference on Computational Intelligence and Games (CIG), pp. 246–253 (Aug 2015)
5. Kolodner, J.L., et al.: Problem-based learning meets case-based reasoning in the middle-school science classroom: Putting learning by design (TM) into practice. J. Learn. Sci. **12**(4), 495–547 (2003)
6. Lindgren, R., Johnson-Glenberg, M.: Emboldened by embodiment: six precepts for research on embodied learning and mixed reality. Educ. Res. **42**(8), 445–452 (2013)
7. Marcopoulos, E., Zhang, Y.: onlineSPARC: a programming environment for answer set programming. TPLP **19**(2), 262–289 (2019)
8. Mayer, R.E.: Cognitive theory of multimedia learning. Camb. Handb. Multimed. Learn. **41**, 31–48 (2005)
9. Nguyen, V.T.: VRASP demo, November 2019. https://github.com/Alex-Nguyen/VRASP
10. Nguyen, V.T., Hite, R., Dang, T.: Learners's technological acceptance of vr content development: a sequential 3-part use case study of diverse post-secondary students. Int. J. Semant. Comput. **13**(03), 343–366 (2019)
11. Pouw, W.T., Van Gog, T., Paas, F.: An embedded and embodied cognition review of instructional manipulatives. Educ. Psychol. Rev. **26**(1), 51–72 (2014)
12. Resnick, M., et al.: Scratch: programming for all. Commun. ACM **52**(11), 60–67 (2009)
13. T. Nguyen, V., Hite, R., Dang, T.: Web-based virtual reality development in classroom: from learner's perspectives. In: 2018 IEEE International Conference on Artificial Intelligence and Virtual Reality (AIVR), pp. 11–18, December 2018
14. Vo, N., Mitra, A., Baral, C.: The NL2KR platform for building natural language translation systems. In: Proceedings of the 53rd Annual Meeting of the Association for Computational Linguistics and the 7th International Joint Conference on Natural Language Processing (Volume 1: Long Papers), pp. 899–908 (2015)
15. Vosinakis, S., Anastassakis, G., Koutsabasis, P.: Teaching and learning logic programming in virtual worlds using interactive microworld representations. Br. J. Educ. Technol. **49**(1), 30–44 (2018)

16. Zhang, Y., Wang, J., Bolduc, F., Murray, W.G.: LP based integration of computing and science education in middle schools. In: Proceedings of the ACM Conference on Global Computing Education, CompEd, 17–19 May 2019, pp. 44–50 (2019)
17. Zhang, Y., Wang, J., Bolduc, F., Murray, W.G., Staffen, W.: A preliminary report of integrating science and computing teaching using logic programming. In: Proceedings of AAAI (2019, to appear)

Memory and Real-Time in Functional Programming

On the Effects of Integrating Region-Based Memory Management and Generational Garbage Collection in ML

Martin Elsman[1]([⊠])[iD] and Niels Hallenberg[2][iD]

[1] University of Copenhagen, Copenhagen, Denmark
mael@di.ku.dk
[2] SimCorp A/S, Copenhagen, Denmark
niels.hallenberg@simcorp.com

Abstract. We present a region-based memory management scheme with support for generational garbage collection. The scheme is implemented in the MLKit Standard ML compiler, which features a compile-time region inference algorithm. The compiler generates native x64 machine code and deploys region types at runtime to avoid write barrier problems and to support partly tag-free garbage collection. We measure the characteristics of the scheme, for a number of benchmarks, and compare it to the Mlton state-of-the-art Standard ML compiler and configurations of the MLKit with and without region inference and generational garbage collection enabled. Although region inference often serves the purpose of generations, we demonstrate that, in some cases, generational garbage collection combined with region inference is beneficial.

Keywords: Region inference · Generational garbage collection

1 Introduction

Region-based memory management allows for programmers to associate the lifetimes of objects with so-called regions and to reason about how and when such regions are allocated and deallocated. Region-based memory management, as it is implemented for instance in Rust [2], can be a valuable tool for constructing critical systems, such as real-time embedded systems [25]. Region inference differs from explicit region-based memory management by taking a non-annotated program as input and producing as output a region-annotated program, including directives for allocating and deallocating regions [27]. The result is a programming paradigm where programmers can learn to write region-friendly code (by following certain patterns [28]) for essential parts of a program and perhaps retain a combination of region inference and garbage collection [17] for programs (or the parts of a program) that are not time critical.

Both region-inference and generational garbage collection have been shown to manage short-lived values well. In this paper we present a framework that combines these techniques, and discuss the effects of the integration.

© Springer Nature Switzerland AG 2020
E. Komendantskaya and Y. A. Liu (Eds.): PADL 2020, LNCS 12007, pp. 95–112, 2020.
https://doi.org/10.1007/978-3-030-39197-3_7

The region-based memory management scheme that we consider is based on the stack discipline. Whenever e is some expression, region inference may decide to replace e with the term `letregion` ρ `in` e' `end`, where e' is the result of transforming the expression e, which includes annotating allocating expressions with particular region variables (e.g., ρ) specifying the region each value should be stored in. The semantics of the `letregion` term is first to allocate a region (initially an empty list of pages) on the region stack, bind the region to the region variable ρ, evaluate e', and, finally, deallocate the region bound to ρ (and its pages). The region type system allows regions to be passed to functions at run time (i.e., functions can be region-polymorphic) and to be captured in closures. The soundness of region inference ensures that a region is not deallocated as long as a value within it may be used by the remainder of the computation. When combining region inference and reference-tracing garbage collection, to remedy for the sometimes overly static approximation of liveness, we must be careful to rule out the possibility of deallocating regions with incoming pointers from live objects. Luckily, it turns out that such pointers can be ruled out by the region type system [8], which means that we can be sure that a tracing garbage collector will not be chasing dangling pointers at run time.

Our generational collector associates two generations with each region. It has the feature that an object is promoted to the old generation of its region (during a collection) only if it has survived a previous collection. Compared to the earlier non-generational collection technique [17], we may run a minor collection by only traversing (and copying) objects in the young generations.

The contributions of this paper are the following:

1. We present a technique for combining region-based memory management with a generational (stop the world) garbage collector, using a notion of typed regions, which allows us to deal with mutable data in minor collections and for tag-free representations of certain kinds of values such as tuples.
2. To demonstrate the absolute feasibility of the technique, we show empirically that the MLKit generates code that, in many cases, is comparable in performance to executables generated with the Mlton compiler (v20180207).
3. We demonstrate empirically that the combination of generational garbage collection and region-based memory management can lead to improved performance over using non-generational garbage collection but also that the increased memory waste (unused memory in region pages), caused by having multiple generations associated with each region, sometimes leads to an overhead compared to when a non-generational collection strategy is used.
4. We demonstrate empirically that when combined with generational garbage collection, region inference will take care of reclaiming most of the data in young generations with the effect that minor collections occur less often.

The study is performed in the context of the MLKit [28]. It generates native x64 machine code for Linux and macOS [9] and implements a number of techniques for refining the representations of regions [4,27], including dividing regions into stack allocated (bounded) regions and heap allocated regions.

The paper is organised as follows. In Sect. 2, we present the generational garbage collection algorithm and how the algorithm is extended to work with mutable and large objects. In Sect. 3, we present a number of experimental results. In Sect. 4, we describe related work, and in Sect. 5, we conclude.

2   Generational Garbage Collection

A *region descriptor* represents an unbounded region and consists of a pointer to the previous region descriptor on the stack (p), a generation descriptor for the young generation (g_y), a generation descriptor for the old generation (g_o), and a list (L) for large objects, which are objects that do not fit in a region page; see Fig. 1. Each *generation descriptor* (g) consists of a pointer to a list of fixed-sized region pages (fp) and an allocation pointer (a).

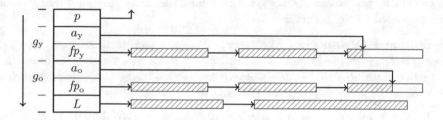

Fig. 1. A region descriptor on the down-growing stack. Region descriptors are linked, through "previous pointers" (p), hold generation descriptors (g_y and g_o), and hold a linked list of large objects (L).

The garbage collector we describe is a *generational* collector, which supports both minor and major collections. In a *minor* collection, only reachable objects allocated in young generations are traversed and *evacuated* (i.e., copied); those allocated in old generations are left untouched. In a *major* collection, all reachable objects are traversed and evacuated. In a minor collection, only reachable objects allocated in young generations are traversed, but a minor collection does not differentiate between in which region an object is stored, as there can be pointers from objects in newer regions to objects in older regions.

Consider a region r_2 above a region r_1 on the stack, with two generations each. This scenario allows for *deep* pointers from r_2 pointing to objects in region r_1 as shown in Fig. 2 (labeled 1 to 4) and *shallow* pointers pointing from objects allocated in region r_1 into objects allocated in region r_2 (labeled 5 to 8). Shallow pointers only exist between regions allocated in the same `letregion` construct, which is a sufficient requirement to rule out the possibility of dangling pointers [8,17]. The scheme that we first describe does not allow for pointers to point from an old generation to a young generation (i.e., the pointers labeled 3 and 7); mutable objects, which may violate this principle, are treated later in Sect. 2.3.

When an object in a young generation of a region is evacuated, the object may be promoted to the old generation of the region. The collector implements

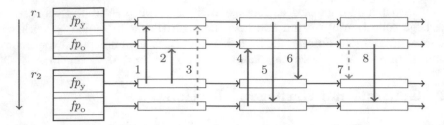

Fig. 2. Possible and impossible pointers. Impossible pointers are those that are dashed. The stack grows downwards. Shallow pointers (e.g., pointers from values in r_1 to values in r_2) are allowed only between regions that are allocated and deallocated simultaneously (e.g., a list's elements are stored independently from the spine of the list.)

the following promotion strategy, which guarantees that only long-living values are promoted to old generations:

Definition 1 (Promotion Strategy). *Promote objects when they have survived precisely one collection. The first time a value in a region r is evacuated, the value stays allocated in the young generation. During the following garbage collection, the value is promoted (moved) to the old generation of r.*

During a minor garbage collection, objects that have survived one collection must be promoted to the old generation, whereas objects that have not yet survived a collection should remain in the young generation. However, the implementation must preserve a *generation upward-closure* property, which states that, after a collection, whenever a value v has been promoted to an old generation, all values v' pointed to by v are also residing in old generations.

Figure 3 shows two regions and their young generations. The *black areas* contain objects that have survived one collection. The *white areas* signify objects that have been allocated since the last collection. Objects allocated in the black areas will be promoted to an old generation and objects allocated in the white area will stay allocated in a young generation. Figure 3 shows different combinations of pointers from white and black areas into white and black areas.

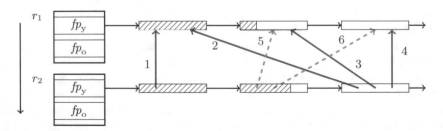

Fig. 3. The black areas contain objects that have survived one collection and white areas contain objects allocated since the last collection.

To implement the promotion strategy, the generation upward-closure invariant must disallow values in black areas to point at values in white areas (pointers 5 and 6 in Fig. 3):

Definition 2 (Generation Upward-Closure). *If a value resides in an old generation and points to a value v' then v' resides in an old generation. If a value resides in a black area in a young generation and points to a value v' then v' resides in an old generation or in a black area in a young generation.*

We now argue that the promotion strategy satisfies the Generation Upward-Closure invariant. The argument is a case-by-case analysis of the possible pointers shown in Fig. 3 (pointers 1, 2, 3, and 4), where each pointer takes the form $v_2 \rightarrow v_1$ and where v_2 is allocated in r_2 and v_1 is allocated in r_1:

Pointer 1. Both v_2 and v_1 reside in black areas, which means that, given v_2 is live, they will both be promoted to old generations according to the promotion strategy. The possibly promoted pointer will thus trivially satisfy Definition 2, part 1.

Pointer 2. If v_2 is live then it will be promoted to the black area of the young generation while v_1 is promoted to the old generation. The possibly promoted pointer will trivially satisfy Definition 2, part 2.

Pointer 3. Both v_2 and v_1 reside in white areas of young generations, which means that, given v_2 is live, they will both be promoted to black areas in young generations. Again, the possibly promoted pointer will trivially satisfy Definition 2, part 2.

Pointer 4. Similar to pointer 3.

Pointer 3 gives rise to some considerations because v_1 is allocated in a region page containing both a black and a white area. How do we mark v_1 as being allocated in a white area? One possibility is that we mark each object as being white or black, which will require that all objects are stored with a tag. A less costful solution, which we shall pursue, is to introduce the notion of a *region page color pointer* (*colorPtr*), which points at the first white value in the region page. Given a value v located at a position p in a region page and the color pointer *colorPtr* associated with the region page, if $p < colorPtr$ then v is allocated in the black area of the region page; otherwise, v is allocated in the white area.[1] Notice, that color pointers are updated and referenced only during a garbage collection; it does not change when allocating new values.

For the scheme to be sound, we need to make sure that pointers of the form of pointer 5 and pointer 6 never occur as the promotion strategy would otherwise lead to pointers from old generations to young generations, which would violate Definition 2. As we have shown, the garbage collector will never introduce such pointers and, luckily, neither will the mutator, except due to mutable data assignment, which we will treat in Sect. 2.3.

---

[1] In the implementation, the color pointer associated with a region page is located in the header of the page. If *colorPtr* points past the page, the entire page is black.

An alternative to the implemented promotion strategy is to add additional generations and let a minor collection traverse all objects except those in an oldest generation. Such a solution, however, could introduce a large amount of unused memory in region pages. Another promotion strategy would be to promote objects when they have survived a number ($N \geq 0$) of collections, which generalises the implemented promotion strategy, but is intractable as it requires tracking of the number of times each object in a young generation has survived a collection.

2.1 Evacuating Objects

The *evacuation* process copies live objects into fresh pages so that the copied-from pages can be reclaimed, including the parts of the pages that hold unreachable values. Definition 2 is implemented as follows. During a major collection, the collector will evacuate objects from old generations into old generations. During a minor collection, however, old generations will be left untouched and the collector will not attempt at traversing values stored in old generation pages. During a major or a minor collection, the collector will evacuate objects in young generation white areas into young generation black areas. Moreover, the collector will evacuate objects in young generation black areas into old generations. The evacuation strategy is implemented by marking all region pages in old generations black, which means that the same algorithm can be used to evacuate objects in minor and major collections. All objects in black areas are copied into black areas in old generations. All objects in white areas are copied into black areas in young generations. All objects allocated between two collections are allocated in white areas in young generations.

Before a major collection, all region pages are assembled to form the from-space as shown in Fig. 4. For a minor collection, from-space is formed from all young generation pages. After a collection (minor or major), the from-space pages are added to the free-list of pages.

old   old   young   young   young

Fig. 4. From-space contains black region pages from old generations, black region pages from young generations, white region pages from young generations, and partly-white region pages from young generations. No white region pages from old generations exist.

To distinguish pointers from non-pointers, integers and other unboxed values (e.g., booleans and enumeration datatypes) are represented as tagged values with the least significant bit set. Records are represented as a vector of values with a prefix tag word, which is used by the collector to identify the number of record components. Pairs and triples, however, are represented without a prefix tag word. Given a pointer to a value in a region page, the collector can determine that the value is a pair or a triple by inspecting the region type associated with the region in which the object resides. In practice, the implementation works with the region types RTY_BOT, RTY_PAIR, RTY_TRIPLE, RTY_DOUBLE, RTY_REF, RTY_ARRAY, and RTY_TOP. Here the region type RTY_TOP is used for specifying regions that can contain values of arbitrary type, except those associated with the other region types. The region type RTY_BOT never occurs at run time, but is used for specifying type and region polymorphic functions. The region unification algorithm will fail to unify two regions with different types (except if one of the region types is RTY_BOT), which provides the guarantee that values stored in a region at run time are classified according to the region type of the region. For efficiency, the region type for a region is stored both in the generation descriptor for the old generation and in the generation descriptor for the young generation.

Values stored in finite regions on the stack are traversed by the garbage collector, but never copied or collected.

2.2   The GC Algorithm

The GC algorithm makes use of a series of auxiliary utility functions:

- in_oldgen_and_minor(p): Returns TRUE if the collection is a minor collection and p points to an object in a region page for which the old-generation bit is set. Returns FALSE otherwise.
- is_int(p): Returns TRUE if the least-significant bit in p is set. Returns FALSE otherwise.
- tag_is_fwd_ptr(w): Returns TRUE if the tag word w is the reserved forward pointer tag, which is different from other tags used for tagged objects. Returns FALSE otherwise.
- is_pairregion(r): Returns TRUE if the runtime type associated with the region descriptor r is REGION_PAIR. Returns FALSE otherwise.
- in_tospace(p): Returns TRUE if p points to an object in a region page for which the to-space bit is set. Returns FALSE otherwise.
- acopy_pair(r,p): Allocates a pair in the region associated with the region descriptor r and copies into the newly allocated memory the two pointers (or integers) contained in the pair pointed to by p.
- obj_sz(w): Returns the size of the object in words, given its tag word.
- gendesc(p): Returns the generation descriptor for the generation in which the object pointed to by p resides. Each region page in the generation has associated with it a generation pointer, pointing at the generation descriptor for the generation. Generation pointers are installed when a new region page is associated with a generation.
- push_scanstack(a): Pushes the allocation pointer a onto the scan stack.
- pop_scanstack(): Pops and returns the top scan pointer from the scan stack. Returns NULL if the scan stack is empty.
- target_gen(g,p): Returns the old generation associated with g's region unless g is a young generation and p appears in a white area in g, in which case it returns g.

A central part of the GC algorithm is the function evacuate, shown in Fig. 5, which copies live values under consideration from-space into to-space. It takes a pointer p and copies the value pointed to into to-space provided it is not already copied and that it is a prospect (i.e., under a minor collection, values in old generations are not copied.) For brevity, only pairs are treated specially; the implementation also treats regions of type RTY_TRIPLE and RTY_REF specially, as also triples and references are represented unboxed.

```
void* evacuate(void* p) {
  if ( is_int(p) ||
       in_oldgen_and_minor(p) )
    return p;
  g = gendesc(p);
  gt = target_gen(g,p);
  if ( is_pairregion(g) ) {
    if ( in_tospace(*(p+1)) )
      return *(p+1); // fwd-ptr
    a = acopy_pair(gt,p);
    *(p+1) = a;        // set fwd-ptr
  } else {
    if ( tag_is_fwd_ptr(*p) )
      return *p;
    a = acopy(gt,p);
    *p = a;            // set fwd-ptr
  }
  if ( gt->status == NONE ) {
    gt->status = SOME;
    push_scanstack(a);
  }
  return a;
}
```

```
void cheney(void* s) {
  g = gendesc(s);
  if ( is_pairregion(g) ) {
    while ( s+1 != g->a ) {
      *(s+1) = evacuate(*(s+1));
      *(s+2) = evacuate(*(s+2));
      s = next_pair(s,g);
    }
  } else {
    while ( s != g->a ) {
      for ( i=1; i<obj_sz(*s); i++ )
        *(s+i) = evacuate(*(s+i));
      s = next_value(s,g);
    }
  }
  g->status = NONE;
}
```

Fig. 5. The function evacuate assumes that the argument p points to an object and that it perhaps resides in from-space and needs to be copied to to-space. After copying, a forward-pointer is installed.

Fig. 6. The function cheney assumes that the argument scan pointer s points to a value that has already been copied to to-space but for which the components have not yet been evacuated. The function is named cheney because it degenerates to Cheney's algorithm if multi-generations are disabled.

Another central function is the cheney function, which takes care of scanning the values that have been copied into to-space. During scanning, the cheney function may call evacuate on values that have themselves not yet been copied, which may cause an update to the generation allocation pointer. Once, for all regions, the scan-pointer reaches the allocation pointer, the collection terminates. The cheney function is shown in Fig. 6. Notice, again, that special treatment is required for dealing with untagged values (only the case for pairs is shown).

The main GC function, called gc is shown in Fig. 7. It evacuates all values in the root set and continues by calling the cheney function on all values on the scan stack. Notice that the evacuate function pushes values that have been copied to to-space onto the scan stack for further processing (the gt->status field is used to ensure that the scan pointer is pushed at most once).

```
void gc(void** rootset) {
  while ( p = next_root(rootset) ) *p = evacuate(*p);
  while ( p = pop_scanstack() ) cheney(p);
}
```

Fig. 7. The main GC function evacuates each of the values in the root set after which the **cheney** function is called with scan pointers from the scan stack as long as there are scan pointers on the stack.

To determines whether a minor or a major collection is run, a so-called *heap-to-live ratio* is maintained, which by default is set to 3.0. Whenever the size of the free-list of pages becomes less than 1/3 of the total region heap, garbage collection is initiated upon the next function entry (i.e., safe point). After each collection, it is ensured that the number of allocated region pages is at least 3.0 times the size of to-space (given the heap-to-live ratio is 3.0). The following rules are deployed for switching between major and minor collections, allowing an arbitrary number of minor collections between two major collections:

1. If the current collection is a major collection, the next collection will be a minor collection. The region heap is enlarged to satisfy the heap-to-live ratio.
2. If the current collection is a minor collection and the heap-to-live ratio is not satisfied after the collection, the next collection will be a major collection.

2.3 Mutable Objects and Large Objects

In the presence of mutable objects, the generation upward closure invariant may be violated during program evaluation. In particular, a reference cell (which are rare in a functional language) residing in an old generation, may be assigned to point at a value residing in a young generation. We refine the generation upward-closure condition as follows:

Definition 3 (Refined Generation Upward-Closure). *For all values v, if v is non-mutable and resides in an old generation then for all values v' pointed to from v, v' resides in an old generation.*

The refined generation upward-closure invariant is safe, if each minor collection traverses all reachable mutable values (even those that reside in old generations). For minor collections we extend the root set to contain, not only live values on the stack, but also all references and tables allocated. How does the collector locate all references and tables? Simply by arranging that such values are stored in regions with distinguished region types. During a minor collection, the region stack is traversed and objects in regions of type RTY_REF and RTY_ARRAY are traversed. Thus, we avoid the implementation of the usual "remembered set" of mutable values that have been updated since the previous collection. This strategy can potentially be more costly than if a proper "remembered set" is maintained, which we leave to future work.

Concerning the treatment of large objects, there are several options. In the implementation, we are currently treating large objects without associating with being either young or old. Large objects are kept in one list associated with a region descriptor. Following this strategy, large objects are not associated with a particular generation (nor need they be associated with a color) and may therefore only be deleted during major collections. However, large objects should be traversed (not copied), when reached, both during major and minor collections.

3   Experimental Results

In this section, we describe a series of experiments that serve to demonstrate the relationship between region inference, non-generational garbage collection, and the generational garbage collection algorithm presented in Sect. 2.

The experiments are performed with MLKit version 4.4.1 and Mlton v20180207. MLKit version 4.4.1 generates native x64 machine code, which is also the case for Mlton v20180207. The two compilers are very different. Whereas Mlton is a whole-program highly-optimising compiler, MLKit features a smart-recompilation system that allows for quick rebuilds upon modification of source code.

All benchmark programs are executed on a MacBook Pro (15-inch, 2016) with a 2.7 GHz Intel Core i7 processor and 16 GB of memory running macOS. Times reported are wall clock times and memory usage is measured using the macOS /usr/bin/time program. Measurements are averages over 10 runs. We use m to specify memory usage (resident set size) and t to specify wall clock execution time (in seconds). Subscripts describe the mode of the compiler, with $*_r$ signifying region inference enabled, $*_g$ signifying garbage collection enabled, and $*_G$ signifying generational garbage collection enabled. Thus, t_{rG} specifies wall clock execution time with region inference and generational garbage collection enabled. We use m_{mlton} and t_{mlton} to signify memory usage and wall clock execution time for executables running code generated by Mlton. The benchmark programs span from micro-benchmarks such as fib37 and tak (7 and 12 lines), which only use the runtime stack for allocation, to larger programs, such as vliw and mlyacc (3676 and 7353 lines), that solve real-world problems. The program msort-rf has been made region-friendly by the programmer.

By *disabling* region inference, we mean instructing region inference to allocate all values that would be allocated in infinite regions in global regions (collapsed according to their region type). Then not a single infinite region is deallocated at run time and the non-generational garbage collection algorithm essentially reduces to Cheney's algorithm. Disabling region inference does not change the property that many values are allocated in finite regions on the stack.

3.1   Comparison with Mlton

In this section, we present base numbers for running the benchmark programs using the MLKit compiler with region inference and non-generational garbage collection enabled. Figure 8 shows wall clock time for MLKit generated executables relative to wall clock time for Mlton (version v20180207) generated executables. We see that for some of the programs, Mlton outperforms the MLKit (with and without garbage collection enabled). Mlton's whole-program compilation strategy, efficient IO-operations, and optimised instruction selection for the x64 architecture, are good candidates for an explanation. Raw numbers for the configurations are shown in Fig. 9, which also shows memory usage for the different configurations. Even though the performance of all but one benchmark is better with region inference alone, for some of the benchmark programs (i.e., those with numbers marked in bold in Fig. 9), region inference alone does not suffice to obtain good memory performance.

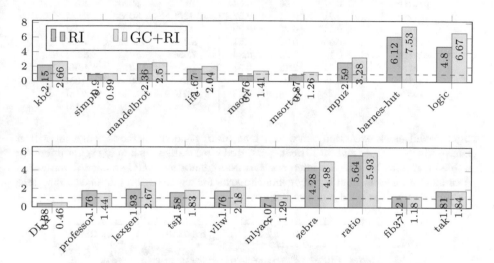

Fig. 8. Wall clock execution times for MLKit generated executables relative to execution times for Mlton generated executables (the dashed red base line). The orange (left) bars show measurements for MLKit with only region inference enabled. The yellow (right) bars show measurements for when both region inference and GC is enabled. (Color figure online)

3.2 Generational Garbage Collection

Measurements showing the effect of non-generational and generational garbage collection in concert with region inference is shown in Fig. 10. First, notice that region inference has a positive influence or no effect on performance in all but one of the benchmarks, namely the Knuth-Bendix completion program, for which region inference adds an excessive number of region parameters to the main mutually recursive functions (explaining the slowdown). Second, generational garbage collection alone (without region inference) performs better than or equivalent to (in all but one case) non-generational garbage collection (the red line). Finally, for six or seven of the benchmarks, the combination of region inference and generational garbage collection performs better than the combination of non-generational garbage collection and region inference. The results are arguably quite sensitive to the heap-to-live ratio (a fair comparison should

Program	t_{mlton}	t_{r}	t_{rg}	m_{mlton}	m_{r}	m_{rg}
kbc	0.10	0.22	0.28	2.5M	**6.9M**	3.4M
simple	0.26	0.24	0.26	6.4M	2.6M	3.4M
mandelbrot	0.09	0.22	0.24	978K	1.4M	1.6M
life	0.54	0.91	1.11	2.6M	**14M**	1.6M
msort	1.09	0.83	1.53	427M	**410M**	137M
msort-rf	0.81	0.70	1.03	652M	102M	124M
mpuz	0.34	0.88	1.11	950K	1.2M	1.3M
barnes-hut	0.14	0.85	1.05	2.2M	**284M**	2.4M
logic	0.11	0.54	0.75	2.4M	**276M**	2.4M
DLX	0.51	0.19	0.23	33M	6.7M	6.9M
professor	0.37	0.66	0.54	1.6M	**10M**	1.4M
lexgen	0.21	0.41	0.57	18M	**50M**	8.1M
tsp	0.14	0.22	0.25	11M	8.3M	13M
vliw	0.05	0.09	0.11	8.4M	**9.7M**	4.6M
mlyacc	0.19	0.20	0.24	7.0M	**66M**	6.6M
zebra	0.51	2.18	2.54	1.6M	**132M**	1.3M
ratio	0.35	1.98	2.08	50M	**38M**	10M
fib37	0.32	0.38	0.38	937K	1.1M	1.1M
tak	0.68	1.23	1.26	938K	1.1M	1.1M

Fig. 9. Wall clock execution times and maximum resident memory usage for Mlton generated executables and for MLKit generated executables with only region inference enabled and with both region inference and non-generational GC enabled (averages of 10 runs). Numbers in bold highlight benchmarks for which region inference alone does not suffice to obtain good memory behavior.

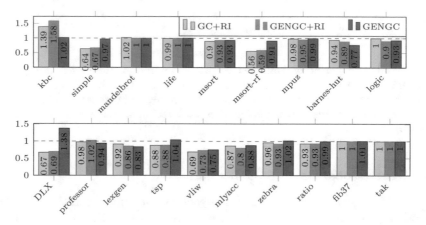

Fig. 10. Wall clock execution times for different configurations of MLKit generated executables relative to execution times for executables with only non-generational GC enabled (the red dashed base line). The green (left) bars show measurements for a configuration with region inference and non-generational GC. The blue (middle) bars show measurements for when both region inference and generational GC is enabled. The violet (right) bars show measurements for when only generational GC is enabled. (Color figure online)

perhaps allow the combination of generational garbage collection and region inference to work with a higher heap-to-live ratio).

Figure 11 shows the garbage collection counts (c_{rg}, c_{rG}, c_g, and c_G) for the different configurations. Notice that the garbage collection counts (and times) are smaller when region inference is enabled. Notice also that the percentage of memory reclaimed by the garbage collector is (close to) invariant to whether the garbage collector is generational or not.

The MLKit features a *region profiling tool* [16], which allows for showing a program's use of regions over time. Figure 12 shows region profiles of MLY-acc computations for four different MLKit runtime configurations. The profiles show that generational garbage collection combined with region inference often requires more memory than when region inference is combined with non-generational garbage collection, but also, that the profile obtained alone with generational garbage collection is similar to the profile obtained with region inference and non-generational garbage collection enabled. The figure also demonstrates a crucial point, namely that the global regions are often those that needs to be collected by the reference tracing collector, which means that schemes that attempt at collecting only the top-most regions will probably fail to be effective.

3.3 Memory Waste

Region inference combined with generational garbage collection results in more memory waste (unused memory in region pages) than when combined with non-generational garbage collection (up to 17% points more). The reason is that, with generational garbage collection, each infinite region contains two lists of region pages (one list for each generation), each of which may not be fully utilised. Figure 13 gives memory waste percentages for the configurations w_{rg} (region inference and non-generational garbage collection), w_{rG} (region inference and generational garbage collection), w_g (non-generational garbage collection), and w_G (generational garbage collection). As expected, the waste is high for the region inference configurations. We also see that generational garbage collection combined with region inference gives rise to the highest degree of waste.

4 Related Work

Most related to this work is the previous work on combining region inference and garbage collection in the MLKit [17]. Compared to the earlier work, the present work investigates how generational garbage collection can be combined with region inference and how the concept of typed regions can be used to implement a generation write barrier. There is a large body of related work concerning general garbage collection techniques [19] and garbage collection techniques for functional languages, including [7,18,23,29].

Incremental, concurrent, and real-time garbage collection techniques for functional languages have recently obtained much attention. In particular, the presence of generations has been shown useful for collecting parts of the heap

Program	c_{rg}	g_{rg}(ms)	p_{rg}	c_{rG}	g_{rG}(ms)		p_{rG}	c_g	g_g(ms)	c_G		g_G(ms)	
kbc	40	5.9	43%	32	(11)	4.9	(1.8)	42%	204	12.6	245	(35)	16.3	(2.2)
simple	7	2.8	7%	10	(5)	3.3	(1.8)	4%	17	8.7	23	(11)	8.7	(5.4)
mandelbrot	1	0.1	0%	1	(0)	0.2	(0.0)	0%	1	0.1	1	(0)	0.1	(0.0)
life	142	6.4	17%	121	(8)	5.4	(0.5)	16%	677	25.4	880	(139)	28.3	(6.8)
msort	33	718.7	53%	47	(23)	762.7	(491.3)	59%	41	1001.1	55	(26)	894.3	(584.0)
msort-rf	23	179.3	6%	35	(17)	270.5	(161.6)	8%	42	1050.2	56	(27)	936.9	(640.9)
mpuz	2	0.3	2%	2	(1)	0.1	(0.0)	2%	2	0.2	2	(1)	0.2	(0.0)
barnes-hut	1948	315.3	63%	1545	(414)	214.0	(79.4)	63%	4272	638.3	4243	(870)	400.4	(143.8)
logic	2276	350.2	100%	2571	(348)	289.7	(55.1)	100%	2306	367.2	2478	(316)	299.3	(54.0)
DLX	5	2.3	0%	6	(3)	3.9	(1.6)	0%	104	119.5	204	(102)	245.8	(109.5)
professor	1218	20.7	27%	1065	(14)	16.0	(0.3)	27%	9821	148.9	8503	(103)	94.3	(2.6)
lexgen	254	148.1	80%	241	(41)	96.4	(25.3)	79%	451	251.6	479	(80)	155.7	(47.1)
tsp	12	16.5	5%	17	(8)	21.3	(7.7)	6%	19	60.5	29	(14)	79.0	(40.9)
vliw	23	8.3	13%	24	(10)	7.5	(3.3)	13%	214	77.6	221	(40)	42.0	(14.4)
mlyacc	115	61.8	69%	88	(18)	36.3	(9.6)	61%	211	104.5	239	(67)	75.0	(35.3)
zebra	5008	90.6	57%	3010	(337)	65.4	(8.4)	56%	17357	274.4	23023	(1001)	310.2	(19.1)
ratio	34	49.2	23%	37	(8)	62.5	(13.8)	22%	110	194.4	99	(13)	180.1	(17.7)
fib37	1	0.1	0%	1	(0)	0.1	(0.0)	0%	1	0.1	1	(0)	0.1	(0.0)
tak	1	0.1	0%	1	(0)	0.1	(0.0)	0%	1	0.1	1	(0)	0.1	(0.0)

Fig. 11. GC counts (c_*) and GC times (g_*) for the different configurations. Reported counts are the total number of collections with the number of major collections and the accumulated major collection time in parentheses. The p_* columns show the percentage of bytes reclaimed by GC (in contrast to region inference).

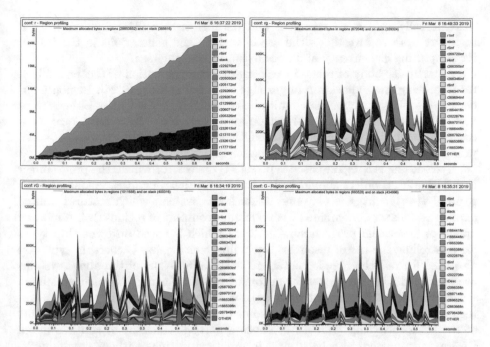

Fig. 12. The top-left MLYacc region profile shows the memory usage over time for a runtime configuration with region inference enabled and reference tracing GC disabled (denoted r). The top-right region profile shows the memory usage for a configuration where non-generational GC is combined with region inference (denoted rg). The configuration for the bottom-left region profile combines generational GC with region inference (denoted rG) whereas the configuration for the bottom-right region profile is using generational GC only (denoted G).

Program	w_{rg} (%)	w_{rG} (%)	w_g (%)	w_G (%)
kbc	42	57	4	8
simple	13	30	2	6
mandelbrot	0	0	0	0
life	8	17	4	9
msort	2	5	2	4
msort-rf	3	6	2	4
mpuz	69	82	47	65
barnes-hut	10	18	2	5
logic	3	6	3	6
DLX	23	32	1	2

Program	w_{rg} (%)	w_{rG} (%)	w_g (%)	w_G (%)
professor	25	38	10	17
lexgen	10	18	1	2
tsp	7	12	5	7
vliw	13	28	1	3
mlyacc	8	21	1	2
zebra	31	38	10	22
ratio	5	7	1	2
fib37	0	0	0	0
tak	0	0	0	0

Fig. 13. Memory waste. The numbers show the average percentage of region waste (unused memory in region pages) measured at each collection.

incrementally and in a concurrent and parallel fashion [3,21,22]. We leave it to future work to investigate the use of regions and generations in the MLKit for supporting concurrency and parallelism in the language.

A particular body of related work investigates the notion of escape analysis for improving stack allocation in garbage collected systems [5,24]. Region inference and MLKit's polymorphic multiplicity analysis [4] allow more objects to be stack allocated than traditional escape analyses, which allows only local, non-escaping values to be stack allocated. Other work investigates the use of static prediction techniques and linear typing for inferring heap space usage [20].

Cyclone [26] is a region-based type-safe C dialect, for which, the programmer can decide if an object should reside in the GC heap or in a region. Another region-based language is Gay and Aiken's RC system, which features limited explicit regions for C, combined with reference counting of regions [15]. A modern language for system programming is Rust, which is based on ownership types for controlling the use of resources, including memory [2]. Ownership types are also used for real-time implementations of Java [6]. None of the above systems are combined with techniques for automatic generational garbage collection.

Also related to the present work is the work by Aiken et al. [1], who show how region inference may be improved for some programs by removing the constraints of the stack discipline, which may cause a garbage collector to run less often. Region inference has also been used in practical settings without combining it with reference-tracing garbage collection. In particular, it has been used as the primary memory management scheme for a web server [10,11,13,14].

5   Conclusion and Future Work

We have presented a technique for combining region inference and generational garbage collection in a functional language. Whereas generational collection by itself is shown (in most cases) to be beneficial compared to a simple Cheney-style non-generational collector, when generational collection is combined with region inference, it turns out that region inference will take care of reclaiming much of the memory that generational garbage collection would otherwise reclaim. There are, however, potential benefits of a generational collector, which, in a few cases, also leads to improved performance. For a more detailed description of the implementation, consult the companion technical report [12].

As a first obvious candidate for future work, the x64 code generator can be improved to generate more efficient code. Second, for making the technique useful for applications that make heavy use of mutable objects, a proper implementation of a "remembered set" would be an appropriate next step. Finally, an obvious candidate for future work is to investigate the possibility of combining region inference and, perhaps, generations, with features for concurrency and parallelism.

References

1. Aiken, A., Fähndrich, M., Levien, R.: Better static memory management: improving region-based analysis of higher-order languages. In: ACM Conference on Programming Languages and Implementation, PLDI, June 1995
2. Aldrich, J., Kostadinov, V., Chambers, C.: Alias annotations for program understanding. In: ACM Conference on Object-Oriented Programming, Systems, Languages, and Applications, OOPSLA (2002)
3. Anderson, T.A.: Optimizations in a private nursery-based garbage collector. In: ACM International Symposium on Memory Management, ISMM (2010)
4. Birkedal, L., Tofte, M., Vejlstrup, M.: From region inference to von Neumann machines via region representation inference. In: ACM Symposium on Principles of Programming Languages, POPL, January 1996
5. Blanchet, B.: Escape analysis: correctness proof, implementation and experimental results. In: ACM Symposium on Principles of Programming Languages (POPL 1998), pp. 25–37. ACM Press, January 1998
6. Boyapati, C., Salcianu, A., Beebee Jr., W., Rinard, M.: Ownership types for safe region-based memory management in real-time Java. In: ACM Conference on Programming Language Design and Implementation, PLDI (2003)
7. Doligez, D., Leroy, X.: A concurrent, generational garbage collector for a multithreaded implementation of ML. In: ACM Symposium on Principles of Programming Languages, POPL (1993)
8. Elsman, M.: Garbage collection safety for region-based memory management. In: ACM Workshop on Types in Language Design and Implementation. TLDI, January 2003
9. Elsman, M., Hallenberg, N.: An optimizing backend for the ML Kit using a stack of regions. Student Project 95-7-8, University of Copenhagen (DIKU), 5 July 1995
10. Elsman, M., Hallenberg, N.: SMLserver–a functional approach to web publishing, 154 p. The IT University of Copenhagen (2002). http://www.smlserver.org
11. Elsman, M., Hallenberg, N.: Web programming with SMLserver. In: Dahl, V., Wadler, P. (eds.) PADL 2003. LNCS, vol. 2562, pp. 74–91. Springer, Heidelberg (2003). https://doi.org/10.1007/3-540-36388-2_7
12. Elsman, M., Hallenberg, N.: Combining region inference and generational garbage collection. Technical report 2019/01, Department of Computer Science, University of Copenhagen (DIKU), ISSN 0107–8283, November 2019
13. Elsman, M., Larsen, K.F.: Typing XHTML web applications in ML. In: Jayaraman, B. (ed.) PADL 2004. LNCS, vol. 3057, pp. 224–238. Springer, Heidelberg (2004). https://doi.org/10.1007/978-3-540-24836-1_16
14. Elsman, M., Munksgaard, P., Larsen, K.F.: Experience report: type-safe multitier programming with Standard ML modules. In: Proceedings of the ML Family Workshop, ML, September 2018
15. Gay, D., Aiken, A.: Language support for regions. In: ACM SIGPLAN Conference on Programming Language Design and Implementation (PLDI 2001). ACM Press, Snowbird, June 2001
16. Hallenberg, N.: A region profiler for a standard ML compiler based on region inference. Student Project 96-5-7, Department of Computer Science, University of Copenhagen (DIKU), June 1996
17. Hallenberg, N., Elsman, M., Tofte, M.: Combining region inference and garbage collection. In: ACM Conference on Programming Language Design and Implementation (PLDI 2002). ACM Press, Berlin, June 2002

18. Huelsbergen, L., Winterbottom, P.: Very concurrent mark-&-sweep garbage collection without fine-grain synchronization. In: ACM International Symposium on Memory Management, ISMM (1998)
19. Jones, R., Hosking, A., Moss, E.: The Garbage Collection Handbook: The Art of Automatic Memory Management. Chapman & Hall/CRC, London (2011)
20. Jost, S., Hammond, K., Loidl, H.W., Hofmann, M.: Static determination of quantitative resource usage for higher-order programs. In: ACM Symposium on Principles of Programming Languages, POPL (2010)
21. Marlow, S., Peyton Jones, S.: Multicore garbage collection with local heaps. In: ACM International Symposium on Memory Management, ISMM (2011)
22. Marlow, S., Peyton Jones, S., Singh, S.: Runtime support for multicore Haskell. In: ACM International Conference on Functional Programming, ICFP (2009)
23. Reppy, J.H.: A high-performance garbage collector for Standard ML. Technical report, AT&T Bell Laboratories, January 1994
24. Salagnac, G., Yovine, S., Garbervetsky, D.: Fast escape analysis for region-based memory management. Electron. Notes Theor. Comput. Sci. **131**, 99–110 (2005)
25. Salagnac, G., Nakhli, C., Rippert, C., Yovine, S.: Efficient region-based memory management for resource-limited real-time embedded systems. In: Workshop on Implementation, Compilation, Optimization of Object-Oriented Languages, Programs and Systems, July 2006
26. Swamy, N., Hicks, M., Morrisett, G., Grossman, D., Jim, T.: Safe manual memory management in cyclone. Sci. Comput. Program. **62**(2), 122–144 (2006)
27. Tofte, M., Birkedal, L., Elsman, M., Hallenberg, N.: A retrospective on region-based memory management. Higher-Order Symb. Comput. **17**(3), 245–265 (2004)
28. Tofte, M., Birkedal, L., Elsman, M., Hallenberg, N., Olesen, T.H., Sestoft, P.: Programming with regions in the MLKit (revised for version 4.3.0). Technical report, IT University of Copenhagen, Denmark, January 2006
29. Ueno, K., Ohori, A.: A fully concurrent garbage collector for functional programs on multicore processors. In: ACM International Conference on Functional Programming, ICFP (2016)

RTMLton: An SML Runtime
for Real-Time Systems

Bhargav Shivkumar[✉][ID], Jeffrey Murphy, and Lukasz Ziarek

SUNY - University at Buffalo, Buffalo, NY, USA
bhargavs@buffalo.edu
https://ubmltongroup.github.io/

Abstract. There is a growing interest in leveraging functional programming languages in real-time and embedded contexts. Functional languages are appealing as many are strictly typed, amenable to formal methods, have limited mutation, and have simple, but powerful concurrency control mechanisms. Although there have been many recent proposals for specialized domain specific languages for embedded and real-time systems, there has been relatively little progress on adapting more general purpose functional languages for programming embedded and real-time systems. In this paper we present our current work on leveraging Standard ML in the embedded and real-time domains. Specifically we detail our experiences in modifying MLton, a whole program, optimizing compiler for Standard ML, for use in such contexts. We focus primarily on the language runtime, re-working the threading subsystem and garbage collector. We provide preliminary results over a radar-based aircraft collision detector ported to SML.

Keywords: Real-time systems · Predictable GC · Functional programming

1 Introduction

With the renewed popularity of functional programming, practitioners have begun re-examining functional programming languages as an alternative for programming embedded and real-time applications [8,9,15,27]. Recent advances in program verification [2,14] and formal methods [1,16] make functional programming languages appealing, as embedded and real-time systems have more stringent correctness criteria. Correctness is not based solely on computed results (logic) but also the predictability of execution (timing). Computing the correct result late is as serious an error as computing the wrong result.

Functional languages can provide a type-safe real-time implementation that, by nature of the language structure prevents common errors and bugs from being expressed, such as buffer under/over flow and null pointer dereferencing. Programmers can thus produce higher fidelity code with lower programmer effort [11]. Additionally, functional programming languages are easier to analyze

© Springer Nature Switzerland AG 2020
E. Komendantskaya and Y. A. Liu (Eds.): PADL 2020, LNCS 12007, pp. 113–130, 2020.
https://doi.org/10.1007/978-3-030-39197-3_8

statically than their object oriented counter parts, and significantly easier than C. As such, they purport to reduce time and effort from a validation and verification perspective. Since many embedded boards are now multi-core, advances in parallel and concurrent programming models and language implementations for functional languages are also appealing as lack of mutable state often results in simpler reasoning about concurrency and parallelism.

There are, however many challenges that need to be addressed prior to being able to leverage a functional language for developing a real-time system. Functional languages must exhibit deterministic behavior under resource constraints, have runtimes that can be bounded in space and time, provide predictable and low latency asynchronous responsiveness, as well as provide a robust concurrency model, to name a few [9]. We surveyed the current state of the art of functional languages and their suitability for developing real-time systems [19], by assessing metrics like the predictability of the language runtime, threading and concurrency support, as well as the ability for the programmer to express real-time constraints. We observed that all of the languages exhibited unpredictable behavior once competition for resources was introduced, specifically in their runtime architectures. The major challenges in providing a predictable language runtime performance for the languages surveyed was their lack of a real-time garbage collection (RTGC) mechanism (predictable memory management).

In this paper we introduce a predictable language runtime for Standard ML (SML) capable of executing real-time applications [17]. We use MLton [18], a whole program optimizing compiler for SML, as a base to implement the constructs necessary for using SML in an embedded and real-time context. We discuss adding a new chunked object model for predictable allocation and non-moving real-time garbage collector with a reservation mechanism. We leverage our previous experience with Multi-MLton [24] and the Fiji real-time virtual machine [21] in guiding our modifications to MLton. Our changes sit below the MLton library level, providing building blocks to explore new programming models. Our system supports running programs built using this system on RT-Linux, a real-time operating system. We present performance measurements, indicating the viability of our prototype, which is publicly available for download at: https://github.com/UBMLtonGroup. This paper is an extension of our previous short workshop paper [15], to which we have added a detailed description of the MLton runtime, the consequences of the design decisions adopted by MLton, and the details of our chunked, concurrent, reservation based real-time GC algorithm. We present additional benchmarks, including a full evaluation of our system on a radar based aircraft collision detector.

2   MLton Architecture and Consequences for Real-Time

MLton is an open-source, whole-program optimizing SML compiler that generates very efficient executables. MLton has a number of features that are well suited for embedded systems and that make it an interesting target for real-time applications.

2.1 MLton Threads

MLton compiled programs consist of only a single OS level thread, over which many green threads are multiplexed. There is a set of three process-wide stack pointers, distinct from the system stack and stored in a monolithic global structure called GC_State, that point to the stack bottom, top and limit of the currently running computation. A thread in MLton is therefore a lightweight data structure that represents a paused computation consisting primarily of a pointer to the thread's stack as well as an index into the stack to allow for unwinding in the case of an exception.

When a thread is paused, the amount of stack space in use is saved from the current process-wide stack to the thread's stack structure (the other two fields are essentially constants and would only change if the stack was moved or grown by the GC). When a thread is resumed, the stack pointers are restored to the process-wide stack fields and computation continues. Thus, thread context switching at its most basic level consists of a pointer swap. An advantage of this implementation is that context switches occur rapidly, and SML stack operations, again being distinct from the system stack, are relatively cheap and facilitate deep recursion. However, this comes at a cost when trying to move to a parallel implementation. The thread runtime semantics are deeply embedded into the compiler and many assumptions are made that are unsafe in a parallel architecture.

MLton provides a logical ready queue from which the next runnable thread is accessed by the scheduler. This is a regular FIFO queue with no notion of priority, however the structure is implicit, relying on continuation chaining and is embedded in the thread switching code itself. This means that there is no single data structure that governs threads nor is there an explicit scheduler. Threading and concurrency libraries (e.g. CML and ACML) build on top of the MLton threading primitives, therefore, introduce their own threading primitives, scheduler, policy, as well as structures for managing ready, suspended, and blocked threads. This layering of low level threading constructs and higher level scheduling constructs opens up a variety of possibilities with respect to rapidly exploring different scheduling models without needing significant compiler retrofitting.

Consequences for Real-Time. The concept of prioritization is useful for ensuring high priority tasks execute accordingly. When adding prioritization to thread scheduling, one approach is to utilize the underlying OS for scheduling. However, as noted in the section above, mapping pools of green threads to OS threads leads to concurrency issues due to MLton's use of a single global structure for state tracking. Another approach is to implement prioritization at the green thread layer. This is not preferable for two reasons. First, there is no notion of pre-emption at the green thread layer. As noted above, MLton threads are essentially chained continuations, and so a thread switch is entirely at the discretion of the currently running thread. While one might argue that this could open the way to the compiler generating a very finely calculated schedule, it would also lead to unacceptable pauses due to I/O.

For example, if syntax is available for specifying timing constraints, then a pre-determined (and validated) schedule can be generated [25], obviating the need for specifying priorities. However, if one of the green threads in the schedule attempts I/O, the underlying OS would pause the entire process until the I/O completes. Therefore, we believe that it is necessary for the compiler's runtime to offer a clean, and safe, mapping of green threads to OS threads so that, for example, I/O operations can be isolated onto a separate OS thread without affecting high priority computations.

2.2 GC Architecture

MLton adopts a hybrid garbage collector that calls upon the runtime memory utilization to decide the strategy it needs to use for collection. All SML objects are allocated in a contiguous heap. All objects are initially allocated in the Nursery section of the heap in bump pointer fashion until the nursery runs out of space, upon which the garbage collector is called. If the ratio of bytes live to nursery size is greater than a predetermined nursery ratio, the runtime uses a minor Cheney copy GC [4]. A minor GC copies objects from nursery to the beginning of the To space (i.e. appending to end of old generation) thus increasing the old generation size and reducing To space and nursery size. When there is no space in the nursery to allocate a new object, a major GC is triggered. It is worthy to note that when there is no memory pressure, the To space is zero size and old generation has the objects that have survived a collection. Therefore, the generational GC isn't triggered until the memory utilization is fairly large, but the garbage collector can still be called for various other tasks like growing the stack.

Major garbage collection is performed in one of the two strategies. If there is enough space to allocate a new heap, the same size of the current heap, then a Cheney copy GC is performed. If there is not enough space for the second semi space, a mark compact GC is performed. The compaction aids in de-fragmenting the heap as well as freeing up more space. After the mark compact phase, the GC falls back to the minor GC for subsequent collections, until it again needs to call a major GC.

MLton's GC architecture is one that implements a "stop the world" (STW) approach. In this approach, all computation threads pause while the garbage collector runs. This design decision was made keeping in mind the single computation model of MLton, that the heap is more prone to corruption if multiple threads are accessing the heap when the GC is copying objects or doing a compaction. Pause times vary depending on the strategy being used for collection, it follows that minor GC takes less time than a major GC. There are four kinds of ML objects: Normal (fixed size) objects, weak objects, arrays and stacks. The arrays and stacks are generally allocated in the old generation as they are more likely to persist longer than the other two kinds of objects. Normal and weak objects are bump pointer allocated in the nursery and then moved to the old generation based on their longevity.

Consequences for Real-Time. In a real-time setting the use of a STW GC is a deal breaker. The cost of performing this GC is directly proportional to the utilization of the heap, and if done during the tasks that have a tight deadline, it could lead to deadline misses. Pre-empting the GC when it runs out of time could make it real-time compatible but it will be useless as it could not be guaranteed that collection would always complete. This could be addressed by implementing incremental collection [20] strategies, but would require the GC to run as a separate thread which is contrary to MLton's single threaded computation model. The multiple GC strategies utilized by MLton further complicates the case by making the maximum pause time more unpredictable, as the strategy used for collection depends on the state of the heap when a collection is triggered.

3 Real-Time Extensions to MLton

To create a version of MLton that supports a real-time computation, we must address the limitations described in the Sect. 2. At a high level, this includes moving concurrency to the OS level, with potential to support parallelism, extending the MLton threading model to support priorities and multiplexing over OS threads, and redesigning the GC to be real-time aware.

3.1 Concurrency and Threading

The first step to having a threading model that supports OS-level concurrency is to split the green threads multiplexed over a single OS thread over multiple OS-level threads. More over, to support real-time execution we also must split green threads based on their priority. In the most simple case there exists at most one green thread (computation) for any given priority supported by the system[1]. Figure 1 shows our concurrency model. An OS-level thread is created for each priority the system supports. Currently we expose only the priorities that the underlying OS or Real-time Operating System (RTOS) expose.

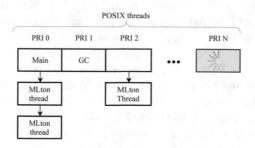

Fig. 1. Priority Based OS/Green Thread Relationship Model

---

[1] Most real-time systems have a specific set of priorities they support.

Migrating to a runtime system that leverages multiple OS-level threads, requires re-engineering how MLton keeps track of the state of the system using the GC_State structure. This structure has numerous fields that store the current position of frontier, current executing green thread, current Stack-Top/StackBottom among others and all these values are accessed at any time by offsetting a pointer to this structure. The decision to use one single structure for storing all the global state was to make the access fast by caching the entire structure on a register. When there is a single thread of execution, there is no need to worry about concurrent access to the GC_State and thus the integrity of the state is maintained. Introducing multiple threads of execution brings in a plethora of changes including the necessity to differentiate between the thread of execution to which the value being stored belongs. Needless to say, threads must also have controlled access to the shared fields in this structure. In RTMLton, we've decided to keep GC_State as a single structure, but implement arrays within it where appropriate. This allows us to be more efficient when it comes to memory utilization – an important consideration when targeting embedded systems. For example, finding the current green thread running within the OS thread, we would refer to the index GC_State->currentThread[osthreadnumber].

3.2   Creating a Real-Time GC

To implement concurrent GC, it is necessary to have the garbage collector execute in its own thread so that it can work independently to mutator threads (program threads). Multi-core implementations of SML like MultiMLton take a different route in handling this separation. They use a per thread heap and thus have a per thread GC which stays coupled to the execution thread. Multiple heaps may pose other complexities (like read/write barrier overheads, global synchronization) in an embedded or real-time system, which is why we chose a single shared heap.

A shared heap implementation is easier but brings us back to the difficult task of pulling out the GC onto a separate thread. In doing so, we need to make sure each thread is responsible for growing its own stack and allocating objects it requires. Although the GC can scan and collect while mutator threads execute, mutator threads must be paused to scan their stacks and construct a root set. This is necessary because MLton stores temporary variables on the stack and if the GC were to run before the stack frame is fully reified, the results would be unpredictable. MLton also will write into a newly created stack frame before finalizing and recording the size of the frame. Without the identification of safe points to pause the threads, the heap will be malformed with potentially live objected considered dead. Fortunately, MLton identifies these safe points for us. GC safe points in MLton are points in code where it is safe for the thread running the code to pause allowing the GC to scan stacks.

Although GC safe points are pre-identified for us, the code generated by the compiler assumes a single threaded model and so we found problematic constructs such as global variables and reliance on caching important pointers in registers for performance. We needed to rework these architectural decisions.

As discussed above, MLton tracks a considerable amount of global state using the GC_State structure so we must refactor this structure, in particular, to make it thread-aware. MLton also uses additional global state, outside of GC_State structure, to implement critical functionality.

Handling Fragmentation. The design of a real-time garbage collector should ensure predictability. To eliminate GC work induced by defragmentation and compacting the heap, we make sure that objects are allocated as fixed-size chunks so that objects will never need to be moved for defragmentation through the use of a hybrid fragmenting GC [22]. This chunked heap is managed by a free list.

Normal and weak objects are represented as linked lists. Since object sizes in MLton are predictable at compile time, we achieve constant access time when allocating these objects by sizing our chunks to fit an object. Arrays are represented as trees, in which each node is fixed-size. Internal nodes have a large number of branches (32 in our implementation), which keeps access time $log_{32}(n)$ and is close to constant. MLton constantly allocates small sized arrays and even zero sized arrays. We represent such arrays as a single leaf to eliminate the overhead of finding the immediate child of the root. During collection, the GC first marks all fixed-size chunks that are currently live. Then it sweeps the heap and returns all unmarked chunks to the free lists. This completely eliminates the need for compaction in order to handle fragmentation.

Heap Layout: In MLton, the size of normal objects, arrays and stacks vary significantly. Since one objective of a unified chunked heap is to prevent moving during GC, we need to have all chunks be of the same size. This does lead to space wastage in each chunk as object sizes vary. However, this opens up room for potential optimizations where we can further explore packing of multiple MLton objects into chunks either based on object sizes or their lifetimes, making the GC much more efficient.

Object Layout: MLton already tries to pack small objects into larger ones. In our empirical study, most normal MLton objects are around 24 bytes and arrays are close to 128 bytes. We choose 154 bytes as the chunk payload that carries MLton object along with an extra 12 bytes overhead associated with normal object chunk management and an extra 56 bytes to manage array chunks. Normal objects that are larger than 154 bytes are split into multiple chunks. In our current implementation, we limit normal objects to two chunks each even though we haven't noticed objects that are greater than 64 bytes. The object layout is depicted in Fig. 2.

In MLton, arrays are passed around using a pointer to its payload. The header and length of an array are retrieved by subtracting the header size and array length size from current pointer. We stick to this representation as much as possible. Array nodes are represented in Fig. 2. Internal nodes carry 32 pointers to their children. We pass an array around via a pointer to its first leaf. A root pointer and a next pointer is embedded in the leaf node. The leaf pointer connects all leaves that actually carry payloads for potential linear traversal optimization.

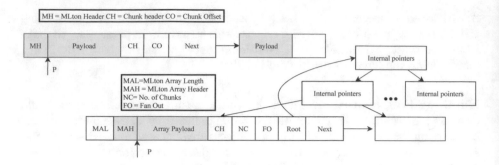

Fig. 2. Chunked object layout

For an array that is 128 bytes or less, we can fit it into 1 leaf chunk. For arrays that span multiple chunks, we construct trees. When accessing an element of an array, we first follow the root pointer to retrieve the root node and then access the array in a top down manner, in which we determine the branch in current node by `index % FO`, then we follow the branch to an alternative internal node. The process is repeated until we finally arrive at a leaf.

Array Limitations. Flattening refers to the multiple optimization passes in MLton that reduces the overhead for accessing nested objects. Unfortunately, it is difficult to reliably decide on an array element size after flattening that can be used at the time of allocation, since tuples can carry elements that differ in size. Our tree-structured array has no information about flattening and the access scheme generated from MLton after flattening cannot work with our chunked array model. Hence, we need to disable some of the flattening optimization passes. We first tried disabling all the flattening passes including local flatten and deep flatten. But in our later investigation, only deep flatten will try to flatten objects in arrays. The local flatten passes are totally compatible with our implementation.

GC Model. For collection, our concurrent GC leverages a traditional non-moving, mark and sweep scheme with a Dijkstra's incremental update write barrier [6]. It is needless to say that our GC thread runs on its own OS thread and operates independently of the mutator, repeating the steps below. Each loop signifies a *GC Cycle*:

Wait for Synchronization - In this phase, the GC is waiting for all the mutator threads to synchronize at the GC checkpoints so that it can continue with its work in a safe manner. MLton performs complicated data flow and control flow analysis to insert GC checkpoints to minimize the number of garbage collections needed. However, the data flow and control flow analysis assumes a single heap model and objects are calculated by number of bytes required (and not chunks), which is incompatible with our model. One solution is to patch up each path in the GC check flow, redirecting all GC checks to our GC runtime function and let the C runtime function decide whether a garbage collection is needed. This method has high overheads in the form of preparing the code to jump to a C call which involves having to save all the temporaries currently live onto the stack as local variables and adding a C_FRAME marker onto the stack all of which not only increases the stack size but also affects overall runtime of the program. In RTMLton, we currently add an optimization pass (*gc-check*) which sums up the allocations in a block and inserts a check to see if there are adequate chunks left. If the block does not allocate objects at all, we ignore it. Such a check only introduces a branch and an inlined integer comparison, which is much faster and more efficient than the former method. Since arrays are allocated by the C runtime, MLton ensures the stack is completely prepared before jumping into GC_arrayAllocate. We can thus safely make GC checks in the array allocation.

Currently, each thread walks its own stacks and marks all chunks that are immediately reachable from its stacks using a tricolor abstraction. All the chunks that are immediately reachable from the stack are marked black (meaning reachable and explored) and the children of the black chunks are shaded gray (reachable but unexplored) and then put into a worklist. It follows that any chunk marked white, or unmarked, is not reachable and hence would be eventually collected. This model where each thread scans only the root set from the stacks and the GC scans the rest and sweeps concurrently, is different from that of MLton's monolithic GC model, in that the mutator doesn't have to wait till the entire heap is scanned. By having each thread scan its own stack, at the end of its period, also contributes to making the GC work incrementally which would give good mutator performance. When all the mutators have finished marking their own stacks at their GC Checkpoints they set a bit to indicate that they have synced and the last mutator to do so would signal the GC to start its process in parallel as all the mutators go about doing their respective jobs.

Start Marking - The GC starts marking the heap when it receives the all synced signal from mutators. All object chunks in the worklist are gray at this point and the GC starts by marking all reachable chunks from each worklist item. Each time a worklist object is picked up, it is marked black and when it has been fully explored, it is removed from the worklist. Marking proceeds as before with the chunk being marked black when reachable and all the chunks immediately reachable from it are shaded gray. The GC aims to collect all reachable objects without wrongfully collecting objects in use. But with the mutator allocating while the GC is marking, it could lead to a rearrangement of the heap by the mutator that invalidates our marking. Which is why we make use of a Dijkstra style incremental update barrier which enforces the strong tricolor invariant. The strong tricolor invariant states that there should be no pointers from black objects to white objects. The write barrier is inserted by the compiler on any pointer store on the heap, and upholds the strong invariant by shading gray, any pointer store that moves a white chunk into a black chunk. The write barrier is made to selectively perform this operation (turned on) only when the GC is running in parallel and at other times only does an atomic comparison to see if it the GC is running or not. When the write barrier is turned on, all new object chunks are allocated gray so as to protect them from collection. Marking phase ends when the worklist is empty.

Sweep - Once the marking is done the GC traverses the heap contiguously and reclaims any unmarked chunks back to the free list. While it sweeps the heap, the GC also unmarks any chunk that is marked in order to prep it for the next GC cycle. Adding a chunk back to the free list is done atomically and involves some small book keeping work like clearing out the chunk headers. Since we are using a chunked heap, we do not need to perform any defragmentation and the addition of chunks back to free list makes it available for reuse almost instantly.

Cleanup and Book Keeping - Before the GC goes back to waiting for synchronization phase, it does some clean up and book keeping like clearing out the sync bits and waking up any mutator that is blocked while waiting for the GC to complete its cycle. In a typical scenario no mutator will be paused while the GC is running except initially to scan its own stack but when the memory is very constrained it may so happen that the mutator does not have enough free chunks to satisfy its allocation requests. Ideally, RTGCs rely on efficient scheduling policies to ensure that the GC runs enough to make sure these scenarios are avoided, but in the absence of such policies we currently block the mutator if it doesn't have enough chunks free and the GC is running. The GC decides to die with an *Insufficient memory* message when it has made no progress(all mutators are blocked) in 2 consecutive GC cycles.

Memory Reservation Mechanism. MLton generated C code is split into basic blocks of code with each block containing multiple statements and ending with a transfer to another code block. These code blocks are translated from the SML functions and an SML function can span multiple C code blocks. When an allocation is done, the allocated objects are pushed into stack slots if the transfer out of the code block has the potential to invoke the GC, failing which may result in the newly allocated object being wrongfully collected. In vanilla MLton, GC can be invoked only from GC safepoints, which ensure that the allocated objects are pushed into appropriate stack slots before the GC runs. In RTMLton however there are two possible places where the GC can be invoked: One, at GC safepoints and two, during allocation when there are no free memory chunks available.

When the GC is invoked at the point of allocation in RTMLton, it leads to an edge case where any previously allocated chunk might be wrongfully collected in very tight memory scenarios, because they were not pushed into stack slots. An allocation statement is not a transfer in MLton's design and therefore it does not expect a GC to happen at that point. Consider the scenarios in Fig. 3:

Scenario 1 and 2 show the cases when the GC is running (i.e. write barrier is turned ON) and Scenario 3 and 4 show the cases when the GC is not running (i.e. write barrier turned OFF). In Scenario 1, you have a code block with 2

Scenario 1 - WriteBarrier turned ON & more than 2 free chunks available

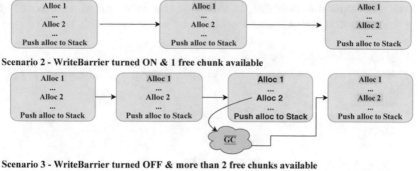

Scenario 2 - WriteBarrier turned ON & 1 free chunk available

Scenario 3 - WriteBarrier turned OFF & more than 2 free chunks available

Scenario 4 - WriteBarrier turned OFF & 1 free chunk available

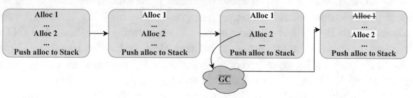

Fig. 3. Allocation scenarios

sequential allocations and there are more than 2 free chunks available. Since the write barrier is ON, both objects are allocated gray and since there is more than 2 free chunks available, no GC is triggered. In Scenario 2, there is just 1 free chunk available. So the first object is allocated gray and when the second allocation happens, the GC is triggered. But since the GC was already running, the first object in shaded and is not wrongfully collected by the GC. Scenario 3 shows the execution when there are more than 2 free memory chunks available. Since the write barrier is turned off, both objects are allocated white. Since there are enough memory chunks available, GC isn't triggered and execution completes normally. When there is only one free chunk available in memory, it leads to the case as in Scenario 4. Since the write barrier is turned OFF (GC isn't running), Alloc1 is allocated white. When control reaches Alloc2, there is a need to invoke the GC as there are no free chunks left. But this time, Alloc1 is not shaded as in the case of Scenario 2 and is therefore wrongfully collected by the GC.

One possible solution to this issue is to convert all allocation into transfers (calls to C functions) and then let MLton appropriately protect all previous allocations by pushing them into stack slots before the next allocation happens. This would involve splitting up each of the C basic blocks further into multiple blocks with each block containing only allocation. We found that this however involves a considerable overhead in terms of the code size as well as the stack space since the number of allocations done by a program isn't trivial.

```
LOCK;
while (free_chunks < (reserved_chunks + reqd_chunks))
{
UNLOCK;
GC_collectAndBlock;
LOCK;
}
reserved_chunks += reqd_chunks;
UNLOCK;
```

Fig. 4. Reservation mechanism snippet

Another way, which we find more efficient, is to guarantee that when a basic block is being executed, it will either receive all the memory chunks it requests for allocation or it will not execute at all. Thus guaranteeing that the GC won't be invoked from an allocation point. MLton already has information about the number of chunks allocated (except allocations by runtime methods) in every block at compile time. We can use this to our advantage by leveraging the *gc-check* pass we put in to do a little more than insert the GC checkpoints. At the point where we insert the GC check, we reserve the number of memory chunks the next code block needs. Reservation is done by atomically incrementing a counter before executing the block and then decrementing it when the object is actually allocated. Figure 4 summarizes the logic involved in reserving allocations before a block is executed.

If the number of free chunks available is lesser than what is already reserved and what is required by the next block, a GC checkpoint is inserted by the optimization pass and the mutator is blocked preventing the execution of the next block until woken up by the GC. If there are enough free chunks available, we simply increment the reserved count by the number of chunks the mutator will need and any subsequent mutator that tries to allocate will know that those many chunks have already been reserved from the free list. It is to note that the pass does not consider array allocations and other allocations like a new thread object or new stack frames since these are decided at runtime. But as discussed before, MLton appropriately manages the stack before transferring into such runtime functions, making it safe to have the runtime do the reservation in these cases thus adhering to the policy of "*No allocation without reservation*". In contrast to the other method of splitting each block to have only one allocation, this method incurs no specific overhead except that of the statements to increment and decrement the reserved count. Currently this check and reservation is done at a per block level but it opens up potential to incorporate some of MLton's complex control and dataflow analysis to find a better place to reserve memory chunks as part of future work.

4 Evaluation

Comparing RTMLton to MLton using the MLton benchmark suite, indicates that RTMLton performs similarly to MLton in tests that do not employ arrays extensively (less than 15% overhead) and performance degrades in tests, like matrix multiplication, that make use of arrays heavily without amortizing these costs. Thus the matrix multiplication benchmark exhibits the worst case performance of our system due to array access overhead (roughly 2x slow down) [15]. We expect to be able to address this overhead by adjusting our array layout in future revisions of our system and reworking MLton's optimization strategies to be real-time compliant. Raw performance, however, is not how real-time systems are evaluated. Predictability is paramount in the system and overheads, as long as they can be accounted for, are ok if the system can meet its target deadlines. We evaluate the predictability of RTMLton on an SML port of a real-time benchmark, the aircraft Collision Detector (CD_x) [13]. CD_x is an airspace analysis algorithm that detects potential collisions between aircrafts based on simulated radar frames and used to evaluate the performance of C and Java based real-time systems. CD_x consists of two main parts namely the Air Traffic Simulator (ATS) and the Collision Detector (CD). The ATS generates radar frames, which contain important information about aircraft, like their callsign and position in 3D space. The ATS produces a user defined number of frames. The CD analyzes frames periodically and it detects a collision in a given frame whenever the distance between any two aircrafts is smaller than a predefined proximity radius. The algorithm for detecting collisions is given in detail in the original paper [13]. The CD performs complex mathematical computations to discover potential collisions and benchmarks various properties of the system like deadline misses and response time for operation. CD processes frames differently based on how far apart planes are in the frames. It does a simple 2D analysis when planes are further away and does a more complicated 3D calculation of relative positions when a collision is imminent. At its core, the benchmark

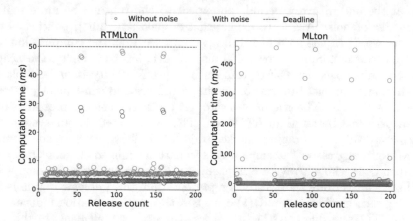

Fig. 5. Performance of RTMLton and MLton on CD_x.

is a single periodic task that repeats the collision detection algorithm over the subsequent radar frames.

We run the CD_x benchmark using a period of 50ms for the CD and leverage a workload that has heavy collisions and measure the computation time for each release of the CD thread. We gather numbers over 2000 releases of the CD thread and graph out the distribution of the computation times and compare it with the deadline for the task. For readability and due to space constraints we highlight a representative 200 releases. To measure the predictability of each system we rerun the same benchmark with a noise making thread, which runs a computation that allocates objects on the same heap as the CD thread. The noise thread is scheduled along with the CD thread. In RTMLton the noise making thread is executed in a separate POSIX thread which allows the OS real-time scheduler to schedule threads preemptively and based on their priority. In vanilla MLton the noise making thread is just a green thread that is scheduled non preemptively (co-operatively) with the CD thread. Thus, in MLton all jitter in the numbers is isolated to the runtime itself as the noise making thread can never interrupt the computation of the CD thread. If the noise making thread would be scheduled preemptively the jitter would increase further since MLton does not have a priority mechanism for threads. All benchmarks are run on an Intel i7-3770 (3.4 GHz) machine with 16 GB of RAM running 32-bit Ubuntu Linux (16.04) with RT-Kernel 4.14.87.

We expect RTMLton to perform more predictably than MLton under memory pressure as the RTMLton GC is concurrent and preemptible. Figure 5 shows the results of running the benchmark on RTMLton and MLton respectively. As expected, RTMLton does not distort the computation time by more than the deadline when the noise thread is running, but does exhibit overhead compared to MLton as we saw in the regular benchmarks. The computation time with the noise thread is a little more than without noise in RTMLton due to the increase in frequency of the CD thread having to mark its own stack, but it is never exceeds the task deadline of 50 ms. When used with a scheduling policy which does incremental GC work, by forcing the mutator to mark its own stack at the end of every period, we expect to the runtime be more uniform irrespective of noise. We leave exploration of such scheduling policies as part of future work. In the case of MLton, we can see that the computation time varies up to a maximum of over 400 ms, when it has to compact the heap in order to make space for CD to run. Such unpredictability is undesirable and leads to a huge impact in terms of missing deadlines and consequently jitter on subsequent releases. The graphs also show that with no memory pressure vanilla MLton performs better than RTMLton. This is expected as our system does induce overhead for leveraging chunked objects. Similarly, we have not yet modified MLton's aggressive flattening passes to flatten chunked objects. Operations that span over whole arrays are implemented in terms of array random access in MLton's basis library. In MLton's representation, this implementation is fast; accessing each element incurs $O(1)$ cost. But this implementation induces overhead in RTMLton due to $O(\log(n))$ access time to each element. In this case, the logarithmic access time is a trade off – predictable performance for GC for slower, but still predictable, array access times[2]. Another source of overhead for RTMLton is the per-block GC check and reservation mechanism. In comparison MLton performs its GC check more conservatively, as discussed in Sect. 3.2, but crucially relies on a lack of OS level concurrency for the correctness of this optimized GC check. Figure 5 shows some frames in RTMLton taking a lot more time than the others even under no memory pressure; these computations represent the worst case performance scenario for RTMLton on the CD benchmark as they are computationally more intensive (due to imminent collisions in the frame) and do significantly more allocations as well, thereby increasing the number of times the mutator needs to scan its stack. Although the benchmark triggers the worst case, RTMLton is still able to meet the task deadline for CD.

To better understand the predictability of object allocation in RTMLton, we implemented a classic fragmentation tolerance benchmark. In this test we allocate a large array of refs, de-allocate half of it, and then time the allocation of another array which is approximately the size of holes left behind by the deallocated objects. Figure 6 shows that when we move closer to the minimum heap required for the program to run, MLton starts takes a lot more time for allocating on the fragmented heap whereas RTMLton, with its chunked model, is more predictable. Since we are allocating arrays in the fragmentation benchmark we expect the high initial overhead of RTMLton as multiple heap objects are allocated for every user defined array since they are chunked. Another reason for the default overhead is because we portray the worst case scenario for RTMLton by having our mutator scan the stacks on every GC checkpoint, irrespective of memory pressure. Despite these overheads, RTMLton manages to perform predictably when heap space is constricted and limited. MLton, however, is inherently optimized for the average case and so the allocation cost degrades when heap pressure is present. We note that most embedded systems run as close to the minimal heap as possible to maximize utilization of memory. Predictable performance as available heap approaches an application's minimum heap is crucial and is highlighted in the shaded region of the Fig. 6.

5   Related Work

Real-Time Garbage Collection: There are roughly three classes of RTGC: (i) *time based* [3] where the GC is scheduled as a task in the system, (ii) *slack based* [22] where the GC is the lowest priority real-time task and executes in the times between release of higher priority tasks, and (iii) *work based* [23] where each allocation triggers an amount of GC work proportional to the allocation request. In each of these RTGC definitions, the overall system designer *must* take into consideration the time requirements to run the RTGC. We currently

---

[2] Almost all dynamically allocated arrays are small and fit into one chunk making them $O(1)$ access and large arrays are statically allocated and their size known up front so the $O(\log(n))$ access time can be taken into consideration when validating the system.

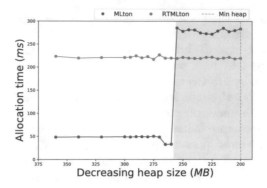

Fig. 6. Fragmentation tolerance

have adopted a slack based approach in the context of real-time MLton, though a work based approach is also worth exploring.

Other Languages with Real-Time Capabilities: Our survey [19] of existing functional languages and their real-time adaptability showed us that most languages we reviewed were found to be lacking in at least one of the key areas we identified in order to provide a predictable runtime system. However, some functional Domain Specific Languages (DSL) were found to be very suitable for hard real-time applications. DSLs, by their nature, offer a reduced set of language and runtime functionality and so are not suitable for general purpose real-time application development. Also notable are efforts such as the real-time specification for Java (RTSJ) [7] and safety critical Java (SCJ) [12], which provide a general purpose approach but burden the developer with having to manage memory directly. For example, both provide definitions for scoped memory [10], a region based automatic memory management scheme where the developer manages the regions. There is also research available on how to lessen the burden by automatically discovering how to infer scoped regions [5]. Finally, there is research in applying a region based memory management approach, while avoiding the use of a GC, in the context of SML [26].

6   Conclusion

In this paper we discussed the challenges of bringing real-time systems programming to a functional language and presented the GC specific implementation challenges we faced while adapting MLton for use on embedded and real-time systems. Specifically, we discussed our chunked model and how it leads to more predictable performance, which is critical for real-time applications, when heap utilization is high. We used an aircraft Collision Detector (CD_x) to benchmark the predictability of our system relative to general purpose MLton and show in our evaluation section that our worst case GC impact is constant which is an important objective to achieve in a real-time language. We observe that while we are slower than generic MLton, it is due to conservative design decisions that can be addressed in future revisions of our system. We believe our biggest contribution in this paper is the integration of a real-time suitable garbage collector into a general purpose, functional language to allow for the targeting of real-time systems.

Acknowledgements. This work has been support in part by National Science Foundation grants: CCF 1749539 and CNS 1823230.

References

1. Arts, T., Benac Earle, C., Derrick, J.: Development of a verified erlang program for resource locking. Int. J. Softw. Tools Technol. Transf. **5**(2), 205–220 (2004)
2. Audebaud, P., Paulin-Mohring, C.: Proofs of randomized algorithms in Coq. Sci. Comput. Program. **74**(8), 568–589 (2009). Special Issue on Mathematics of Program Construction (MPC 2006)
3. Bacon, D.F., Cheng, P., Rajan, V.T.: Controlling fragmentation and space consumption in the metronome, a real-time garbage collector for Java. In: Proceedings of the 2003 ACM SIGPLAN Conference on Language, Compiler, and Tool for Embedded Systems, LCTES 2003, pp. 81–92. ACM, New York (2003)
4. Cheney, C.J.: A nonrecursive list compacting algorithm. Commun. ACM **13**(11), 677–678 (1970)
5. Deters, M., Cytron, R.K.: Automated discovery of scoped memory regions for real-time Java. In: Proceedings of the 3rd International Symposium on Memory Management, ISMM 2002, pp. 132–142. ACM, New York (2002)
6. Dijkstra, E.W., Lamport, L., Martin, A.J., Scholten, C.S., Steffens, E.F.M.: On-the-fly garbage collection: An exercise in cooperation. Commun. ACM **21**(11), 966–975 (1978)
7. Gosling, J., Bollella, G.: The Real-Time Specification for Java. Addison-Wesley Longman Publishing Co., Inc., Boston (2000)
8. Hammond, K.: The dynamic properties of Hume: A functionally-based concurrent language with bounded time and space behaviour. In: Mohnen, M., Koopman, P. (eds.) IFL 2000. LNCS, vol. 2011, pp. 122–139. Springer, Heidelberg (2001). https://doi.org/10.1007/3-540-45361-X_8
9. Hammond, K.: Is it time for real-time functional programming? In: Gilmore, S. (ed.) Revised Selected Papers from the Fourth Symposium on Trends in Functional Programming, TFP 2003, Edinburgh, United Kingdom, 11–12 September 2003. Trends in Functional Programming, vol. 4, pp. 1–18. Intellect (2003)
10. Hamza, H., Counsell, S.: Region-based RTSJ memory management: State of the art. Sci. Comput. Program. **77**(5), 644–659 (2012)
11. Hughes, J.: Why functional programming matters. Comput. J. **32**(2), 98–107 (1989)
12. JSR 302: Safety Critical Java Technology (2007)
13. Kalibera, T., Hagelberg, J., Pizlo, F., Plsek, A., Titzer, B., Vitek, J.: CDX: A family of real-time Java benchmarks. In: Proceedings of the 7th International Workshop on Java Technologies for Real-Time and Embedded Systems, JTRES 2009, pp. 41–50. ACM, New York (2009)

14. Kumar, R., Myreen, M.O., Norrish, M., Owens, S.: CakeML: A verified implementation of ML. In: Proceedings of the 41st ACM SIGPLAN-SIGACT Symposium on Principles of Programming Languages, POPL 2014, pp. 179–191. ACM, New York (2014)

15. Li, M., McArdle, D.E., Murphy, J.C., Shivkumar, B., Ziarek, L.: Adding real-time capabilities to a SML compiler. SIGBED Rev. **13**(2), 8–13 (2016)

16. López, N., Núñez, M., Rubio, F.: Stochastic process algebras meet Eden. In: Butler, M., Petre, L., Sere, K. (eds.) IFM 2002. LNCS, vol. 2335, pp. 29–48. Springer, Heidelberg (2002). https://doi.org/10.1007/3-540-47884-1_3

17. Milner, R., Tofte, M., Macqueen, D.: The Definition of Standard ML. MIT Press, Cambridge (1997)

18. MLton. http://www.mlton.org

19. Murphy, J.C., et al.: A survey of real-time capabilities in functional languages and compilers. Concurr. Comput.: Pract. Exp. **31**(4), e4902 (2019)

20. Nettles, S., O'Toole, J.: Real-time replication garbage collection. In: Proceedings of the ACM SIGPLAN 1993 Conference on Programming Language Design and Implementation, PLDI 1993, pp. 217–226. ACM, New York (1993)

21. Pizlo, F., Ziarek, L., Blanton, E., Maj, P., Vitek, J.: High-level programming of embedded hard real-time devices. In: Proceedings of the 5th European Conference on Computer Systems, EuroSys 2010, pp. 69–82. , ACM, New York (2010)

22. Pizlo, F., Ziarek, L., Maj, P., Hosking, A.L., Blanton, E., Vitek, J.: Schism: fragmentation-tolerant real-time garbage collection. In: Proceedings of the 2010 ACM SIGPLAN Conference on Programming Language Design and Implementation, PLDI 2010, pp. 146–159. ACM, New York (2010)

23. Siebert, F.: Realtime garbage collection in the JamaicaVM 3.0. In: Proceedings of the 5th International Workshop on Java Technologies for Real-Time and Embedded Systems, JTRES 2007, pp. 94–103. ACM, New York (2007)

24. Sivaramakrishnan, K.C., Ziarek, L., Jagannathan, S.: MultiMLton: A multicore-aware runtime for standard ML. J. Funct. Program. **24**, 613–674 (2014)

25. Timber: A gentle introduction. http://www.timber-lang.org/index_gentle.html

26. Tofte, M., Talpin, J.P.: Region-based memory management. Inf. Comput. **132**(2), 109–176 (1997)

27. Wan, Z., Taha, W., Hudak, P.: Real-time FRP. In: Proceedings of the Sixth ACM SIGPLAN International Conference on Functional Programming, ICFP 2001, pp. 146 156. ACM, New York (2001)

A Timed IO Monad

David Janin[(✉)]

LaBRI, Bordeaux INP, University of Bordeaux, 33 405 Talence, France
`janin@labri.fr`

Abstract. Programming with explicit timing information is often tedious and error prone. This is especially visible in music programming where, when played, the specified durations of notes and rests must be shortened in order to compensate the actual duration of all surrounding processing. In this paper, we develop the notion of timed extension of a monad that aims at relieving programmers from such a burden. We show how, under simple conditions, such extensions can be built, and how useful features of monad programming such as asynchronous concurrency with promises or data-flow programming with monadic streams can be uniformly lifted to the resulting timed programming framework. Even though presented and developed in the abstract, the notion of timed extension of a monad is nevertheless illustrated by two concrete instances: a default timed IO monad where programmers specify durations in microseconds, and a musically timed IO monad, where programmers specify durations in number of beats, the underlying tempo, that is, the speed of the music in beats per minute, possibly changed whenever needed.

1 Introduction

Timed programming. The simplest example of timed programming is probably a program that plays some music. Assume a function $f :: Int \rightarrow Note$ that tells which note is to be played at any instant n from start. Assume that we want to play each of these notes for one second, with one second of silence (or rest) between each note. With duration arguments expressed in seconds, in Haskell's IO monad, one could expect that the program:

$$playMusic :: (Int \rightarrow Notes) \rightarrow Int \rightarrow IO\ ()$$
$$playMusic\ f\ n = \mathbf{do}\ \{playNote\ (f\ n)\ 1; delay\ 1; playMusic\ f\ (n+1)\}$$

realizes such an expected behavior when launched by $playMusic\ f\ 0$. While this program *should* be correct, for it is defined with the correct timing specification, it is *actually not*, for it relies on the false assumption that every other computations but those that are specified with a given duration are instantaneous.

More precisely, one can define the *time drift* of this program as the difference between the actual instant a note is played and the specified instant it should have been played. Then one can observe that, when ran, the time drift of the program above is unbounded. Indeed, it increases, note after note, at least by

© Springer Nature Switzerland AG 2020
E. Komendantskaya and Y. A. Liu (Eds.): PADL 2020, LNCS 12007, pp. 131–147, 2020.
https://doi.org/10.1007/978-3-030-39197-3_9

the actual duration of the computation of each note. In other words, such a program, when run in the IO Monad yields a *time leak*. Playing correctly such a music requires at least reducing the *specified* duration of each note or rest by the *actual* duration of the surrounding computations, implicitly but wrongly assumed to be of neglectable duration, not mentioning the time inaccuracy of actions such as delays.

Though simple, the explicit programming of such reductions in order to achieve a correct scheduling in time is repetitive, tedious and therefore error prone. We aim at relieving programmers from such a burden. One way to achieve this is to treat the program above as correct, for it specifies correct *specified durations*, and, instead, to change the way it is executed at runtime, that is, to change the underlying monad.

A Timed IO Monad. It is a well established fact that, thanks to monad modeling, pure functional programming can be safely extended to programming with side effects [15,19]. Observing that *passing time* is a *side effect*, we thus aim at designing some timed monad that freely allows the programmer to assume that many actions are instantaneous, even if they certainly are not, and assume that all other actions have a specified positive duration, even if their actual durations will be shortened for achieving a correct scheduling.

This can be done by extending monads to timed monads in such a way that there is a clean distinction between:

(1) the *specified temporal scheduling*, automatically derived from the *specified durations* of the timed actions contained in a program,
(2) the *actual temporal scheduling* observed when running that program in the underlying monad, induced by the *actual durations* of these timed actions,

in such a way that, if possible and within reasonable bound, the actual temporal scheduling matches the specified temporal scheduling.

Observe that such a distinction between specified and actual temporal scheduling is fairly standard in music. The specified scheduling is described in the music score, as written by the composer, the actual scheduling is observed during the music performance, as defined by the musicians.

Organization of the Paper. The notion of timed extension of a monad is defined in Sect. 2 via a type class and some equational properties every instance of that class shall satisfy. We also discuss the validity of these equations, fairly sensitive in presence of measured time.

In Sect. 3, we show how a monad can be uniformly extended into a timed monad as soon as it is equipped with basic timing primitives. This is achieved by extending the (implicit) monad state by an (explicit) timestamp that refers to the *expected* or *specified* timestamp in that state. Under simple conditions of the existing basic timing primitives, the *time drift* is provably positive in any state. Applied to the IO monad, this yields a timed IO monad with duration measured in microseconds.

Considering multi-scales approach, we provide in Sect. 4 another uniform timed extension of a monad, with basic timing primitives defined over one duration type, that yields a timed monad extension defined over another duration type. Applied to the IO monad, this yields a musically timed IO monad with duration measured in number of beats, a dynamically changeable tempo defining the beat rate w.r.t. to the underlying physical duration type.

Last, we show how various monadic programming features, when available in the underlying monads, can be lifted to their timed extensions. This includes asynchronous concurrent programming with promises (Sect. 5), or data-flow programming with monadic streams (Sect. 6). Related works are then discussed in Sect. 7 before examining some potential followups in Sect. 8.

2   Timed Monad Class

We describe below the notion of timed extension of a monad. The monads we shall consider are *assumed to be strict*, that is, when executing a bind $m \ggg f$, the action m is always evaluated before evaluating f on the returned value, i.e. the bind is strict in its first argument.

2.1   Timestamp, Duration, Time Scale and Time Drift

We briefly review here (our encoding of) basic timed concepts. A *timestamp* is defined here as the *duration* elapsed from some fixed but unknown initial time. We expect timestamps, therefore durations as well, to be totally ordered in a *time scale*. In Haskell, this is done by putting:

> **newtype** *Time d* = *Time d* **deriving** (*Eq, Ord*)

where d is the duration type and *Time d* is the timestamp type. While the sum of two durations makes perfect sense, the sum of two timestamps does not, so we (only) equip timescales with the following primitives:

> $duration :: Num\ d \Rightarrow Time\ d \rightarrow Time\ d \rightarrow d$
> $duration\ (Time\ d_1)\ (Time\ d_2) = (d_1 - d_2)$
> $shift :: Num\ d \Rightarrow Time\ d \rightarrow d \rightarrow Time\ d$
> $shift\ (Time\ d_1)\ d_2 = Time\ (d_1 + d_2)$

that measures the (relative) duration between two timestamps, and that shifts a timestamp by some duration.

As already mentioned in the introduction, a key point of our proposal lays in the distinction between:

(1) *expected* timestamps used for scheduling specification,
(2) *actual* timestamps observed along scheduling realization.

This distinction induces a timing performance measure: the *time drift* defined as the difference between the actual timestamp and the expected timestamp.

It is a desirable property that, in a running timed program, the time drift is kept *positive* so that no action is actually scheduled before its specified time, and *bounded* so that any specified duration above that bound can accurately be handled by the underlying scheduler.

2.2   Timed Monad

Simply said, a timed monad is a monad where every action has some specified (possibly dynamic) duration. The interface of a timed monad is detailed by the following type class:

class $(Ord\ d, Num\ d, Monad\ m, Monad\ t)$
$\quad \Rightarrow TimedMonad\ m\ d\ t\ |\ t \rightarrow m, t \rightarrow d$ **where**
$\quad now :: t\ (Time\ d)$
$\quad drift :: t\ d$
$\quad delay :: d \rightarrow t\ ()$
$\quad lift :: m\ a \rightarrow t\ a$
$\quad run :: t\ a \rightarrow m\ a$

that describes a timed monad $t :: * \rightarrow *$ that extends a monad $m :: * \rightarrow *$ with duration measured over some type $d :: *$. There, the functional dependencies $t \rightarrow m$ and $t \rightarrow d$ ensure that both the initial monad m and the duration space d are uniquely determined by the timed monad t.

The meaning of these primitives is detailed below. Let us mention however that *now* shall return the current *specified* timestamp, *drift* shall return the current time drift, the actual or real timestamp being defined by the following derived action:

$\quad realNow :: TimedMonad\ m\ d\ t \Rightarrow t\ (Time\ d)$
$\quad realNow = \textbf{do}\ \{t \leftarrow now; d \leftarrow drift; return\ (shift\ t\ d)\}$

insisting again, if ever needed, on such a crucial distinction we are making between specified and actual timing information.

We provide below some equational laws that every timed monad instance shall satisfy. For such laws to be stated smoothly enough, we define the following timed monad action that, parameterized by a timed action m, returns its *specified* duration, that shall always be *positive*.

$\quad dur :: TimedMonad\ m\ d\ t \Rightarrow t\ a \rightarrow t\ d$
$\quad dur\ m = \textbf{do}\ \{t_0 \leftarrow now; \_ \leftarrow m; t_1 \leftarrow now; return\ (duration\ t_1\ t_0)\}$

Observe that computing such a specified duration implies running the action together with its side-effects but dropping its returned value. This means that, in practice, it shall be of little use. We will later see, in Sect. 5, another way to retrieve the specified duration of a running timed action for using it elsewhere in a program.

2.3   Timed Monad Laws

The semantics of timed primitives is detailed more formally by the following invariant laws that shall be satisfied by any monad m extended into a timed monad t over a duration type d. The reader shall keep in mind that *dur* measures *specified* durations, not real ones, most of the laws being obviously false when precise enough real durations are considered.

Monad primitives. First, since the timed monad t is first a monad, the usual monad laws shall be satisfied:

$$return\ a \ggg f \equiv f\ a \tag{1}$$

$$m \ggg return \equiv m \tag{2}$$

$$(m \ggg f) \ggg g \equiv m \ggg (\lambda x \to f\ x \ggg g) \tag{3}$$

with the following duration laws for monad primitives:

$$dur\ (return\ a) \equiv return\ 0 \tag{4}$$

$$dur\ (m \gg m') \equiv dur\ m \ggg \lambda d \to dur\ m' \ggg \lambda d' \to return\ (d + d') \tag{5}$$

for every value $a :: a$, action $m :: t\ a$, action $m' :: t\ b$ and function $f :: a \to t\ b$. In other words, return actions take no time and the duration of two actions composed by the bind operator is the sum of the durations of these actions. As a derived law, since $fmap\ f\ m = m \ggg (return \circ f)$, we also have:

$$dur\ m \equiv dur\ (fmap\ f\ m) \tag{6}$$

for every action $m :: t\ a$ and function $f :: a \to b$. In other words, in a timed setting, functors preserve specified durations, time measurement acting over types as a fibration [10].

Current (Specified) Time and Drift. The action now shall instantaneously return the current specified timestamp as evaluated by accumulating the specified durations of the action performed before that one. The action $drift$ shall instantaneously return the current time drift, that is, the difference between the actual timestamp (as measured by the underlying runtime) and the specified timestamp (as stored in the underlying timed monad state). By instantaneous, we mean that the following equations shall be satisfied:

$$dur\ (now) \equiv return\ 0 \tag{7}$$
$$dur\ (drift) \equiv return\ 0 \tag{8}$$

These equations also imply that neither now nor $drift$ have any side effect.

Delays. The action $delay\ d$ shall wait until the current specified timestamp (as returned by now) shifted by the given positive duration d is eventually passed *for real* therefore, in optimal cases, reducing the time drift to a minimal value. The following laws shall be satisfied:

$$dur\ (delay\ d) \equiv delay\ d \gg return\ d \tag{9}$$

$$delay\ (d_1 + d_2) \equiv delay\ d_1 \gg delay\ d_2 \tag{10}$$

$$delay\ (-d) \equiv return\ () \tag{11}$$

for every *positive* duration $d\ d_1\ d_2 :: d$. The first law states that the specified duration of $delay\ d$ is the parameter d, the second one states that $delay$

restricted to positive durations is additive with respect to bind, the third one states that delays with negative durations have no effects at all. As we shall observe in Sect. 5.3, as safer assumption could be that a delay of negative duration creates a *temporal causality error*.

Instantaneous Lift. The function *lift* shall turn an action of the underlying monad m to an action in the timed monad t with the following laws that shall be satisfied:

$$lift \circ return \equiv return \tag{12}$$

$$lift\ (m \ggg f) \equiv lift\ m \ggg (lift \circ f) \tag{13}$$

$$dur\ (lift\ (m)) \equiv lift\ m \gg return\ 0 \tag{14}$$

for any $m :: m\ a$ and $f :: a \rightarrow m\ b$. The first two laws are the usual laws for monad transformers. Any instance (*TimedMonad m d t*) *is* a transformation of the monad m into the monad t. However, we have not specified here a monad transformer since only specific monads, equipped with some timing primitives, can be transformed this way. The third law states that, by *definition*, the specified duration of the timed action *lift m* :: $t\ a$ with $m :: m\ a$ is zero, *regardless* of the actual duration of the action m.

In practice, this assumption means that *lift* shall only be used on actions that are reasonably instantaneous, e.g. *printChar c* in the IO monad, but should not be used on actions that are visibly not instantaneous, e.g. *getChar* in the IO monad as this would immediately yield an unbounded time drift. As we shall see below a timed lift function is available for that latter case.

Runs. The function *run* allows for moving a timed action back into the underlying untimed monad with:

$$run \circ lift \equiv id \tag{15}$$

i.e. *lift* preserves the essence of the actions it lifts. Observe that over timed actions, the reverse direction does not hold since we have

$$lift\ (run\ m) \not\equiv m \tag{16}$$

as soon as the timed action m has a *non-zero* duration.

Timed Lift. Deriving from these primitives, we can lift any monad action from the underlying monad to the timed monad taking into account its actual duration[1] by:

```
timedLift :: TimedMonad m d t ⇒ m a → t a
timedLift m = do { a ← lift m; d ← drift; delay d; return a }
```

Such a timed lifting is then applicable to visibly non-instantaneous such as blocking actions, e.g. *getChar* in the IO monad.

---

[1] A careful reading of this code shows that the resulting specified duration of a timed lifted action is, more precisely, the actual duration of its execution minus the existing time drift right before its execution.

2.4 On the Validity of Timed Monad Extensions

One may wonder if there exists any timed extension of a monad at all that fulfills the properties stated above. Strictly speaking, with unrestricted usage of *drift* combined with an accurate measurement of physical time, the answer is no ! Indeed, given two distinct but equivalent timed actions m_1 and m_2, we have:

$$m_1 \gg drift \not\equiv m_2 \gg drift \qquad (17)$$

unless m_1 and m_2 have the same *actual* duration, which is very unlikely.

This suggests that, unless measuring time drift for testing purposes, the function *drift* shall not be used. However, such a suggestion is not applicable for, as seen above, the function *timedLift*, necessarily defined with *drift*, is needed for lifting monad action with unbounded real duration. In other words, when extending an untimed monad into a timed one, there necessarily are functions such as *timedLift* that do not preserve (untimed) monad action equivalence. This implies that the validity of all timed equations but (15) shall only be observed in a timed setting. In some sense, timed and untimed worlds shall be kept distinct and incomparable, each of them being equipped with its own induced action equivalence.

3 Default Timed Monad Instances

We provide below a default instance of a timed extension of a monad that can be defined as soon as that monad admits enough primitives for time handling.

3.1 Monads with Timer

Monads with timing informations are defined by the following class type:

> **class** $(Ord\ d,\ Num\ d,\ Monad\ m) \Rightarrow HasTimer\ m\ d$ **where**
> $\quad getRealTime :: m\ (Time\ d)$
> $\quad waitUntil :: Time\ d \to m\ ()$
> $\quad getDrift :: (Time\ d) \to m\ d$
> $\quad getDrift\ t = \textbf{do}\ \{r \leftarrow getRealTime;\ return\ (duration\ r\ t)\}$

where *getRealTime* shall return the real timestamp measured over the duration type d, *waitUntil* shall wait until the specified time stamps is passed (for real), and the derived action *getDrift* shall therefore compute the difference between the real current timestamp and the one passed in parameter. Any monad with timing information shall satisfy the following properties:

(1) **Time monotonicity**: for every action $m :: m\ a$, the action

$$getRealTime \ggg \lambda t_1 \to m \gg getRealTime \ggg \lambda t_2 \to return\ (t_0, t_1)$$

shall return (t_1, t_2) with $t_1 \leqslant t_2$,

(2) **Coherent waits**: for every timestamp t_1 the action

$$waitUntil\ t_1 \gg getRealTime$$

shall return t_2 with $t_1 \leqslant t_2$.

The first property states that time shall flow from the past to the future. The second one states that a *waitUntil* action shall never resume before the expected timestamp is actually passed *for real*.

The IO Example. As an instance example, thanks to the *System.Clock* and *Control.Concurrent* libraries in Haskell, one can put:

> **newtype** *Micro* = *Micro Int* **deriving** (*Show*, *Eq*, *Ord*, *Num*)
>
> *getSystemTime* :: *IO* (*Time Micro*)
> *getSystemTime* = **do** { $t \leftarrow getTime\ Monotonic$;
>   (*return* ∘ *Time* ∘ *fromInteger*) (*div* (*toNanoSecs t*) 1000) }
>
> **instance** *HasTimer IO Micro* **where**
>   *getRealTime* = *getSystemTime*
>   *waitUntil* (*Time d*) = **do** { *Time* $r \leftarrow getSystemTime$;
>   (*threadDelay* ∘ *fromInteger* ∘ *toInteger*) ($d - r$) }

where *Micro* is a type of durations measured in microseconds.

3.2   Derived Timed Monad Instance

Deriving a timed monad instance from a monad with timing information can then be achieved by extending the (implicit) monad state by an explicit timestamp. More precisely, we define the timed action data type:

> **data** *TA m d a* = *TA* (*Time d* → *m* (*Time d, a*))

over a monad $m :: * \rightarrow *$ and a duration type $d :: *$, from which we derive:

> **instance** (*Monad m*, *HasTimer m d*) ⇒ *Monad* (*TA m d*) **where**
>   *return a* = *TA* ($\lambda s \rightarrow return\ (s, a)$)
>   *TA m* $\gg f$ = *TA* ($\lambda s \rightarrow m\ s \gg \lambda(s_1, a) \rightarrow$ **let** (*TA* m_1) = *f a* **in** $m_1\ s_1$)

and

> **instance** (*Monad m*, *HasTimer m d*)
>   ⇒ *TimedMonad m d* (*TA m d*) **where**
>   *now* = *TA* ($\lambda s \rightarrow return\ (s, s)$)
>   *drift* = *TA* $\$\ \lambda s \rightarrow getDrift\ s \gg \lambda d \rightarrow return\ (s, d)$
>   *delay d* | $d \leqslant 0$ = *return* ()
>   *delay d* | $d > 0$ = *TA* $\$\ \lambda s \rightarrow$ **do**
>   { $dr \leftarrow getDrift\ s$; *waitUntil* (*shift s* ($d - dr$)); *return* (*shift s d*, ()) }
>   *lift m* = *TA* $\$\ \lambda s \rightarrow m \gg \lambda a \rightarrow return\ (s, a)$
>   *run* (*TA m*) = *getRealTime* $\gg m \gg \lambda(\_, a) \rightarrow return\ a$

This eventually provides the expected default timed monad extension of a monad m with timing information.

The correctness of such a construction, that is, the fact that laws (1)–(15) are satisfied by $TA\ m\ d$ under the restriction described in Sect. 2.4, can easily be proved from the above code and the hypothesis made on m, d and t. More precisely, the standard monad laws follow directly from the fact that $TA\ m\ d$ is a simple variation on a classical state monad transformer. Thanks to property (1) assumed for $getRealTime$, durations are always positive. Then, timed laws follow from the way all the above defined functions act on timestamps.

3.3 More on Temporal Correctness Issues

One can observe that run initializes the time drift with a positive (if not zero) value since the initial specified timestamp is set to the actual timestamp. Thanks to property (2) on $waitUntil$, one can also observe that delays always resume after the specified timestamp is actually passed for real. It follows that the time drift after a delay is always positive. Since every other primitive timed action has an actual duration greater than its specified duration, it follows that:

(1) *the time drift is always positive,*

as easily proved by induction on the syntactic complexity of timed monad actions built from timed monad primitives. In other words, the action scheduling in the default instance is made in such a way that no action is actually scheduled before its specified scheduling time.

Temporal correctness also requires that such a time drift is bounded. Here, we can only observe that, obviously, in the general case:

(2) *nothing ensures the time drift is bounded.*

Indeed, as already mentioned, lifting a blocking IO action as an instantaneous one immediately induces an unbounded time drift. We shall discuss such an issue in the conclusion.

The IO Example. As a particular case, the default timed extension of the IO monad, we call TIO, is simply defined by:

> **type** $TIO = TA\ IO\ Micro$

with the instance $TimedMonad\ IO\ Micro\ TIO$ deriving from the above instance $HasTimer\ IO\ Micro$.

4 Symbolic Timed Extension of a Monad

We consider now the case of a time scale for the programmer distinct from the timescale of the underlying monad. More precisely, given an inner time scale, e.g. the physical time, measured by some inner duration type i, we aim at offering a symbolic timescale measured by some outer duration type o. This requires having some type s for measuring the possible speed (or tempo) of outer durations w.r.t. to inner durations.

4.1   Inner and Outer Durations with Tempi

The relationship between duration types i, o and tempo s, when time speed is assumed to be piecewise constant, is conveniently modeled by the following type class:

> **class** $(Num\ i, Num\ o, Num\ s) \Rightarrow ScaleChange\ i\ o\ s \mid s \rightarrow i, s \rightarrow o$ **where**
> $initialSpeed :: s$
> $step :: s \rightarrow i \rightarrow o$
> $backStep :: s \rightarrow o \rightarrow i$

where $initialSpeed$ is some fixed initial speed value, $step\ s\ i$ that essentially computes the outer duration obtained by "multiplying" the speed s by the inner duration i, and $backStep\ s\ o$ that essentially computes the inner duration obtained by "dividing" the outer duration o by (some non zero) speed s.

The way these "multiplication" and "division" are actually performed shall depend on the chosen types. In the abstract, the following equations shall be satisfied by any instances:

$$backStep\ s\ (step\ s\ i) \equiv i \tag{18}$$

$$step\ d\ (backStep\ d\ o) \equiv o \tag{19}$$

for any inner duration i, outer duration o and non zero speed s, up to the possible rounding errors due to changes of numerical types.

As a consequence, the function mapping the inner timescale $Time\ i$ to the outer timescale $Time\ o$ shall be bijective (up to rounding) and, in case $step$ and $backStep$ functions are truly implemented as some multiplication and division, piecewise linear.

The IO Example. As an instance example, one can define:

> **newtype** $Beat = Beat\ Double$ **deriving** $(Eq, Ord, Show, Num)$
> **newtype** $BPM = BPM\ Double$ **deriving** $(Eq, Ord, Show, Num)$
> **instance** $ScaleChange\ Micro\ Beat\ BPM$ **where**
> $initialSpeed = BPM\ 60$
> $step\ (BPM\ t)\ (Micro\ d) = Beat\ \$\ t * ((fromInteger \circ toInteger)\ d)/ratio$
> $backStep\ (BPM\ t)\ (Beat\ d) = Micro\ \$\ fromInteger\ (floor\ (d * ratio/t))$

with $ratio = 60 * 10^6$, the time speed being expressed in beats per minutes (bpm).

4.2   Derived Symbolic Timed Monad Instance

A symbolic timed extension of a monad can then be built quite like the default timed extension described above. Indeed, we define symbolic timed states by:

> **data** $ST\ i\ o\ s = ST\ \{innerTime :: Time\ i, outerTime :: Time\ o, speed :: s\}$

with symbolic timed actions defined by:

data $STA\ m\ i\ o\ s\ a = STA\ (ST\ i\ o\ s \rightarrow m\ (ST\ i\ o\ s, a))$

This eventually yields the instance $TimedMonad\ m\ o\ (STA\ m\ i\ o\ s)$, defined essentially like the instance of $TA\ m\ d$, taking care however to maintain coherent inner and outer timestamps in every symbolic timed state. This can be done without any real difficulty, laws (18)–(19) ensuring, for a given time speed s, coherent back and forth translation between duration types i and o.

The IO Example. As a particular case, the promised musically timed extension of the IO monad is defined by:

type $MusicIO = STA\ IO\ Micro\ Beat\ BPM$

The underlying tempo can be changed at any time by the following parameterized timed action:

$setTempo :: BPM \rightarrow MusicIO\ ()$
$setTempo\ t\ |\ t \leqslant 0 = error\ \$\ $ `"setTempo : forbidden negative tempo"`
$setTempo\ t$
$\quad = STA\ \$\ \lambda s \rightarrow$ **let** $ST\ ti\ to\quad = s$ **in** $return\ (ST\ ti\ to\ t, ())$

Given function $f :: Int \rightarrow Note$, our initial example can then simply and correctly be encoded by:

$playInIO = run\ playMusic$

$playMusic :: (Int \rightarrow Notes) \rightarrow Int \rightarrow MusicIO\ ()$
$playMusic\ f\ n$
$\quad =$ **do** $\{\ lift\ (playNote\ (f\ n))\ 1;\ delay\ 1;\ playMusic\ f\ (n+1)\ \}$
$playNote :: Note \rightarrow Beat \rightarrow MusicIO\ ()$
$playNote\ n\ d = startNote\ n \gg delay\ d \gg stopNote\ n$

By construction, the tempo has been initialized to 60 bpm, that is, one beat per second.

5   Timed Promises

One may ask how robust our constructions of timed monads are, or, more precisely, to which extent additional features of a given monad can be lifted to its timed extension. We shall describe here the case of asynchronous concurrent promises that can uniformly be lifted from any monad where they are defined to its (default) timed extension when there is one.

5.1   Monad References

Since the 70s, there is the concept of promises that successfully extends functional programming to asynchronous concurrent features. Simply said, a promise is a place holder returned by a forked program that is eventually fulfilled by the value returned by that program [6].

In Haskell, the notion of promise is conveniently replaced by the notion of monad references [11] specified as follows:

class *Monad m* ⇒ *MonadRef m* **where**
    type *Ref m* :: * → *
    fork :: *m a* → *m* (*Ref m a*)
    read :: *Ref m a* → *m a*
    tryRead :: *Ref m a* → *m* (*Maybe a*)
    parRead :: *Ref m a* → *Ref m b* → *m* (*Either a b*)

where the action *fork m* shall fork the monad action *m* and *immediately* returns a reference to that action, the action *read r* shall return the value produced by the running action referenced by *r as soon as* it is available, the action *tryRead r* shall be a non blocking version of *read r* and the action *parRead* r_1 r_2 shall take two monad references r_1 and r_2 as parameters and return the value of the *first referenced action that terminates*, or either of the values if both are already terminated or are terminating at the same (or indistinguishable) time.

The basic (non-concurrent) semantics of monad reference basic primitives is governed by the following laws:

$$(fork\ m) \ggg read \equiv m \tag{20}$$

$$fork \circ read \equiv return \tag{21}$$

$$fork\ (m \ggg f) \equiv (fork\ m) \ggg \lambda r \to fork\ (read\ r \ggg f) \tag{22}$$

for every *m* :: *m a*, *f* :: *a* → *m b*. Other laws, specifying the expected concurrent semantics of monad references are detailed in the companion article [11].

5.2 Timed Monad References

Equipping a timed extension of monad by monad references, as soon as the underlying monad itself has references, is (almost) easy as shown by the following instance:

data *TRef m d a* = *TRef* (*Time d*) (*Ref m* (*Time d, a*))

instance (*MonadRef m, HasTimer m d*) ⇒ *MonadRef* (*TA m d*) **where**
    type *Ref* (*TA m d*) = *TRef m d*
    fork (*TA m*) = *TA* $ λ*s* → **do** { *r* ← *fork* (*m s*); *return* (*s, TRef s r*) }
    read (*TRef _ r*) = *TA* $ λ*s* → **do** { (*t, a*) ← *read r*; *return* (*max s t, a*) }
    tryRead (*TRef _ r*) = *TA* $ λ*s* → **do** { *c* ← *tryRead r*; **case** *c* **of**
        Nothing → *return* (*s, Nothing*)
        Just (*t, a*) → *return* (*max s t, Just a*) }
    parRead (*TRef _ r_1*) (*TRef _ r_2*) = *TA* $ λ*s* → **do** { *c* ← *parRead* r_1 r_2;
      case *c* **of** { *Left* (*t, a*) → *return* (*max s t, Left a*);
           Right (*t, b*) → *return* (*max s t, Right b*) } }

One can observe that in all read actions above, variable *t* refers to the (specified) timestamp at which the referenced action is eventually completed while variable

s refers to the (specified) timestamp at which the read action is called. As these two timestamps refer to independant events, we need to compute the (specified) timestamp $max\ s\ t$ right after which these two events have occured. Then, one can check that equations (20)–(22) are satisfied, even though this requires equivalent actions to also have the same (specified) duration.

Remark. With the above proposed instance, nothing ensures the function *parRead* returns the value of the soonest terminated action *as specified* by termination timestamps. Indeed, the function *parRead* is non deterministic in two cases, the first one being when two referenced actions are already terminated, the second one being when there are terminating *almost* at the same time. Clearly, the first case can easily be solved by performing a *tryRead* on the second reference right after the first one is received and, if terminated, sorting the returned values according to their timestamp. However, the second case is more tricky to solve. One solution is to ensure that function *tryRead* returns *Nothing* only in the case the referenced action *provably* terminates later than the specified time at which *tryRead* is launched. Such a possibility is however yet not implemented.

5.3   Time Specific Action on Timed Monad References

The reader may have observed that, in the code above, we do not use the timestamp recorded in a timed reference when forking an action. Its relevance appears in the function *durRef* given below, from which various timed specific actions are derived.

$$durRef :: TRef\ m\ d\ a \rightarrow TA\ m\ d\ d$$
$$durRef\ (TRef\ t_0\ r)$$
$$= TA\ (\lambda s \rightarrow \mathbf{do}\ \{(t, \_) \leftarrow read\ r; return\ (max\ s\ t, duration\ t\ t_0)\})$$
$$replayRef :: TRef\ m\ d\ a \rightarrow TA\ m\ d\ a$$
$$replayRef\ r = \mathbf{do}\ \{t_1 \leftarrow now; d \leftarrow durRef\ r; a \leftarrow read\ r; t_2 \leftarrow now;$$
$$delay\ (d - duration\ t_2\ t_1); return\ a\}$$
$$expandRef :: (d \rightarrow d) \rightarrow TRef\ m\ d\ a \rightarrow TA\ m\ d\ a$$
$$expandRef\ f\ r = \mathbf{do}\ \{t_1 \leftarrow now; d \leftarrow durRef\ r; a \leftarrow read\ r; t_2 \leftarrow now;$$
$$\mathbf{let}\ d_1 = f\ d - duration\ t_2\ t_1\ \mathbf{in}\ delay\ d_1; return\ a\}$$

where *durRef* returns, when finished, the specified duration of a referenced action, *replayRef* replays the referenced action from start, with the same duration but no side effect, and *expandRef* replays a referenced action but expanding (or shrinking) its duration by applying some function parameter f.

Observe that all these actions can be used as soon as their parameters are available therefore even before the referenced actions are terminated and there specified durations are known. This means that shrinking a duration may fail to be done correctly as illustrated by $fork\ m \ggg expandRef\ (\ /2)$ that unsuccessfully tries to replay twice faster a just forked action. Such a resulting action is not temporal causal or, equivalently, duration d_1 in the code of *expandRef* is strictly negative hence no delay is applied. Executing a negative delay is here a clear sign of a causality error, an error that could well be raised as such.

As already observed in music experiments conducted along a previous modeling of interactive music by temporal tiles [1], programming interactive music systems, these functions yield a completely new branch of realtime musical effects, such has repeating every note with its same duration, an effect that is essentially not available in the existing reactive music application software.

6   Data Flow Programming with Timed Monad Streams

Defining data flows by means of nested monad actions is a technique that is getting more and more popular for data-flow-like programming within generic functional programming languages as illustrated by Snoyman's *Conduit* library. Following the (simpler) definition of monad streams recently (re)defined and developed for audio processing and control [12], there is the type constructor:

newtype *Stream f a = Stream { next :: f (Maybe (a, Stream f a))}*

either defining monad streams with $f = m$ for some monad m, or defining references to (running) monad streams with $f = Ref\ m$ for some monad m with references [11]. Then, as a derived function example, we have:

merge :: MonadRef m
  $\Rightarrow$ *Stream m a* $\rightarrow$ *Stream m b* $\rightarrow$ *Stream m (Either a b)*

that merges two monad streams by order of arrival of their elements. Applied to timed monad and timed monad references, these kind of functions have clear application in timed data flow programming, especially for handling asynchronous control flows as recently illustrated [12].

In other words, timed data flow programming automatically derives from timed monads and timed monad references. This somehow illustrates the fundational nature of these two concepts that both extend monads.

7   Related Works

In functional programming languages, there already are many proposals for programming timed reactive concurrent systems ranging from the synchronous language family [18], possibly extended with modern polymorphism as with Reactive ML [14], to the many variants of functional reactive program (FRP) series initiated with FRAN [3,4,20]. However, to the best of our knowledge, most of these approaches consider a qualitative timing, as defined by series of events, instead of a quantitative timing, as proposed here, a quantitative timing the programmer may specify and refer to.

More precisely, the synchronous language approach mostly aims at defining timed programs over symbolic time scales (series of clock ticks) for which the actual duration between any two ticks is provably bounded. This eventually led to the successful development of programming languages such as Lustre or Esterel [18] that allows programmers to implement (provably correct) synchronous realtime applications. Yet, programming timed applications with weaker but quantitative time specification seems to go out of the application scope of these languages, despite interesting extensions toward polymorphic and higher-order timing mechanisms [2].

The FRP approach, somewhat more theoretical, aims at defining an adequate API for programming with timed signal. Initially designed to cope with arbitrary timescale [3], concrete implementations of FRP are mostly limited to reactive programming, though with some exceptions [16]. In practice, timescales are defined by event arrivals, that act as qualitative clock ticks, function between signals being restricted to Mealy machines. There, the initially proposed API with signals defined as functions from timestamps to values yields (fairly easily) memory leaks which are avoided by such a restriction, either by syntactic means [17] or by modal type mechanisms [13]. Our timed extension of monads, with derived timed monad streams, brings back qualitative time measurement between clock ticks without the associated time leaks.

The multitime scale approach, presented in Sect. 4 is an example of a fairly simple (piece-wise linear and locally finite) hybrid (bijective) signal. Along the lines proposed in [16], it can probably be extended for defining more general hybrid signals, with their associated monitoring actions.

Our approach is also influenced by Hudak's aim at defining temporal objects by means of the properties their combinators shall satisfy [7]. Though our proposal eventually diverges from Hudak's polymorphic temporal media, it nevertheless inherits from its underlying intention to bridge the gap between theory and practice, as already illustrated by Euterpea [9].

Last, the initial motivation for the present development of timed monads was to define an efficient and more generic programming interface for encoding temporal tiles [1,8]. As a matter of fact, all interactive music experiments conducted with such a model are easily and more efficiently re-implemented within the proposed timed monad framework.

8   Conclusion

Along these pages, we have proposed and instantiated a fairly generic notion of timed extension of a monad. We have also shown how additional programming features of monads can simply be lifted into these extension. This timed extension relies on distinguishing specified and actual duration: a distinction already put in practice in interactive music systems, the musician and the computer interacting one with the other [1]. Of course, the topic is far from being closed, how to add timing information into interactive programs being a vast subject. Several issues remain to be solved. On the positive side, our proposal allows for clearly identifying what are the yet unsolved timing problems and where to look for solutions.

As already observed in Sect. 3.3, nothing ensures that the time drift is bounded in a timed monad action. The reader might be disappointed by such a fact. However, ensuring that a given program has a bounded time drift is a well-known tricky issue, undecidable in the general case. What restrictions on programs may yield timed actions with provably bounded time drift is a long standing research problem [18]. Clearly, recursively defined action shall only be allowed when each recursive call is both terminal, in order to avoid memory leaks, and guarded by some sufficient long delays, in order to avoid time leaks. One possibility could be to extend modal types [13] with quantified durations. Existing results in quantitative temporal logic may help. Also, extending the underlying monad actions type by some bound on their actual durations might help as well. This would allow checking that actions are properly lifted with adequate delays. Indeed, as already observed, lifting a blocking action as an instantaneous action is nonsense. Similar techniques should probably be used for detecting temporally non causal transformations as illustrated in Sect. 5.3 example.

As also observed in Sect. 2.4, two actions in a base monad m can be equivalent while their timed lifting is not. Indeed, with durations measured in microseconds, it is very unlikely that two distinct but equivalent actions have the same duration. Real time measurement is a property killer. One partial solution might be to measure time drift with less accuracy. In a music system, with symbolic time, such a problem is well-known. It arises when aiming at translating back realtime performances into music scores, as in score followers [5]. Rephrased in terms of timed monad, the implementation of *drift* is the key to handling such a problem. Is there any time drift between two different musicians performing the same score? Measurements say yes, but listeners say no. The measurement of the time drift should follow listeners.

Of course, developing programming languages towards application in music may sound a bit pointless compared to applications with more economical impact such as, say, autonomous vehicles or connected objects. Is that so ? Clearly, experiments are easier to conduct in music than in most other application fields, with less dramatic consequences in case of errors. Moreover, time is known and handled by musicians for centuries. As illustrated throughout, various musical concepts can be generalized or abstracted into useful timed programming concepts. Moreover, our approach is abstract enough to be potentially applicable to other areas. Timed programming, with its need for automatic handling of time drift, is surely in the close neighborhood of spacetime programming, with its need for automatic handling of spacetime drift.

References

1. Archipoff, S., Janin, D.: Structured reactive programming with polymorphic temporal tiles. In: ACM Workshop on Functional Art, Music, Modeling and Design (FARM). ACM Press (2016)
2. Colaço, J.-L., Girault, A., Hamon, G., Pouzet, M.: Towards a higher-order synchronous data-flow language. In: International Conference on Embedded Software (EMSOFT), pp. 230–239. ACM (2004)
3. Elliott, C., Hudak, P.: Functional reactive animation. In: International Conference on Functional Programming (ICFP). ACM (1997)

4. Elliott, C.M.: Push-pull functional reactive programming. In: Symposium on Haskell, pp. 25–36. ACM (2009)
5. Giavitto, J.-L., Echeveste, J., Cont, A., Cuvillier, P.: Time, timelines and temporal scopes in the Antescofo DLS v1.0. In: International Computer Music Conference (ICMC) (2017)
6. Halstead Jr., R.H.: Multilisp: a language for concurrent symbolic computation. ACM Trans. Program. Lang. Syst. **7**(4), 501–538 (1985)
7. Hudak, P.: An algebraic theory of polymorphic temporal media. In: Jayaraman, B. (ed.) PADL 2004. LNCS, vol. 3057, pp. 1–15. Springer, Heidelberg (2004). https://doi.org/10.1007/978-3-540-24836-1_1
8. Hudak, P., Janin, D.: From out-of-time design to in-time production of temporal media. Research report, LaBRI, Université de Bordeaux (2015)
9. Hudak, P., Quick, D.: The Haskell School of Music : From Signals to Symphonies. Cambridge University Press, Cambridge (2018)
10. Janin, D.: Spatio-temporal domains: an overview. In: Fischer, B., Uustalu, T. (eds.) ICTAC 2018. LNCS, vol. 11187, pp. 231–251. Springer, Cham (2018). https://doi.org/10.1007/978-3-030-02508-3_13
11. Janin, D.: An equational modeling of asynchronous concurrent programming. Technical report, LaBRI, Université de Bordeaux (2019)
12. Janin, D.: Screaming in the IO monad. In: ACM Workshop on Functional Art, Music, Modeling and Design (FARM). ACM (2019)
13. Krishnaswami, N.R.: Higher-order functional reactive programming without space-time leaks. In: International Conference on Functional Programming (ICFP) (2013)
14. Mandel, L., Pouzet, M.: ReactiveML, a reactive extension to ML. In: International Symposium on Principles and Practice of Declarative Programming (PPDP). ACM (2005)
15. Moggi, E.: A modular approach to denotational semantics. In: Pitt, D.H., Curien, P.-L., Abramsky, S., Pitts, A.M., Poigné, A., Rydeheard, D.E. (eds.) CTCS 1991. LNCS, vol. 530, pp. 138–139. Springer, Heidelberg (1991). https://doi.org/10.1007/BFb0013462
16. Nilsson, H., Peterson, J., Hudak, P.: Functional hybrid modeling. In: Dahl, V., Wadler, P. (eds.) PADL 2003. LNCS, vol. 2562, pp. 376–390. Springer, Heidelberg (2003). https://doi.org/10.1007/3-540-36388-2_25
17. van der Ploeg, A., Claessen, K.: Practical principled FRP: forget the past, change the future, FRPNow! In: International Conference on Functional Programming (ICFP), pp. 302–314. ACM (2015)
18. de Simone, R., Talpin, J.-P., Potop-Butucaru, D.: The synchronous hypothesis and synchronous languages. In: Embedded Systems Handbook. CRC Press (2005)
19. Wadler, P.: Comprehending monads. In: Conference on LISP and Functional Programming (LFP), New York. ACM (1990)
20. Winograd-Cort, D., Hudak, P.: Settable and non-interfering signal functions for FRP: how a first-order switch is more than enough. In: International Conference on Functional Programming (ICFP), pp. 213–225. ACM (2014)

Reasoning and Efficient Implementation

Exploiting Database Management Systems and Treewidth for Counting

Johannes K. Fichte[1]([⊠]) [iD], Markus Hecher[2,3]([⊠]) [iD], Patrick Thier[2]([⊠]),
and Stefan Woltran[2]([⊠]) [iD]

[1] TU Dresden, Dresden, Germany
johannes.fichte@tu-dresden.de
[2] TU Wien, Vienna, Austria
{hecher,thier,woltran}@dbai.tuwien.ac.at
[3] University of Potsdam, Potsdam, Germany
hecher@uni-potsdam.de

Abstract. Bounded treewidth is one of the most cited combinatorial
invariants, which was applied in the literature for solving several counting problems efficiently. A canonical counting problem is #SAT, which
asks to count the satisfying assignments of a Boolean formula. Recent
work shows that benchmarking instances for #SAT often have reasonably
small treewidth. This paper deals with counting problems for instances
of small treewidth. We introduce a general framework to solve counting questions based on state-of-the-art database management systems
(DBMS). Our framework takes explicitly advantage of small treewidth
by solving instances using dynamic programming (DP) on tree decompositions (TD). Therefore, we implement the concept of DP into a DBMS
(PostgreSQL), since DP algorithms are already often given in terms of
table manipulations in theory. This allows for elegant specifications of DP
algorithms and the use of SQL to manipulate records and tables, which
gives us a natural approach to bring DP algorithms into practice. To the
best of our knowledge, we present the first approach to employ a DBMS
for algorithms on TDs. A key advantage of our approach is that DBMS
naturally allow to deal with huge tables with a limited amount of main
memory (RAM), parallelization, as well as suspending computation.

Keywords: Dynamic programming · Parameterized algorithmics ·
Bounded treewidth · Database systems · SQL · Relational algebra ·
Counting

1 Introduction

Counting solutions is a well-known task in mathematics, computer science, and
other areas [8,17,24,38]. In combinatorics, for instance, one characterizes the

Our system dpdb is available under GPL3 license at github.com/hmarkus/dp_on_dbs.
The work has been supported by the Austrian Science Fund (FWF), Grants Y698,
P26696, and P32830, and the German Science Fund (DFG), Grant HO 1294/11-1.

E. Komendantskaya and Y. A. Liu (Eds.): PADL 2020, LNCS 12007, pp. 151–167, 2020.
https://doi.org/10.1007/978-3-030-39197-3_10

number of solutions to problems by means of mathematical expressions, e.g., generating functions [18]. One particular counting problem, namely *model counting* (#SAT) asks to output the number of solutions of a given Boolean formula. Model counting and variants thereof have already been applied for solving a variety of real-world applications [8,10,19,44]. Such problems are typically considered rather hard, since #SAT is complete for the class #P [3,35], i.e., one can simulate any problem of the polynomial hierarchy with polynomially many calls [41] to a #SAT solver. Taming this high complexity is possible with techniques from parameterized complexity [12]. In fact, many of the publicly available #SAT instances show good structural properties after using regular preprocessors like pmc [29], see [23]. By good structural properties, we mean that graph representations of these instance have reasonably small *treewidth*. The measure treewidth is a structural parameter of graphs which models the closeness of the graph to being a tree and is one of the most cited combinatorial invariants studied in parameterized complexity [12], and subject of recent competitions [15].

This observation gives rise to a general framework for counting problems that leverages treewidth. The general idea to develop such frameworks is indeed not new, since there are both, specialized solvers [9,23,25], as well as general systems like D-FLAT [5], Jatatosk [4], and sequoia [31], that exploit treewidth. Some of these systems explicitly use *dynamic programming (DP)* to directly exploit treewidth by means of so-called *tree decompositions (TDs)*, whereas others provide some kind of declarative layer to model the problem (and perform decomposition and DP internally). In this work, we solve (counting) problems by means of explicitly specified DP algorithms, where essential parts of the DP algorithm are specified in form of SQL SELECT queries. The actual run of the DP algorithm is then delegated to our system dpdb, which employs *database management systems (DBMS)* [43]. This has not only the advantage of naturally describing and manipulating the tables that are obtained during DP, but also allows dpdb to benefit from decades of database technology in form of the capability to deal with huge tables using limited amount of main memory (RAM), dedicated database joins, as well as query optimization and data-dependent execution plans.

Contribution. We implement a system dpdb for solving counting problems based on dynamic programming on tree decompositions, and present the following contributions. (i) Our system dpdb uses database management systems to handle table operations needed for performing dynamic programming efficiently. The system dpdb is written in Python and employs PostgreSQL as DBMS, but can work with other DBMSs easily. (ii) The architecture of dpdb allows to solve general problems of bounded treewidth that can be solved by means of table operations (in form of relational algebra and SQL) on tree decompositions. As a result, dpdb is a generalized framework for dynamic programming on tree decompositions, where one only needs to specify the essential and problem-specific parts of dynamic programming in order to solve (counting) problems. (iii) Finally, we show how to solve the canonical problem #SAT with the help of dpdb, where it seems that the architecture of dpdb is particularly well-suited. Concretely, we compare the runtime of our system with state-of-the-art model counters, where we observe competitive behavior and promising indications for future work.

2 Preliminaries

We assume familiarity with terminology of graphs and trees. For details, we refer to the literature and standard textbooks [16].

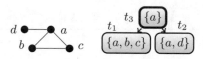

Fig. 1. Graph G (left) with a TD $\mathcal{T}$ of graph G (right).

Boolean Satisfiability. We define Boolean formulas and their evaluation in the usual way, cf., [26]. A literal is a Boolean variable x or its negation $\neg x$. A *CNF formula* φ is a set of *clauses* interpreted as conjunction. A clause is a set of literals interpreted as disjunction. For a formula or clause X, we abbreviate by $\text{var}(X)$ the variables that occur in X. An *assignment* of φ is a mapping $I : \text{var}(\varphi) \to \{0,1\}$. The formula $\varphi(I)$ *under assignment I* is obtained by removing every clause c from φ that contains a literal set to 1 by I, and removing from every remaining clause of φ all literals set to 0 by I. An assignment I is *satisfying* if $\varphi(I) = \emptyset$. Problem #SAT asks to output the number of satisfying assignments of a formula.

Tree Decomposition and Treewidth. A *tree decomposition (TD)* [12,27] of a given graph G is a pair $\mathcal{T} = (T, \chi)$ where T is a rooted tree and χ is a mapping which assigns to each node $t \in V(T)$ a set $\chi(t) \subseteq V(G)$, called *bag*, such that (i) $V(G) = \bigcup_{t \in V(T)} \chi(t)$ and $E(G) \subseteq \{\{u,v\} \mid t \in V(T), \{u,v\} \subseteq \chi(t)\}$; and (ii) for each $r, s, t \in V(T)$, such that s lies on the path from r to t, we have $\chi(r) \cap \chi(t) \subseteq \chi(s)$. We let $\text{width}(\mathcal{T}) := \max_{t \in V(T)} |\chi(t)| - 1$. The *treewidth* $\text{tw}(G)$ of G is the minimum $\text{width}(\mathcal{T})$ over all TDs $\mathcal{T}$ of G. For a node $t \in V(T)$, we say that type(t) is *leaf* if t has no children and $\chi(t) = \emptyset$; *join* if t has children t' and t'' with $t' \neq t''$ and $\chi(t) = \chi(t') = \chi(t'')$; *intr* ("introduce") if t has a single child t', $\chi(t') \subseteq \chi(t)$ and $|\chi(t)| = |\chi(t')| + 1$; *rem* ("removal") if t has a single child t', $\chi(t') \supseteq \chi(t)$ and $|\chi(t')| = |\chi(t)| + 1$. If for every node $t \in V(T)$, type$(t) \in \{leaf, join, intr, rem\}$, then the TD is called *nice*.

Example 1. Figure 1 depicts a graph G and a TD $\mathcal{T}$ of G of width 2. The treewidth of G is also 2 since G contains a complete graph with 3 vertices [27]. ∎

Relational Algebra. We use relational algebra [11] for manipulation of relations, which forms the theoretical basis of the database standard *Structured Query Language (SQL)* [43] on tables. An *attribute a* is of a certain finite

---

Algorithm 1. Table algorithm $S(t, \chi(t), \varphi_t, \langle \tau_1, \ldots, \tau_\ell \rangle)$ for #SAT [36] using nice TD.

In: Node t, bag $\chi(t)$, clauses φ_t, sequence $\langle \tau_1, \ldots \tau_\ell \rangle$ of child tables. **Out:** Table τ_t.

1 **if** type(t) = *leaf* **then** $\tau_t := \{\langle \emptyset, 1 \rangle\}$
2 **else if** type(t) = *intr, and* $a \in \chi(t)$ *is introduced* **then**
3 $\quad | \quad \tau_t := \{\langle J, c \rangle \qquad\qquad | \langle I, c \rangle \in \tau_1, J \in \{I^+_{a \mapsto 0}, I^+_{a \mapsto 1}\}, \varphi_t(J) = \emptyset\}$
4 **else if** type(t) = *rem, and* $a \notin \chi(t)$ *is removed* **then**
5 $\quad | \quad \tau_t := \{\langle I^-_a, \Sigma_{\langle J, c \rangle \in \tau_1 : I^-_a = J^-_a} c \rangle \qquad\qquad | \langle I, \cdot \rangle \in \tau_1\}$
6 **else if** type(t) = *join* **then**
7 $\quad | \quad \tau_t := \{\langle I, c_1 \cdot c_2 \rangle \qquad\qquad | \langle I, c_1 \rangle \in \tau_1, \langle I, c_2 \rangle \in \tau_2\}$

$S^-_e := S \setminus \{e \mapsto 0, e \mapsto 1\}$, $S^+_s := S \cup \{s\}$.

domain dom(a). Then, a *tuple* r over set att(r) of attributes is a set of pairs of the form (a, v) with $a \in$ att(r), $v \in$ dom(a) s.t. for each $a \in$ att(r), there is exactly one $v \in$ dom(a) with $(a, v) \in r$. A *relation* R is a finite set of tuples r over set att(R) := att(r) of attributes. Given a relation R over att(R). Then, we let dom(R) := $\bigcup_{a \in \text{att}(R)}$ dom(a), and let relation R *projected to* $A \subseteq$ att(R) be given by $\Pi_A(R) := \{r_A \mid r \in R\}$, where $r_A := \{(a, v) \mid (a, v) \in r, a \in A\}$. This concept can be lifted to *extended projection* $\dot{\Pi}_{A,S}$, where we assume in addition to $A \subseteq$ att(R), a set S of expressions of the form $a \leftarrow f$, such that $a \in$ att(R)$\setminus A$, and f is an arithmetic function that takes a tuple $r \in R$, such that there is at most one expression in S for each $a \in$ att(R)$\setminus A$. Formally, we define $\dot{\Pi}_{A,S}(R) := \{r_A \cup r^S \mid r \in R\}$ with $r^S := \{(a, f(r)) \mid a \in$ att(r), $(a \leftarrow f) \in S\}$. Later, we use *aggregation by grouping* $_AG_{(a \leftarrow g)}$, where we assume $A \subseteq$ att(R), $a \in$ att(R) $\setminus A$ and a so-called *aggregate function* g, which takes a relation $R' \subseteq R$ and returns a value of domain dom(a). Therefore, we let $_AG_{(a \leftarrow g)}(R) := \{r \cup \{(a, g(R[r]))\} \mid r \in \Pi_A(R)\}$, where $R[r] := \{r' \mid r' \in R, r \subseteq r'\}$. We define *renaming* of R given set A of attributes, and a bijective mapping $m :$ att(R) $\rightarrow A$ s.t. dom(a) = dom($m(a)$) for $a \in$ att(R), by $\rho_m(R) := \{(m(a), v) \mid (a, v) \in R\}$. *Selection* of rows in R according to a given Boolean formula φ with equality[1] is defined by $\sigma_\varphi(R) := \{r \mid r \in R, \varphi(r^E) = \emptyset\}$, where r^E is a truth assignment over var(φ) such that for each $v, v', v'' \in$ dom(R) $\cup$ att(R) (1) $r^E(v \approx v') = 1$ if $(v, v') \in r$, (2) $r^E(v \approx v) = 1$, (3) $r^E(v \approx v') = r^E(v' \approx v)$, and (4) if $r^E(v \approx v') = 1$, and $r^E(v' \approx v'') = 1$, then $r^E(v \approx v'') = 1$. Given a relation R' with att(R') $\cap$ att(R) $= \emptyset$. Then, we refer to the *cross-join* by $R \times R' := \{r \cup r' \mid r \in R, r' \in R'\}$. Further, a θ-*join* (according to φ) corresponds to $R \bowtie_\varphi R' := \sigma_\varphi(R \times R')$.

3   Towards Relational Algebra for Dynamic Programming

A solver based on *dynamic programming (DP)* evaluates the input $\mathcal{I}$ in parts along a given TD of a graph representation G of the input. Thereby, for each node t of the TD, intermediate results are stored in a *table* τ_t. This is achieved

---

[1] We allow for φ to contain expressions $v \approx v'$ as variables for $v, v' \in$ dom(R) $\cup$ att(R), and we abbreviate for $v \in$ att(R) with dom(v) = $\{0, 1\}$, $v \approx 1$ by v and $v \approx 0$ by $\neg v$.

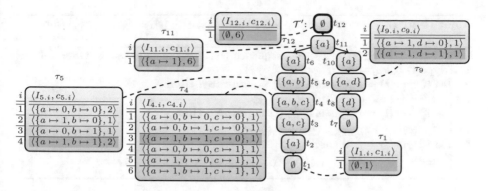

Fig. 2. Selected tables obtained by DP on $\mathcal{T}'$ for φ of Example 2 using algorithm S. (Color figure online)

by running a so-called *table algorithm* A, which is designed for a certain graph representation, and stores in τ_t results of problem parts of $\mathcal{I}$, thereby considering tables $\tau_{t'}$ for child nodes t' of t. DP works for many problems $\mathcal{P}$ as follows.

1. Construct a graph representation G of the given input instance $\mathcal{I}$.
2. Heuristically compute a tree decomposition $\mathcal{T} = (T, \chi)$ of G.
3. Traverse the nodes in $V(T)$ in post-order, i.e., perform a bottom-up traversal of T. At every node t during post-order traversal, execute a table algorithm A that takes as input t, bag $\chi(t)$, a *local problem* $\mathcal{P}(t, \mathcal{I}) = \mathcal{I}_t$ depending on $\mathcal{P}$, as well as previously computed child tables of t and stores the result in τ_t.
4. Interpret table τ_n for the root n of T in order to output the solution of $\mathcal{I}$.

For solving problem $\mathcal{P} = \#\text{SAT}$, we need the following graph representation. The *primal graph* G_φ [36] of a formula φ has as vertices its variables, where two variables are joined by an edge if they occur together in a clause of φ. Given formula φ, a TD $\mathcal{T} = (T, \chi)$ of G_φ and a node t of T. Sometimes, we refer to the treewidth of the primal graph of a given formula by the *treewidth of the formula*. Then, we let local problem $\#\text{SAT}(t, \varphi) = \varphi_t$ be $\varphi_t := \{ c \mid c \in \varphi, \text{var}(c) \subseteq \chi(t) \}$, which are the clauses entirely covered by $\chi(t)$.

Table algorithm S as presented in Algorithm 1 shows all the cases that are needed to solve $\#\text{SAT}$ by means of DP over nice TDs. Each table τ_t consist of rows of the form $\langle I, c \rangle$, where I is an assignment of φ_t and c is a counter. Nodes t with type$(t) = leaf$ consist of the empty assignment and counter 1, cf., Line 1. For a node t with introduced variable $a \in \chi(t)$, we guess in Line 3 for each assignment β of the child table, whether a is set to true or to false, and ensure that φ_t is satisfied. When an atom a is removed in node t, we project assignments of child tables to $\chi(t)$, cf., Line 5, and sum up counters of the same assignments. For join nodes, counters of common assignments are multiplied, cf., Line 7.

Example 2. Consider formula $\varphi := \{\overbrace{\{\neg a, b, c\}}^{c_1}, \overbrace{\{a, \neg b, \neg c\}}^{c_2}, \overbrace{\{a, d\}}^{c_3}, \overbrace{\{a, \neg d\}}^{c_4}\}$. Satisfying assignments of formula φ are, e.g., $\{a \mapsto 1, b \mapsto 1, c \mapsto 0, d \mapsto 0\}$,

Algorithm 2. Alternative table algorithm $S_{\mathsf{RAlg}}(t, \chi(t), \varphi_t, \langle \tau_1, \ldots, \tau_\ell \rangle)$ for #SAT.

In: Node t, bag $\chi(t)$, clauses φ_t, sequence $\langle \tau_1, \ldots \tau_\ell \rangle$ of child tables. **Out:** Table τ_t.

1 **if** type$(t) = $ *leaf* **then** $\tau_t := \{\{(\mathrm{cnt}, 1)\}\}$
2 **else if** type$(t) = intr$, *and* $a \in \chi(t)$ *is introduced* **then**
3 $\quad | \quad \tau_t := \tau_1 \bowtie_{\varphi_t} \{\{([\![a]\!], 0)\}, \{([\![a]\!], 1)\}\}$
4 **else if** type$(t) = rem$, *and* $a \notin \chi(t)$ *is removed* **then**
5 $\quad | \quad \tau_t := {}_{\chi(t)}G_{\mathrm{cnt}\leftarrow\mathrm{SUM}(\mathrm{cnt})}(\Pi_{\mathrm{att}(\tau_1)\setminus\{[\![a]\!]\}}\tau_1)$
6 **else if** type$(t) = join$ **then**
7 $\quad | \quad \tau_t := \dot{\Pi}_{\chi(t),\{\mathrm{cnt}\leftarrow\mathrm{cnt}\cdot\mathrm{cnt}'\}}(\tau_1 \bowtie_{\bigwedge_{a\in\chi(t)}[\![a]\!]\approx[\![a]\!]'} \rho_{\bigcup_{a\in\mathrm{att}(\tau_2)}\{[\![a]\!]\mapsto[\![a]\!]'\}}\tau_2)$

$\{a \mapsto 1, b \mapsto 0, c \mapsto 1, d \mapsto 0\}$ or $\{a \mapsto 1, b \mapsto 1, c \mapsto 1, d \mapsto 1\}$. In total, there are 6 satisfying assignments of φ. Observe that graph G of Fig. 1 actually depicts the primal graph G_φ of φ. Intuitively, $\mathcal{T}$ of Fig. 1 allows to evaluate formula φ in parts. Figure 2 illustrates a nice TD $\mathcal{T}' = (\cdot, \chi)$ of the primal graph G_φ and tables $\tau_1, \ldots, \tau_{12}$ that are obtained during the execution of S on nodes $t_1, \ldots, t_{12}$. We assume that each row in a table τ_t is identified by a number, i.e., row i corresponds to $u_{t.i} = \langle I_{t.i}, c_{t.i} \rangle$.

Table $\tau_1 = \{\langle \emptyset, 1 \rangle\}$ has type$(t_1) = $ *leaf*. Since type$(t_2) = intr$, we construct table τ_2 from τ_1 by taking $I_{1.i} \cup \{a \mapsto 0\}$ and $I_{1.i} \cup \{a \mapsto 1\}$ for each $\langle I_{1.i}, c_{1.i} \rangle \in \tau_1$. Then, t_3 introduces c and t_4 introduces b. $\varphi_{t_1} = \varphi_{t_2} = \varphi_{t_3} = \emptyset$, but since $\chi(t_4) \subseteq \mathrm{var}(c_1)$ we have $\varphi_{t_4} = \{c_1, c_2\}$ for t_4. In consequence, for each $I_{4.i}$ of table τ_4, we have $\{c_1, c_2\}(I_{4.i}) = \emptyset$ since S enforces satisfiability of φ_t in node t. Since type$(t_5) = rem$, we remove variable c from all elements in τ_4 and sum up counters accordingly to construct τ_5. Note that we have already seen all rules where c occurs and hence c can no longer affect interpretations during the remaining traversal. We similarly create $\tau_6 = \{\langle \{a \mapsto 0\}, 3 \rangle, \langle \{a \mapsto 1\}, 3 \rangle\}$ and $\tau_{10} = \{\langle \{a \mapsto 1\}, 2 \rangle\}$. Since type$(t_{11}) = join$, we build table τ_{11} by taking the intersection of τ_6 and τ_{10}. Intuitively, this combines assignments agreeing on a, where counters are multiplied accordingly. By definition (primal graph and TDs), for every $c \in \varphi$, variables $\mathrm{var}(c)$ occur together in at least one common bag. Hence, since $\tau_{12} = \{\langle \emptyset, 6 \rangle\}$, we can reconstruct for example model $\{a \mapsto 1, b \mapsto 1, c \mapsto 0, d \mapsto 1\} = I_{11.1} \cup I_{5.4} \cup I_{9.2}$ of φ using highlighted (yellow) rows in Fig. 2. On the other hand, if φ was unsatisfiable, τ_{12} would be empty ($\emptyset$). ∎

Alternative: Relational Algebra. Instead of using set theory to describe how tables are obtained during dynamic programming, one could alternatively use relational algebra. There, tables τ_t for each TD node t are pictured as relations, where τ_t distinguishes a unique column (attribute) $[\![x]\!]$ for each $x \in \chi(t)$. Further, there might be additional attributes required depending on the problem at hand, e.g., we need an attribute cnt for counting in #SAT, or an attribute for modeling costs or weights in case of optimization problems. Algorithm 2 presents a table algorithm for problem #SAT that is equivalent to Algorithm 1, but relies on relational algebra only for computing tables. This step from set notation to relational algebra is driven by the observation that in these table algorithms one

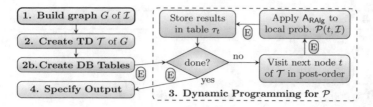

Fig. 3. Architecture of Dynamic Programming with Databases. Steps highlighted in red are provided by the system depending on specification of yellow and blue parts, which is given by the user for specific problems $\mathcal{P}$. The yellow "E"s represent events that can be intercepted and handled by the user. The blue part concentrates on table algorithm A_{RAlg}, where the user specifies how SQL code is generated in a modular way. (Color figure online)

can identify recurring patterns, and one mainly has to adjust problem-specific parts of it (highlighted by coloring in Algorithm 1). In particular, one typically derives for nodes t with type$(t) = $ *leaf*, a fresh initial table τ_t, cf., Line 1 of Algorithm 2. Then, whenever an atom a is introduced, such algorithms often use θ-joins with a fresh initial table for the introduced variable a representing potential values for a. In Line 3 the selection of the θ-join is performed according to φ_t, i.e. corresponding to the local problem of #SAT. Further, for nodes t with type$(t) = $ *rem*, these table algorithms typically need projection. In case of Algorithm 2, Line 5 also needs grouping in order to maintain the counter, as several rows of τ_1 might collapse in τ_t. Finally, for a node t with type$(t) = $ *join*, in Line 7 we use extended projection and θ-joins, where we join on the same truth assignments, which allows us later to leverage advanced database technology. Extended projection is needed for multiplying the counters of the two rows containing the same assignment.

4   Dynamic Programming on TDs Using Databases and SQL

In this section, we present a general architecture to model table algorithms by means of database management systems. The architecture is influenced by the DP approach of the previous section and works as depicted in Fig. 3, where the steps highlighted in yellow and blue need to be specified depending on the problem $\mathcal{P}$. Steps outside Step 3 are mainly setup tasks, the yellow "E"s indicate *events* that might be needed to solve more complex problems on the polynomial hierarchy. For example, one could create and drop auxiliary sub-tables for each node during Step 3 within such events. Observe that after the generation of a TD $\mathcal{T} = (T, \chi)$, Step 2b automatically creates tables τ_t for each node t of T, where the corresponding table schema of τ_t is specified in the blue part, i.e., within A_{RAlg}. The *default schema* of such a table τ_t that is assumed in this

---

Listing 3. Template of $\mathsf{A}_{\mathsf{RAlg}}(t, \chi(t), \mathcal{I}_t, \langle \tau_1, \ldots, \tau_\ell \rangle)$ of Figure 3 for problem $\mathcal{P}$.

In: Node t, bag $\chi(t)$, instance $\mathcal{I}_t$, sequence $\langle \tau_1, \ldots \tau_\ell \rangle$ of child tables. **Out:** Table τ_t.

```
1  if type(t) = leaf then τ_t := #εTab#
2  else if type(t) = intr, and a ∈ χ(t) is introduced then
3  │    τ_t := Π̇_{χ(t),#extProj#}(τ_1 ⋈_{#localProbFilter#} #intrTab#)
4  else if type(t) = rem, and a ∉ χ(t) is removed then
5  │    τ_t := _{χ(t)}G_{#aggrExp#}(Π_{att(τ_1)\{[[a]]}}τ_1)
6  else if type(t) = join then
7  │    τ_t := Π̇_{χ(t),#extProj#}(τ_1 ⋈_{⋀_{a∈χ(t)}[[a]]≈[[a]]'} ρ_{∪{[[a]]↦[[a]]'}}τ_2)
                                                    a∈att(τ_2)
```

---

section foresees one column for each element of the bag $\chi(t)$, where additional columns such as counters or costs can be added.

Actually, the core of this architecture is focused on the table algorithm $\mathsf{A}_{\mathsf{RAlg}}$ executed for each node t of T of TD $\mathcal{T} = (T, \chi)$. Besides the definition of table schemes, the blue part concerns specification of the table algorithm by means of a procedural *generator template* that describes how to dynamically obtain SQL code for each node t thereby oftentimes depending on $\chi(t)$. This generated SQL code is then used internally for manipulation of tables τ_t during the tree decomposition traversal in Step 3 of dynamic programming. Listing 3 presents a general template, where parts of table algorithms for problems that are typically problem-specific are replaced by colored placeholders of the form #placeHolder#, cf., Algorithm 2. Observe that Line 3 of Listing 3 uses extended projection as in Line 7. This is needed for some problems requiring changes on vertex introduction.

Note, however, that the whole architecture does not depend on certain normalization or forms of TDs, e.g., whether it is nice or not. Instead, a table algorithm of any TD is simply specified by handling *problem-specific* implementations of the placeholders of Listing 3, where the system following this architecture is responsible for interleaving and overlapping these cases within a node t. In fact, we discuss an implementation of a system according to this architecture next, where it is crucial to implement non-nice TDs to obtain higher efficiency.

4.1 System dpdb: Dynamic Programming with Databases

We implemented the proposed architecture of the previous section in the prototypical dpdb system. The system is open-source[2], written in Python 3 and uses PostgreSQL as DBMS. We are convinced though that one can easily replace PostgreSQL by any other state-of-the-art relational database that uses SQL. In the following, we discuss implementation specifics that are crucial for a performant system that is still extendable and flexible.

Computing TDs. TDs are computed mainly with the library *htd* version 1.2 with default settings [2], which finds TDs extremely quick also for interesting instances [23] due to heuristics. Note that dpdb directly supports the TD format

---

[2] Our system dpdb is available under GPL3 license at github.com/hmarkus/dp_on_dbs.

of recent competitions [15], i.e., one could easily replace the TD library. It is important though to not enforce htd to compute nice TDs, as this would cause a lot of overhead later in dpdb for copying tables. However, in order to benefit from the implementation of θ-joins, query optimization and state-of-the-art database technology in general, we observed that it is crucial to limit the number of child nodes of every TD node. Then, especially when there are huge tables involved, θ-joins among child node tables cover at most a limited number of child node tables. In consequence, the query optimizer of the database system still has a chance to come up with meaningful execution plans depending on the contents of the table. Note that though one should consider θ-joins with more than just two tables, since such binary θ-joins already fix in which order these tables shall be combined, thereby again limiting the query optimizer. Apart from this trade-off, we tried to outsource the task of joining tables to the DBMS, since the performance of database systems highly depends on query optimization. The actual limit, which is a restriction from experience and practice only, highly depends on the DBMS that is used. For PostgreSQL, we set a limit of at most 5 child nodes for each node of the TD, i.e., each θ-join covers at most 5 child tables.

Towards non-nice TDs. Although this paper presents the algorithms for nice TDs (mainly due to simplicity), the system dpdb interleaves these cases as presented in Listing 3. Concretely, the system executes one query per table τ_t for each node t during the traversal of TD $\mathcal{T}$. This query consists of several parts and we briefly explain its parts from outside to inside. First of all, the inner-most part concerns the *row candiates* for τ_t consisting of the θ-join as in Line 7 of Listing 3, including parts of Line 3, namely cross-joins for each introduced variable, involving #intrTab# without the filtering on #localProbFilter#. Then, there are different configurations of dpdb concerning these row candidates. For debugging (see below) one could (1) actually materialize the result in a table, whereas for performance runs, one should use (2) *common table expressions (CTEs or WITH-queries)* or (3) *sub-queries (nested queries)*, which both result in one nested SQL query per table τ_t. On top of these row candidates, projection[3] and grouping involving #aggrExp# as in Line 5 of Listing 3, as well as selection according to #localProbFilter#, cf., Line 3, is specified. It turns out that PostgreSQL can do better with sub-queries, where the query optimizer oftentimes pushes selection and projection into the sub-query if needed, which is not the case for CTEs, as discussed in the PostgreSQL manual [1, Sec. 7.8.1]. On different DBMS or other vendors, e.g., Oracle, it might be better to use CTEs instead.

Example 3. Consider again Example 2 and Fig. 1. If we use table algorithm S_{RAlg} with dpdb on formula φ of TD $\mathcal{T}$ and Option (3): sub-queries, where the row candidates are expressed via a sub-queries. Then, for each node t_i of $\mathcal{T}$, dpdb generates a view vi as well as a table τ_i containing in the end the content of vi. Observe that each view only has one column $[\![a]\!]$ for each variable a of φ since the truth assignment of the other variables are not needed later. This

---

[3] Actually, dpdb keeps only columns relevant for the table of the parent node of t.

keeps the tables compact, only τ_1 has two rows, τ_2, and τ_3 have only one row. We obtain the following views.

```
CREATE VIEW v1 AS SELECT a, sum(cnt) AS cnt FROM
 (WITH intrTab AS (SELECT 1 AS val UNION ALL SELECT 0)
   SELECT i1.val AS a, i2.val AS b, i3.val AS c, 1 AS cnt
          FROM intrTab i1, intrTab i2, intrTab i3)
WHERE (NOT a OR b OR c) AND (a OR NOT b OR NOT c) GROUP BY a

CREATE VIEW v2 AS SELECT a, sum(cnt) AS cnt FROM
 (WITH intrTab AS (SELECT 1 AS val UNION ALL SELECT 0)
   SELECT i1.val AS a, i2.val AS d, 1 AS cnt FROM intrTab i1, intrTab i2)
WHERE (a OR d) AND (a OR NOT d) GROUP BY a

CREATE VIEW v3 AS SELECT a, sum(cnt) AS cnt FROM
 (SELECT τ₁.a, τ₁.cnt * τ₂.cnt AS cnt FROM τ₁, τ₂ WHERE τ₁.a = τ₂.a)
GROUP BY a                                                        ■
```

Parallelization. A further reason to not over-restrict the number of child nodes within the TD, lies in parallelization. In dpdb, we compute tables in parallel along the TD, where multiple tables can be computed at the same time, as long as the child tables are computed. Therefore, we tried to keep the number of child nodes in the TD as high as possible. In our system dpdb, we currently allow for at most 24 worker threads for table computations and 24 database connections at the same time (both pooled and configurable). On top of that we have 2 additional threads and database connections for job assignments to workers, as well as one dedicated watcher thread for clean-up and connection termination, respectively.

Logging, Debugging and Extensions. Currently, we have two versions of the dpdb system implemented. One version aims for performance and the other one tries to achieve comprehensive logging and easy debugging of problem (instances), thereby increasing explainability. The former for instance does neither keep intermediate results nor create database tables in advance (Step 2b), as depicted in Fig. 3, but creates tables according to an SQL SELECT statement. In the latter we keep all the intermediate results, we record database timestamps before and after certain nodes, provide statistics as, e.g., width, number of rows, etc. Further, since for each table τ_t, exactly one SQL statement is executed for filling this table, we also have a dedicated view of the SQL SELECT statement, whose result is then inserted in τ_t. Together with the power and flexibility of SQL queries, we observed that this helps in finding errors in the table algorithm specifications.

Besides convenient debugging, system dpdb immediately contains an extension for *approximation*. There, we restrict the table contents to a maximum number of rows. This allows for certain approximations on counting problems or optimization problems, where it is infeasible to compute the full tables. Further, dpdb foresees a dedicated *randomization* on these restricted number of rows such that we obtain different approximate results on different random seeds.

Note that dpdb can be easily extended. Each problem can overwrite existing default behavior and dpdb also supports problem-specific argument parser for each problem individually. Out-of-the-box, we support the formats DIMACS sat and DIMACS graph [32] as well as the common format for TDs [15].

4.2 Table Algorithms With dpdb for Selected Problems

The system dpdb allows for *easy protyping* of DP algorithms on TDs. This covers decision problems, counting problems as well as optimization problems. As a proof of concept, we present the relevant parts of table algorithm specification according to the template in Listing 3 for a selection of problems below[4]. To this end, we assume in this section a not necessarily nice TD $\mathcal{T} = (T, \chi)$ of the corresponding graph representation of our given instance $\mathcal{I}$. Further, for the following specifications of the table algorithm using the template A_{RAlg} in Algorithm 2, we assume any node t of T and its child nodes $t_1, \ldots, t_\ell$.

Problem #SAT. Given instance formula $\mathcal{I} = \varphi$. Then, specific parts for #SAT for node t with $\varphi_t = \{\{l_{1,1}, \ldots, l_{1,k_1}\}, \ldots, \{l_{n,1}, \ldots, l_{n,k_n}\}\}$.

- #εTab#:   SELECT 1 AS cnt
- #intrTab#:   SELECT 1 AS val UNION ALL 0
- #localProbFilter#: $(l_{1,1}$ OR ... OR $l_{1,k_1})$ AND ... AND $(l_{n,1}$ OR ... OR $l_{n,k_n})$
- #aggrExp#:   SUM(cnt) AS cnt
- #extProj#: τ_1.cnt * ... * τ_ℓ.cnt AS cnt

Observe that for the corresponding decision problem SAT, where the goal is to decide only the existence of a satisfying assignment for given formula φ, #εTab# returns the empty table and parts #aggrExp#, #extProj# are just empty since there is no counter needed.

Problem #o-COL. For given input graph $\mathcal{I} = G = (V, E)$, a *o-coloring* is a mapping $\iota : V \to \{1, \ldots, o\}$ such that for each edge $\{u, v\} \in E$, we have $\iota(u) \neq \iota(v)$. Problem #o-COL asks to count the number of o-colorings of G. Local problem #o-COL(t,G) is defined by the graph $G_t := (V \cap \chi(t), E \cap \lceil \chi(t) \times \chi(t) \rceil)$.

Specific parts for #o-COL for node t with $E(G_t) = \{\{u_1, v_1\}, \ldots, \{u_n, v_n\}\}$.

- #εTab#:   SELECT 1 AS cnt
- #intrTab#:   SELECT 1 AS val UNION ALL ... UNION ALL o
- #localProbFilter#: NOT ($[\![u_1]\!] = [\![v_1]\!]$) AND ... AND NOT ($[\![u_n]\!] = [\![v_n]\!]$)
- #aggrExp#:   SUM(cnt) AS cnt
- #extProj#: τ_1.cnt * ... * τ_ℓ.cnt AS cnt

Problem MINVC. Given input graph $\mathcal{I} = G = (V, E)$, a *vertex cover* is a set of vertices $C \subseteq V$ of G such that for each edge $\{u, v\} \in E$, we have $\{u, v\} \cap C \neq \emptyset$. Then, MINVC asks to find the minimum cardinality $|C|$ among all vertex covers C, i.e., C is such that there is no vertex cover C' with $|C'| < |C|$. Local problem MINVC$(t, G) := G_t$ is defined as above. We use an additional column card for storing cardinalities.

Problem MINVC for node t with $E(G_t) = \{\{u_1, v_1\}, \ldots, \{u_n, v_n\}\}$ and $\chi(t) = \{a_1, \ldots, a_k\}$ can be specified as follows.

---

[4] Implementation for problems #SAT as well as MINVC is readily available in dpdb.

- #εTab#:   `SELECT 0 AS card`
- #intrTab#:   `SELECT 1 AS val UNION ALL 0`
- #localProbFilter#: $([\![u_1]\!]$ `OR` $[\![v_1]\!])$ `AND` $\ldots$ `AND` $([\![u_n]\!]$ `OR` $[\![v_n]\!])$
- #aggrExp#:   `MIN(card) AS card`
- #extProj#: $\tau_1.\texttt{card} + \ldots + \tau_\ell.\texttt{card} - (\Sigma_{i=1}^{\ell}|\chi(t_i) \cap \{a_1\}| - 1) *$
                   $\tau_1.[\![a_1]\!] - \ldots - (\Sigma_{i=1}^{\ell}|\chi(t_i) \cap \{a_k\}| - 1) * \tau_1.[\![a_k]\!]$

Observe that #ExtProj# is a bit more involved on non-nice TDs, as, whenever the column for a vertex a is set to 1, i.e., vertex a is in the vertex cover, we have to consider a only with cost 1, also if a appears in several child node bags.

Note that concrete implementations could generate and apply parts of this specification, as for example in #localProbFilter# only edges involving newly introduced vertices need to be checked.

Similar to MinVC and #o-Col one can model several other (graph) problems. One could also think of counting the number of solutions of problem MinVC, where both a column for cardinalities and one for counting is used. There, in addition to grouping with `GROUP BY` in dpdb, we additionally could use the `HAVING` construct of SQL, where only rows are kept, whose column `card` is minimal.

5   Experiments

We conducted a series of experiments using publicly available benchmark sets for #Sat. Our tested benchmarks [22] are publicly available, and our results are also on github at github.com/hmarkus/dp_on_dbs/padl2020.

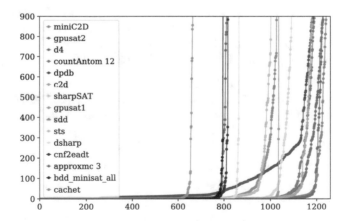

Fig. 4. Runtime for the top 15 solvers over all #Sat instances. The x-axis refers to the number of instances and the y-axis depicts the runtime sorted in ascending order for each solver individually.

Table 1. Number of solved #SAT instances, preprocessed by pmc and grouped by intervals of upper bounds of the treewidth. time[h] is the cumulated wall clock time in hours, where unsolved instances are counted as 900 s.

solver	0-20	21-30	31-40	41-50	51-60	>60	best	unique	∑	time[h]
miniC2D	1193	29	10	2	1	7	13	0	**1242**	**68.77**
gpusat2	**1196**	**32**	1	0	0	0	250	2	1229	71.27
d4	1163	20	10	2	4	28	52	1	1227	76.86
countAntom 12	1141	18	10	5	4	13	101	0	1191	84.39
dpdb	1159	19	5	2	0	0	2	1	1185	100.99
c2d	1124	31	10	3	3	10	20	0	1181	84.41
sharpSAT	1029	16	10	2	4	30	253	1	1091	106.88
gpusat1	1020	16	0	0	0	0	106	1	1036	114.86
sdd	1014	4	7	1	0	2	0	0	1028	124.23
sts	927	4	8	**7**	5	**52**	73	**21**	1003	128.43
dsharp	853	3	7	2	0	0	83	0	865	157.87
cnf2eadt	799	3	7	2	0	7	**328**	0	818	170.17
approxmc 3	794	3	7	2	0	6	10	0	812	173.35
bdd_minisat_all	791	4	1	0	0	0	99	0	796	175.09
cachet	624	3	8	2	3	24	3	0	664	209.26
approxmc 2	447	3	0	0	0	0	1	0	450	265.31
sharpCDCL	340	3	0	0	0	0	0	0	343	289.17

(rows dpdb through sharpCDCL grouped under side-label: preprocessed by pmc [29])

5.1   Setup

Measure & Resources. We mainly compare wall clock time and number of time-outs. In the time we include *preprocessing time* as well as *decomposition time* for computing a TD with a fixed random seed. For parallel solvers we allowed access to 24 physical cores on machines. We set a timeout of 900 s and limited available RAM to 14 GB per instance and solver.

Benchmark Instances. We considered a selection of overall 1494 instances from various publicly available benchmark sets #SAT consisting of fre/meel benchmarks[5] (1480 instances), and c2d benchmarks[6] (14 instances). However, we considered instances preprocessed by regular #SAT preprocessor *pmc* [29], similar to results of recent work on #SAT [23], where it was also shown that more than 80% of the #SAT instances have primal treewidth below 19 after preprocessing.

Benchmarked system dpdb. We used PostgreSQL 9.5 for our system dpdb, which was available on our benchmark described hardware below. However, we expect major performance increases if higher versions are used, which was not available on our benchmark machines. In particular, parallel queries, where a query is evaluated in parallel, were added and improved in every version greater than 9.6.

Other benchmarked systems. In our experimental work, we present results for the most recent versions of publicly available #SAT solvers, namely, *c2d* 2.20 [13],

---

[5] See: tinyurl.com/countingbenchmarks.
[6] See: reasoning.cs.ucla.edu/c2d.

d4 1.0 [30], *DSHARP* 1.0 [33], *miniC2D* 1.0.0 [34], *cnf2eadt* 1.0 [28], *bdd_minisat_all* 1.0.2 [42], and *sdd* 2.0 [14], which are all based on knowledge compilation techniques. We also considered rather recent approximate solvers *ApproxMC2*, *ApproxMC3* [7] and *sts* 1.0 [20], as well as CDCL-based solvers *Cachet* 1.21 [37], *sharpCDCL*[7], and *sharpSAT* 13.02 [40]. Finally, we also included multi-core solvers *gpusat* 1.0 and *gpusat* 2.0 [23], which both are based on dynamic programming, as well as *countAntom* 1.0 [6] on 12 physical CPU cores, which performed better than on 24 cores. Experiments were conducted with default solver options.

Benchmark Hardware. Almost all solvers were executed on a cluster of 12 nodes. Each node is equipped with two Intel Xeon E5-2650 CPUs consisting of 12 physical cores each at 2.2 GHz clock speed, 256 GB RAM and 1 TB hard disc drives (*not* an SSD) Seagate ST1000NM0033. The results were gathered on Ubuntu 16.04.1 LTS machines with disabled hyperthreading on kernel 4.4.0-139. As we also took into account solvers using a GPU, for gpusat1 and gpusat2 we used a machine equipped with a consumer GPU: Intel Core i3-3245 CPU operating at 3.4 GHz, 16 GB RAM, and one Sapphire Pulse ITX Radeon RX 570 GPU running at 1.24 GHz with 32 compute units, 2048 shader units, and 4 GB VRAM using driver amdgpu-pro-18.30-641594 and OpenCL 1.2. The system operated on Ubuntu 18.04.1 LTS with kernel 4.15.0-34.

5.2　Results

Figure 4 illustrates the top 15 solvers, where instances are preprocessed by pmc, in a cactus-like plot, which provides an overview over all the benchmarked #SAT instances. The x-axis of these plots refers to the number of instances and the y-axis depicts the runtime sorted in ascending order for each solver individually. Overall, dpdb seems to be quite competitive and beats most of the solvers, as for example gpusat1, sharpSAT, dsharp, approxmc as well as cachet. Surprisingly, our system shows a different runtime behavior than the other solvers. We believe that the reason lies in an initial overhead caused by the creation of the tables that seems to depend on the number of nodes of the used TD. There, *I/O operations* of writing from main memory to hard disk seem to kick in. Table 1 presents more detailed runtime results, showing a solid fifth place for dpdb as our system solves the vast majority of the instances. Assume we only have instances up to an upper bound[8] of treewidth 35. Then, if instances with TDs up to width 35 are considered, dpdb solves even slightly more instances than countAntom.

6　Final Discussion and Conclusions

We presented a generic system dpdb for explicitly exploiting treewidth by means of dynamic programming on databases. The idea of dpdb is to use database

---

[7] See: tools.computational-logic.org.

[8] These upper bounds were obtained via decomposer htd in at most two seconds.

management systems (DBMS) for table manipulation, which makes it (1) easy and elegant to perform *rapid prototyping* for problems, and (2) allows to leverage from decades of database theory and database system tuning. It turned out that all the cases that occur in dynamic programming can be handled quite elegantly with plain SQL queries. Our system dpdb can be used for both decision and counting problems, thereby also considering optimization. We see our system particularly well-suited for counting problems, especially, since it was shown that for model counting (#Sat) instances of practical relevance typically have small treewidth [23]. In consequence, we carried out preliminary experiments on publicly available instances for #Sat, where we see competitive behavior compared to most recent solvers.

Future Work. Our results give rise to several research questions. First of all, we want to push towards PostgreSQL 12, but at the same time also consider other vendors and systems, e.g., Oracle. In particular, the behavior of different systems might change, when we use different strategies on how to write and evaluate our SQL queries, e.g., sub-queries vs. common table expressions. Currently, we do not create or use any indices, as preliminary tests showed that *meaningful B*tree indices* are hard to create and oftentimes cost too much time to create. Further, the exploration of bitmap indices, as available in Oracle *enterprise DBMS* would be worth trying in our case (and for #Sat), since one can efficiently combine database columns by using extremely *efficient bit operations*.

It might be worth to rigorously test and explore our extensions on limiting the number of rows per table for *approximating* #Sat or other counting problems, cf., [8,19,39]. Another interesting research direction is to study whether efficient data representation techniques on DBMS can be combined with dynamic programming in order to lift our solver to quantified Boolean formulas. Finally, we are also interested in extending this work to projected model counting [21].

References

1. Postgresql documentation 12 (2019). https://www.postgresql.org/docs/12/queries-with.html
2. Abseher, M., Musliu, N., Woltran, S.: htd – a free, open-source framework for (customized) tree decompositions and beyond. In: Salvagnin, D., Lombardi, M. (eds.) CPAIOR 2017. LNCS, vol. 10335, pp. 376–386. Springer, Cham (2017). https://doi.org/10.1007/978-3-319-59776-8_30
3. Bacchus, F., Dalmao, S., Pitassi, T.: Algorithms and complexity results for #SAT and Bayesian inference. In: FOCS 2003, pp. 340–351. IEEE Computer Society (2003)
4. Bannach, M., Berndt, S.: Practical access to dynamic programming on tree decompositions. Algorithms **12**(8), 172 (2019)
5. Bliem, B., Charwat, G., Hecher, M., Woltran, S.: D-flat^2: subset minimization in dynamic programming on tree decompositions made easy. Fundam. Inform. **147**(1), 27–61 (2016)

6. Burchard, J., Schubert, T., Becker, B.: Laissez-Faire caching for parallel #SAT solving. In: Heule, M., Weaver, S. (eds.) SAT 2015. LNCS, vol. 9340, pp. 46–61. Springer, Cham (2015). https://doi.org/10.1007/978-3-319-24318-4_5

7. Chakraborty, S., Fremont, D.J., Meel, K.S., Seshia, S.A., Vardi, M.Y.: Distribution-aware sampling and weighted model counting for SAT. In: AAAI 2014, pp. 1722–1730. The AAAI Press (2014)

8. Chakraborty, S., Meel, K.S., Vardi, M.Y.: Improving approximate counting for probabilistic inference: From linear to logarithmic sat solver calls. In: IJCAI 2016, pp. 3569–3576. The AAAI Press (2016)

9. Charwat, G., Woltran, S.: Expansion-based QBF solving on tree decompositions. Fundam. Inform. **167**(1–2), 59–92 (2019)

10. Choi, A., Van den Broeck, G., Darwiche, A.: Tractable learning for structured probability spaces: a case study in learning preference distributions. In: IJCAI 2015. The AAAI Press (2015)

11. Codd, E.F.: A relational model of data for large shared data banks. Commun. ACM **13**(6), 377–387 (1970)

12. Cygan, M., et al.: Parameterized Algorithms. Springer, Switzerland (2015). https://doi.org/10.1007/978-3-319-21275-3

13. Darwiche, A.: New advances in compiling CNF to decomposable negation normal form. In: ECAI 2004, pp. 318–322. IOS Press (2004)

14. Darwiche, A.: SDD: a new canonical representation of propositional knowledge bases. In: IJCAI 2011, pp. 819–826. AAAI Press/IJCAI (2011)

15. Dell, H., Komusiewicz, C., Talmon, N., Weller, M.: The PACE 2017 parameterized algorithms and computational experiments challenge: the second iteration. In: IPEC 2017, Leibniz International Proceedings in Informatics (LIPIcs), vol. 89, pp. 30:1–30:12. Dagstuhl Publishing (2018)

16. Diestel, R.: Graph Theory. Graduate Texts in Mathematics, vol. 173, 4th edn. Springer, Heidelberg (2012). https://doi.org/10.1007/978-3-662-53622-3

17. Domshlak, C., Hoffmann, J.: Probabilistic planning via heuristic forward search and weighted model counting. J. Artif. Intell. Res. **30**, 565–620 (2007)

18. Doubilet, P., Rota, G.C., Stanley, R.: On the foundations of combinatorial theory (VI): the idea of generating function. In: Berkeley Symposium on Mathematical Statistics and Probability, vol. 2, pp. 267–318 (1972)

19. Dueñas-Osorio, L., Meel, K.S., Paredes, R., Vardi, M.Y.: Counting-based reliability estimation for power-transmission grids. In: AAAI 2017, pp. 4488–4494. The AAAI Press (2017)

20. Ermon, S., Gomes, C.P., Selman, B.: Uniform solution sampling using a constraint solver as an oracle. In: UAI 2012, pp. 255–264. AUAI Press (2012)

21. Fichte, J.K., Hecher, M., Morak, M., Woltran, S.: Exploiting treewidth for projected model counting and its limits. In: Beyersdorff, O., Wintersteiger, C.M. (eds.) SAT 2018. LNCS, vol. 10929, pp. 165–184. Springer, Cham (2018). https://doi.org/10.1007/978-3-319-94144-8_11

22. Fichte, J.K., Hecher, M., Woltran, S., Zisser, M.: A benchmark collection of #SAT instances and tree decompositions (benchmark set), June 2018. https://doi.org/10.5281/zenodo.1299752

23. Fichte, J.K., Hecher, M., Zisser, M.: An improved GPU-based SAT model counter. In: Schiex, T., de Givry, S. (eds.) CP 2019. LNCS, vol. 11802, pp. 491–509. Springer, Cham (2019). https://doi.org/10.1007/978-3-030-30048-7_29

24. Gomes, C.P., Sabharwal, A., Selman, B.: Chapter 20: Model counting. In: Handbook of Satisfiability, Frontiers in Artificial Intelligence and Applications, vol. 185, pp. 633–654. IOS Press (2009)

25. Kiljan, K., Pilipczuk, M.: Experimental evaluation of parameterized algorithms for feedback vertex set. In: SEA. LIPIcs, vol. 103, pp. 12:1–12:12. Schloss Dagstuhl (2018)

26. Kleine Büning, H., Lettman, T.: Propositional Logic: Deduction and Algorithms. Cambridge University Press, Cambridge (1999)

27. Kloks, T.: Treewidth: Computations and Approximations. LNCS, vol. 842. Springer, Heidelberg (1994). https://doi.org/10.1007/BFb0045375

28. Koriche, F., Lagniez, J.M., Marquis, P., Thomas, S.: Knowledge compilation for model counting: affine decision trees. In: IJCAI 2013. The AAAI Press (2013)

29. Lagniez, J., Marquis, P.: Preprocessing for propositional model counting. In: AAAI, pp. 2688–2694. AAAI Press (2014)

30. Lagniez, J.M., Marquis, P.: An improved decision-DDNF compiler. In: IJCAI 2017, pp. 667–673. The AAAI Press (2017)

31. Langer, A., Reidl, F., Rossmanith, P., Sikdar, S.: Evaluation of an MSO-solver. In: Proceedings of ALENEX. pp. 55–63. SIAM/Omnipress (2012)

32. Liu, J., Zhong, W., Jiao, L.: Comments on "the 1993 DIMACS graph coloring challenge" and "energy function-based approaches to graph coloring". IEEE Trans. Neural Netw. **17**(2), 533 (2006)

33. Muise, C., McIlraith, S.A., Beck, J.C., Hsu, E.I.: DSHARP: fast d-DNNF compilation with sharpSAT. In: Kosseim, L., Inkpen, D. (eds.) AI 2012. LNCS (LNAI), vol. 7310, pp. 356–361. Springer, Heidelberg (2012). https://doi.org/10.1007/978-3-642-30353-1_36

34. Oztok, U., Darwiche, A.: A top-down compiler for sentential decision diagrams. In: IJCAI 2015, pp. 3141–3148. The AAAI Press (2015)

35. Roth, D.: On the hardness of approximate reasoning. Artif. Intell. **82**(1–2), 273–302 (1996)

36. Samer, M., Szeider, S.: Algorithms for propositional model counting. J. Discrete Algorithms **8**(1), 50–64 (2010)

37. Sang, T., Bacchus, F., Beame, P., Kautz, H., Pitassi, T.: Combining component caching and clause learning for effective model counting. In: SAT 2004 (2004)

38. Sang, T., Beame, P., Kautz, H.: Performing Bayesian inference by weighted model counting. In: AAAI 2005. The AAAI Press (2005)

39. Sharma, S., Roy, S., Soos, M., Meel, K.S.: GANAK: a scalable probabilistic exact model counter. In: IJCAI, pp. 1169–1176. ijcai.org (2019)

40. Thurley, M.: sharpSAT – counting models with advanced component caching and implicit BCP. In: Biere, A., Gomes, C.P. (eds.) SAT 2006. LNCS, vol. 4121, pp. 424–429. Springer, Heidelberg (2006). https://doi.org/10.1007/11814948_38

41. Toda, S.: PP is as hard as the polynomial-time hierarchy. SIAM J. Comput. **20**(5), 865–877 (1991)

42. Toda, T., Soh, T.: Implementing efficient all solutions SAT solvers. ACM J. Exp. Algorithmics **21**, 1–12 (2015). special Issue SEA 2014

43. Ullman, J.D.: Principles of Database and Knowledge-Base Systems, vol. II. Computer Science Press (1989)

44. Xue, Y., Choi, A., Darwiche, A.: Basing decisions on sentences in decision diagrams. In: AAAI 2012. The AAAI Press (2012)

Whitebox Induction of Default Rules Using High-Utility Itemset Mining

Farhad Shakerin[✉] and Gopal Gupta

The University of Texas at Dallas, Richardson, TX 75080, USA
{farhad.shakerin,gopal.gupta}@utdallas.edu

Abstract. We present a fast and scalable algorithm to induce *non-monotonic* logic programs from statistical learning models. We reduce the problem of search for best clauses to instances of the *High-Utility Itemset Mining* (HUIM) problem. In the HUIM problem, feature values and their importance are treated as transactions and utilities respectively. We make use of TreeExplainer, a fast and scalable implementation of the Explainable AI tool SHAP, to extract locally important features and their weights from ensemble tree models. Our experiments with UCI standard benchmarks suggest a significant improvement in terms of classification evaluation metrics and training time compared to ALEPH, a state-of-the-art *Inductive Logic Programming* (ILP) system.

Keywords: Inductive logic programming · Machine learning · Explainable AI · Negation as failure · Answer set programming · Data mining

1 Introduction

The FOIL algorithm by Quinlan [14] is a popular ILP algorithm that incorporates heuristics from information theory called *weighted information gain* to guide the search for best clauses. The use of a greedy heuristic makes FOIL fast and scalable. However, scalability comes at the expense of losing accuracy if the algorithm is stuck in a local optima and/or when the number of examples is insufficient. Figure 1 demonstrates how the local optima results in discovering sub-optimal rules that does not necessarily coincide with the real underlying sub-concepts of the data.

Unlike FOIL, statistical machine learning algorithms are bound to find the relevant features because they optimize an objective function with respect to global constraints. This results in models that are inherently complex and cannot explain what features account for a classification decision on any given data sample. The Explainable AI techniques such as LIME [15] and SHAP [10] have been proposed that provide explanations for any given data sample. Each explanation is a set of feature-value pairs that would locally determine what features

Authors are partially supported by NSF Grants IIS 1718945 and IIS 1910131.

E. Komendantskaya and Y. A. Liu (Eds.): PADL 2020, LNCS 12007, pp. 168–176, 2020.
https://doi.org/10.1007/978-3-030-39197-3_11

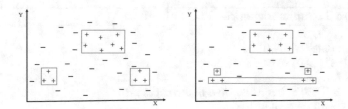

Fig. 1. Optimal sequential covering with 3 Clauses (Left), Sub-Optimal sequential covering with 4 Clauses (Right)

and how strongly each feature, relative to other features, contributes to the classification decision. To capture the global behavior of a black-box model, however, an algorithm needs to group similar data samples (i.e., data samples for which the same set of feature values are responsible for the choice of classification) and cover them with the same clause. While in FOIL, the search for a clause is guided by heuristics, in our novel approach, we adapt *High Utility Item-set Mining* (HUIM) [5]—a popular technique from data mining—to find clauses. We call this algorithm SHAP-FOLD from here on. The advantage of SHAP-FOLD over heuristics-based algorithms such as FOIL is that:

1. SHAP-FOLD does not get stuck in a local optima
2. SHAP-FOLD distinguishes exceptional cases from noisy samples
3. SHAP-FOLD learns a reasonable number of non-monotonic rules in the form of default theories
4. SHAP-FOLD is fast and scalable compared to conventional ILP algorithms

This paper makes the following novel contribution: We present a new ILP algorithm capable of learning *non-monotonic* logic programs from local explanations of black-box models provided by SHAP. Our experiments on UCI standard benchmark data sets suggest that SHAP-FOLD outperforms ALEPH [17] in terms of classification evaluation metrics, running time, and providing more concise explanations measured in terms of number of clauses induced.

2   Background

2.1   The FOIL Algorithm

FOIL is a top-down ILP algorithm that follows a *sequential covering* scheme to induce a hypotheses. The FOIL algorithm is summarized in Algorithm 1. This algorithm repeatedly searches for clauses that score best with respect to a subset of positive and negative examples, a current hypothesis and a heuristic called *information gain* (IG).

The inner loop searches for a clause with the highest information gain using a general-to-specific hill-climbing search. To specialize a given clause c, a refinement operator ρ under θ-subsumption [13] is employed. The most general clause

---
Algorithm 1. Summarizing the FOIL algorithm

Input: $target, B, E^+, E^-$
Output: Initialize $H \leftarrow \emptyset$
1: **while** $(|E^+| > 0)$ **do**
2:     $c \leftarrow (target :- true.)$
3:         **while** $(|E^-| > 0 \land c.length < max\_length)$ **do**
4:             **for** all $c' \in \rho(c)$ **do**
5:                 compute $score(E^+, E^-, H \cup \{c'\}, B)$
6:             **end for**
7:             let $\hat{c}$ be the $c' \in \rho(c)$ with the best score
8:                 $E^- \leftarrow covers(\hat{c}, E^-)$
9:         **end while**
10:        add $\hat{c}$ to H
11:            $E^+ \leftarrow E^+ \setminus covers(\hat{c}, E^+)$
12: **end while**
13: **return** H
---

is the following: $p(X_1, ..., X_n) \leftarrow true.$, where the predicate p/n is the predicate being learned and each X_i is a variable. The refinement operator specializes the current clause $h \leftarrow b_1, ...b_n$. This is realized by adding a new literal l to the clause yielding $h \leftarrow b_1, ...b_n, l$. The heuristic based search uses information gain.

2.2 SHAP

SHAP [10] (SHapley Additive exPlanations) is a unified approach with foundations in game theory to explain the output of any machine learning model. Given a dataset and a trained model, the SHAP framework computes a matrix of the shape $(\#samples, \#features)$ representing the Shapley value of each feature for each data sample. Each row sums to the difference between the model output for that sample and the expected value of the model output. This difference explains why the model is inclined to predict a specific class outcome.

Example 1. *The UCI heart dataset contains features such as patient's blood pressure, chest pain, thallium test results, number of major vessels blocked, etc. The classification task is to predict whether the subject suffers from heart disease or not. Figure 2 shows how SHAP would explain a model's prediction over a data sample. For this sample, SHAP explains why the model predicts heart disease by returning the top features along with their Shapley values (importance weight). According to SHAP, the model predicts "heart disease" because of the values of "thalium test" and "maximum heart rate achieved" which push the prediction from the base (expected) value of 0.44 towards a positive prediction (heart disease). On the other hand, the feature "chest pain" would have pushed the prediction towards negative (healthy), but it is not strong enough to turn the prediction.*

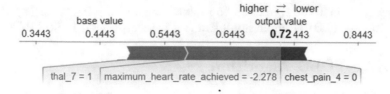

Fig. 2. Shap values for a UCI heart prediction

2.3 High-Utility Itemset Mining

The problem of *High-Utility Itemset Mining* (HUIM) is an extension of an older problem in data mining known as *frequent pattern mining* [1]. Frequent pattern mining is meant to find frequent patterns in transaction databases. A *transaction database* is a set of records (transactions) indicating the items purchased by customers at different times. A *frequent itemset* is a group of items that appear in many transactions. For instance, {noodles, spicy sauce} being a frequent itemset, can be used to take marketing decisions such as co-promoting noodles with spicy sauce. Finding frequent itemsets is a well-studied problem with an efficient algorithm named Apriori [2]. However, in some applications frequency is not always the objective. For example, the pattern {milk,bread} may be highly frequent, but it may yield a low profit. On the other hand, a pattern such as {caviar, champagne} may not be frequent but may yield a high profit. Hence, to find interesting patterns in data, other aspects such as profitability is considered.

Mining high utility itemsets can be viewed as a generalization of the frequent itemset mining where each item in each transaction has a utility (importance) associated with it and the goal is to find itemsets that generate high profit when for instance, they are sold together. The user has to provide a value for a threshold called *minimum utility*. A high utility itemset mining algorithm outputs all the high-utility itemsets with at least *minimum utility* profit. Table 1 shows a transaction database consisting of 5 transactions. Left column shows the transaction Identifier. Middle column contains the items included in each transaction and right column contains each item's respective profit. If the *minimum utility* is set to 25, the result of a high utility itemset mining algorithm is shown in

Table 1. Left: an HUIM Problem Instance. Right: Solution for minutil = 25

Transactions	Items	Profits
T_0	a b c d e	5 10 1 6 3
T_1	b c d e	8 3 6 3
T_2	a c d	5 1 2
T_3	a c e	10 6 6
T_4	b c e	4 2 3

High Utility Itemsets	
{a, c}: 28	{a, c, e}: 31
{a, b, c, d, e}: 25	{b, c}: 28
{b, c, d}: 34	{b, c, d, e}: 40
{b, c, e}: 37	{b, d}: 30
{b, d, e}: 36	{b, e}: 31
{c, e}: 27	

the right table in Table 1. In order to rank the high utility itemsets, Top-K High Utility Itemset (THUI) mining problem [18] is incorporated in SHAP-FOLD.

3   SHAP-FOLD Algorithm

SHAP-FOLD learns a concept in terms of a default theory [16]. In Logic Programming, default theories are represented using *negation-as-failure* (NAF) semantics [3].

Example 2. *The following default theory "Normally, birds fly except penguins which do not", is represented as:*

```
flies(X) :- bird(X), not ab_bird(X).
ab_bird(X) :- penguin(X).
```

The SHAP-FOLD algorithm adapts the FOIL style sequential covering scheme. Therefore, it iteratively learns single clauses, until all positive examples are covered. To learn one clause, SHAP-FOLD first finds common patterns among positive examples. If the resulted clause (default) covers a significant number of negative examples, SHAP-FOLD swaps the current positive and negative examples and recursively calls the algorithm to learn common patterns in negative examples (exceptions). As shown in Example 2, the exceptions are ruled out using negation-as-failure. Learning exceptions allow our SHAP-FOLD algorithm to distinguish between noisy samples and exceptional cases.

To search for "best" clause, SHAP-FOLD tightly integrates the High Utility Itemset Mining (HUIM) and the SHAP technique. In this novel approach, the SHAP system is employed to find relevant features as well as their importance. To find the "best" clause SHAP-FOLD creates instances of HUIM problem. Each instance, contains a subset of examples represented as a set of "transactions" as shown in Table 1. Each "transaction" contains a subset of feature values along with their corresponding utility (i.e., feature importance). The feature importance $\phi_i \in [0, 1]$ for all i distinct feature values. Therefore, a *high-utility itemset* in any set of "transactions" represents strongest features that would contribute to the classification of a significant number of examples, because, otherwise, that itemset would not have been selected as a high-utility itemset. To find the itemset with highest utility, the HUIM algorithm Top-K [18] is invoked with K set to 1.

SHAP-FOLD takes a target predicate name (G), a tabular dataset (D) with m rows and two different labels $+1$ and -1 for positive examples and negative examples respectively. E^+ and E^- represent these examples in the form of target atoms. It also takes a "transaction" database. Each row of T contains a subset of an example's feature-values (z_i) along with their Shapley values (ϕ_i). This "transaction" database is passed along to create HUIM instance and find the itemset with highest utility every time Top-K algorithm is invoked. The summary of SHAP-FOLD's pseudo-code is shown in Algorithm 2.

In the function FOIL (lines 1–8), *sequential covering* loop to cover positive examples is realized. On every iteration, a default clause (and possibly multiple

---

Algorithm 2. Summary of SHAP-FOLD Algorithm

Input: G: Target Predicate to Learn

          B: Background Knowledge

          $D\ \ = \{\ (x_1, y_1), ..., (x_m, y_m)\}:\ y_i \in \{-1, +1\}$

          $E^+ = \{\ x_i \mid x_i \in D \wedge y_i = 1\}:\ \text{Positive Examples}$

          $E^- = \{\ x_i \mid x_i \in D \wedge y_i = -1\}:\ \text{Negative Examples}$

          $T\ \ = \{\ (z_i, \phi_i) \mid z_i \subseteq x_i \wedge x_i \in D \wedge \phi_i\ \text{is}\ z_i\text{'s Shapley values}\ \}$

Output: $D\ \ = \{\ C_1, ..., C_n\}$ ▷ default clauses

          $AB\ = \{\ ab_1, ..., ab_m\}$ ▷ exceptions/abnormal clauses

 1: **function** FOIL(E^+, E^-)

 2:    **while** ($|E^+| > 0$) **do**

 3:       $C_{def+exc} \leftarrow$ LEARN_ONE_RULE(E^+, E^-)

 4:       $E^+ \leftarrow E^+ \setminus covers(C_{def+exc}, E^+, B)$

 5:       $D \leftarrow D \cup \{C_{def+exc}\}$

 6:    **end while**

 7:    **return** D, AB ▷ returns sets of defaults and exceptions

 8: **end function**

 9: **function** LEARN_ONE_RULE(E^+, E^-)

10:    - let Item-Set be $\{(f_1, ...f_n), (\phi_1, ..., \phi_n)\} \leftarrow$ TOP-K(K=1,E^+,T)

11:    $C_{def} \leftarrow (G \text{ :- } f_1, ..., f_n)$

12:    $FP \leftarrow covers(C_{def}, E^-)$ ▷ FP denotes False Positives

13:    **if** $FP > 0$ **then**

14:       $C_{def+exc} \leftarrow$ LEARN_EXCEPTIONS(C_{def}, E^-, E^+)

15:    **end if**

16:    **return** $C_{def+exc}$

17: **end function**

18: **function** LEARN_EXCEPTIONS(C_{def}, E^+, E^-)

19:    $\{C_1, ..., C_k\} \leftarrow$ FOIL(E^+, E^-)   ▷ Recursive Call After Swapping

20:    $ab\_index \leftarrow GENERATE\_UNIQUE\_AB\_INDEX()$

21:    **for** $i \leftarrow 1$ **to** k **do**

22:       $AB \leftarrow AB \cup \{ab_{ab\_index} \text{ :- } bodyof(C_i)\}$

23:    **end for**

24:    **return** $C_{def+exc} \leftarrow (headof(C_{def}) \text{ :- } bodyof(C_{def}),\ \textbf{not}(ab_{ab\_index}))$

25: **end function**

---

exceptions) - denoted by $C_{def+exc}$ - is learned and added to the hypothesis. Then, the covered examples are removed from the remaining examples. In the function LEARN_ONE_RULE (lines 9–17), Top-K algorithm with $k = 1$ is invoked and a high-utility itemset (i.e., a subset of features-values and their corresponding Shapley values) is retrieved. These subset of features create the default part of a new clause. Next, if the default clause covers false positives, the current positive and negative examples are swapped to learn exceptions. In the function LEARN_EXCEPTIONS (lines 18–25), the algorithm recursively calls itself to learn clauses that would cover exceptional patterns. When the recursive call returns, for all learned clauses, their head is replaced by an abnormality predicate. To manufacture the complete default theory, the abnormality predicate preceded by negation-as-failure (not) is added to the default part. Example 3 shows how SHAP-FOLD learns a concise logic program from an XGBoost trained model.

Example 3. *The "UCI Cars" dataset contains 1728 different cars and their acceptability based on features such as buying price, maintenance cost, trunk size, capacity, number of doors, and safety. SHAP-FOLD generates the following program from a trained XGBoost model:*

```
DEF(1): acceptable(A):- safety(A,high), not ab0(A).
EXCEPTIONS(1): ab0(A):- persons(A,2).
               ab0(A):- maintenance(A,very_high).
DEF(2): acceptable(A):- persons(A,4), safety(A,medium), not ab1(A).
EXCEPTIONS(2): ab1(A):- price(A,very_high), trunk(A,small).
               ab1(A):- price(A,high), maintenance(A,very_high).
DEF(3): acceptable(A):- trunk(A,big), safety(A,medium),
                        persons(A,>5).
```

On first iteration, the clause DEF(1) is generated. Since it covers a significant number of negative examples, E^+ and E^- are swapped and algorithm recursively calls itself. Inside LEARN_EXCEPTIONS, the recursive call returns with EXCEPTIONS(1) clauses. The head predicate ab0 replaces their head and finally in line 24, the negation of abnormality is appended to the default to create the following default clause: "A car is considered acceptable if its safety is high, unless it only fits two persons or its maintenance cost is high".

4 Experiments

In this section, we present our experiments on UCI standard benchmarks [8].[1] The ALEPH system [17] is used as a baseline. We set ALEPH to use the heuristic enumeration strategy, and the maximum number of branch nodes to be explored in a branch-and-bound search to 500K. We also configured ALEPH to allow up to 50 false examples covered by each clause while each clause is at least 80% accurate. We use precision, recall, accuracy and F_1 score to compare the results.

The SHAP-FOLD requires a statistical model as input to the SHAP technique. While computing the Shapley values is slow, there is a fast and exact implementation called TreeExplainer [9] for ensemble tree models. XGBoost [4] is a powerful ensemble tree model that perfectly works with TreeExplainer. Thus, we trained an XGBoost model for each of the reported experiments in this paper. Table 2 presents the comparison between ALEPH and SHAP-FOLD on classification evaluation of each UCI dataset. The best performer is highlighted with boldface font. In terms of the running time, SHAP-FOLD scales up much better. In case of "King-Rook vs. King-Pawn", while ALEPH discovers 283 clauses in 836 seconds, SHAP-FOLD does much better. It finishes in 8 seconds discovering only 3 clauses that cover the knowledge underlying the model. Similarly, in case of "UCI kidney", SHAP-FOLD finds significantly fewer clauses. Thus,

---

[1] Full implementation is available at: https://github.com/fxs130430/SHAP_FOLD.

Table 2. Evaluation of SHAP_FOLD on UCI datasets

Data set	Shape	Algorithm Aleph					SHAP-FOLD				
		Precision	Recall	Accuracy	F1	Time (s)	Precision	Recall	Accuracy	F1	Time (s)
Cars	(1728, 6)	0.83	0.63	0.85	0.72	73	**0.84**	**0.94**	**0.93**	**0.89**	**5**
Credit-a	(690, 15)	0.78	0.72	0.78	0.75	180	**0.90**	**0.74**	**0.84**	**0.81**	**7**
Breast-w	(699, 9)	0.92	0.87	0.93	0.89	10	**0.92**	**0.95**	**0.95**	**0.93**	**2**
Kidney	(400, 24)	**0.96**	0.92	0.93	0.94	5	0.93	**0.95**	0.93	0.94	**1**
Voting	(435, 16)	0.97	0.94	0.95	0.95	25	**0.98**	**0.98**	0.95	**0.96**	**1**
Autism	(704, 17)	0.73	0.43	0.79	0.53	476	**0.96**	**0.83**	**0.95**	**0.89**	**2**
Ionosphere	(351, 34)	**0.89**	0.87	0.85	0.88	113	0.87	**0.91**	0.85	**0.89**	**2**
Heart	(270, 13)	0.76	0.75	0.78	0.75	28	0.76	**0.83**	**0.81**	**0.80**	**1**
kr vs. kp	(3196, 36)	0.92	0.99	0.95	0.95	836	0.92	0.99	0.95	0.95	**8**

not only SHAP-FOLD's performance is much better, it discovers more succinct programs. Also, scalability is a major problem in ILP, that our SHAP-FOLD algorithm solves: its execution performance is orders of magnitude better.

SHAP-FOLD almost always achieves a higher Recall score. This suggests that the proper use of *negation-as-failure* leads to better coverage. The absence of negation from ALEPH hypothesis space forces the algorithm to create too specific clauses which leaves many positive examples uncovered. In contrast, our SHAP-FOLD algorithm emphasizes on better coverage via finding high-utility patterns of important features first. If the result turns out to cover too many negative examples to tolerate, by learning exceptions and ruling them out (via the same algorithm applied recursively), SHAP-FOLD maintains the same coverage as it rules out exceptional negative examples.

5   Related Works and Conclusions

A survey of ILP can be found in [12]. In ILP community, researchers have tried to combine statistical methods with ILP techniques. Support Vector ILP [11] uses ILP hypotheses as kernel in dual form of the SVM algorithm. kFOIL [7] learns an incremental kernel for SVM algorithm using a FOIL style specialization. nFOIL [6] integrates the Naive-Bayes algorithm with FOIL. The advantage of our research over all of the above mentioned research work is that, first it is model agnostic, second it is scalable thanks to the fast and scalable HUIM algorithm and SHAP TreeExplainer, third it enjoys the power of *negation-as-failure* which is absent from the above mentioned works.

In this paper, we presented a fast and scalable ILP algorithm to induce default theories from statistical machine learning models. In this novel approach, irrelevant features are filtered out by SHAP, a technique from explainable AI. Then, the problem of searching for "best" clause is reduced to a *High-Utility Itemset Mining* problem. Our experiments on benchmark datasets suggest a significant improvement in terms of the classification evaluation metrics and running time.

References

1. Aggarwal, C.C., Han, J.: Frequent Pattern Mining. Springer, Heidelberg (2014)
2. Agrawal, R., Srikant, R.: Fast algorithms for mining association rules in large databases. In: Proceedings of 20th International Conference on Very Large Data Bases, VLDB 1994, pp. 487–499. Morgan Kaufmann Publishers Inc., CA (1994)
3. Baral, C.: Knowledge Representation, Reasoning and Declarative Problem Solving. Cambridge University Press, Cambridge/New York/Melbourne (2003)
4. Chen, T., Guestrin, C.: Xgboost: a scalable tree boosting system. In: Proceedings of the 22nd ACM SIGKDD, KDD 2016, pp. 785–794 (2016)
5. Gan, W., Lin, J.C., Fournier-Viger, P., Chao, H., Hong, T., Fujita, H.: A survey of incremental high-utility itemset mining. Wiley Interdiscip. Rev. Data Min. Knowl. Discov. $8(2)$, e1242 (2018)
6. Landwehr, N., Kersting, K., Raedt, L.D.: nFOIL: integrating naïve bayes and FOIL. In: Proceedings, The Twentieth National Conference on Artificial Intelligence and the Seventeenth Innovative Applications of Artificial Intelligence Conference, Pittsburgh, Pennsylvania, USA, 9–13 July 2005, pp. 795–800 (2005)
7. Landwehr, N., Passerini, A., Raedt, L.D., Frasconi, P.: kFOIL: learning simple relational kernels. In: Proceedings, The Twenty-First National Conference on Artificial Intelligence and the Eighteenth Innovative Applications of Artificial Intelligence Conference, MA, USA, 16–20 July 2006, pp. 389–394 (2006)
8. Lichman, M.: UCI, ml repository (2013). http://archive.ics.uci.edu/ml
9. Lundberg, S.M., Erion, G.G., Lee, S.I.: Consistent individualized feature attribution for tree ensembles. arXiv preprint arXiv:1802.03888 (2018)
10. Lundberg, S.M., Lee, S.I.: A unified approach to interpreting model predictions. In: Advances in Neural Information Processing Systems, pp. 4765–4774 (2017)
11. Muggleton, S., Lodhi, H., Amini, A., Sternberg, M.J.E.: Support vector inductive logic programming. In: Hoffmann, A., Motoda, H., Scheffer, T. (eds.) DS 2005. LNCS (LNAI), vol. 3735, pp. 163–175. Springer, Heidelberg (2005). https://doi.org/10.1007/11563983_15
12. Muggleton, S., et al.: Ilp turns 20. Mach. Learn. $86(1)$, 3–23 (2012)
13. Plotkin, G.D.: A further note on inductive generalization, in machine intelligence, vol. 6, pp. 101–124 (1971)
14. Quinlan, J.R.: Learning logical definitions from relations. Mach. Learn. 5, 239–266 (1990)
15. Ribeiro, M.T., Singh, S., Guestrin, C.: "why should I trust you?" Explaining the predictions of any classifier. In: Proceedings of the 22nd ACM SIGKDD 2016, pp. 1135–1144 (2016)
16. Shakerin, F., Salazar, E., Gupta, G.: A new algorithm to automate inductive learning of default theories. TPLP $17(5-6)$, 1010–1026 (2017)
17. Srinivasan, A.: The Aleph Manual (2001). https://www.cs.ox.ac.uk/activities/programinduction/Aleph/aleph.html
18. Tseng, V.S., Wu, C.W., Fournier-Viger, P., Philip, S.Y.: Efficient algorithms for mining top-k high utility itemsets. IEEE Trans. Knowl. Data Eng. $28(1)$, 54–67 (2016)

Small Languages and Implementation

Explanations for Dynamic Programming

Martin Erwig[(✉)], Prashant Kumar, and Alan Fern

Oregon State University, Corvallis, USA
{erwig,kumarpra,alan.fern}@oregonstate.edu

Abstract. We present an approach for explaining dynamic programming that is based on computing with a granular representation of values that are typically aggregated during program execution. We demonstrate how to derive more detailed and meaningful explanations of program behavior from such a representation than would otherwise be possible. To illustrate the practicality of this approach we also present a Haskell library for dynamic programming that allows programmers to specify programs by recurrence relationships from which implementations are derived that can run with granular representation and produce explanations. The explanations essentially answer questions of why one result was obtained instead of another. While usually the alternatives have to be provided by a user, we will show that with our approach such alternatives can be in some cases anticipated and that corresponding explanations can be generated automatically.

1 Introduction

The need for program explanations arises whenever a program execution produces a result that differs from the user's expectation. The difference could be due to a bug in the program or to an incorrect expectation on part of the user. To find out, a programmer may employ a debugger to gain an understanding of the program's behavior [1,2]. However, debugging is very costly and time consuming [3]. Moreover, the focus on fault localization makes debuggers not the most effective tools for program understanding, since they force the user to think in terms of low-level implementation details. In fact, debuggers typically already assume an understanding of the program by the programmer [4]. The work on customizable debugging operations is additional testimony to the limitations of generic debugging approaches [5,6]. Finally, debugging is not an option for most users of software, simply because they are not programmers. Therefore, to generate program explanations we need to consider alternative methods.

One approach to producing explanations is to track data that is aggregated during a computation and keep the unaggregated representation that can later be queried to illustrate the effects of the performed computation. Specifically, as we illustrate in Sect. 2 we can maintain *value decompositions* of those data that are the basis for decisions in computations that might require explanations.

This work is partially supported by DARPA under the grant N66001-17-2-4030 and by the National Science Foundation under the grant CCF-1717300.

E. Komendantskaya and Y. A. Liu (Eds.): PADL 2020, LNCS 12007, pp. 179–195, 2020.
https://doi.org/10.1007/978-3-030-39197-3_12

Since our goal is to facilitate systematic explanations of decisions made by dynamic programming algorithms, we show in Sect. 3 how dynamic programming algorithms can be expressed as recurrence equations over semirings, and we present a Haskell implementation to demonstrate that the idea is feasible in practice. In Sect. 4 we demonstrate how to use this implementation to operate with value decompositions and produce explanations.

Value decompositions produce explanations for decisions. Specifically, they are used to answer questions such as "Why was A chosen over alternative B?" Alternatives against which decisions are to be explained are typically provided by users, but as we demonstrate in Sect. 5, sometimes they can be anticipated, which means that comparative explanations can be generated automatically. Finally, we compare our approach with related work in Sect. 6 and present some conclusions in Sect. 7. The main contributions of this paper are as follows.

- A framework based on semirings for expressing *dynamic programming algorithms* that supports the *computation with value decompositions*.
- An extension of the framework for the *automatic generation of explanations*.
- A method for the *automatic generation of examples* in explanations.
- An implementation of the approach as a *Haskell library*.

2   Explaining Decisions with Value Decompositions

Many decision and optimization algorithms select one or more alternatives from a set based on data gathered about different aspects for each alternative. For example, to decide between two vacation destinations one may rank weather (W), food (F), and price (P) on a point scale from 1 (poor) to 10 (great) and compute a total point score for each possible destination and then pick the one with the highest score.

This view can be formalized using the concepts of *value decomposition* and *valuation*. Given a set of categories C, a mapping $v : C \to \mathbb{R}$ is called a *value decomposition* (with respect to C). The (total) *value* of a value decomposition is defined as the sum of its components, that is, $\hat{v} = \sum_{(c,x) \in v} x$. A *valuation* for a set S (with respect to C) is a function φ that maps elements of S to corresponding value decompositions, that is, $\varphi : S \to \mathbb{R}^C$. We write $\hat{\varphi}(A)$ to denote the total value of A's value decomposition. In our example scenario lets consider two destinations $S = \{X, Y\}$ with the respective value decompositions $v_X = \{W \mapsto 7, F \mapsto 8, P \mapsto 1, \}$ and $v_Y = \{W \mapsto 4, F \mapsto 4, P \mapsto 9, \}$, which yields the valuation $\varphi = \{X \mapsto v_X, Y \mapsto v_Y\}$.

The elements of S can be ordered based on the valuation totals in an obvious way:

$$\forall A, B \in S.\ A > B \Leftrightarrow \hat{\varphi}(A) > \hat{\varphi}(B)$$

When a user asks about a program execution why A was selected over B, the obvious explanation is $\hat{\varphi}(A) > \hat{\varphi}(B)$, reporting the valuation totals. However, such an answer might not be useful, since it ignores the categories that link the raw numbers to the application domain and thus lacks a context for the user to interpret the numbers. In our example, destination Y would be selected since $\hat{\varphi}(Y) = 17 > \hat{\varphi}(X) = 16$, which might be surprising because X seems clearly so much better than Y in terms of weather and food.

If the value decomposition is maintained during the computation, we can generate a more detailed explanation. First, we can rewrite $\hat{\varphi}(A) > \hat{\varphi}(B)$ as $\hat{\varphi}(A) - \hat{\varphi}(B) > 0$, which suggests the definition of the *valuation difference* between two elements A and B as follows.

$$\delta(A, B) = \{(c, x - y) \mid (c, x) \in \varphi(A) \wedge (c, y) \in \varphi(B)\}$$

The total of the value difference $\hat{\delta}(A, B)$ is given by the sum of all components, just like the total of a value decomposition. In our example we have $\delta(Y, X) = \{W \mapsto -3, F \mapsto -4, P \mapsto 8\}$. It is clear that the value difference generally contains positive and negative entries and that for $\delta(A, B) > 0$ to be true the sum of the positive entries must exceed the absolute value of the sum of the negative entries. We call the negative components of a value difference its *barrier*. It is defined as follows.

$$\beta(A, B) = \{(c, x) \mid (c, x) \in \delta(A, B) \wedge x < 0\}$$

The total value $\hat{\beta}(A, B)$ is again the sum of all the components. In our example we have $\beta(Y, X) = \{W \mapsto -3, F \mapsto -4\}$ and $\hat{\beta}(Y, X) = -7$.

The decision to select A over B does not necessarily need as support all of the positive components of $\delta(A, B)$; any subset whose total is larger than $|\hat{\beta}(A, B)|$ will suffice. We call such a subset a *dominator*:[1]

$$\Delta(A, B) = \{D \mid D \subseteq \delta(A, B) \wedge \hat{D} > |\hat{\beta}(A, B)|\}$$

The only dominator in our toy example is $\Delta(Y, X) = \{P \mapsto 8\}$.

The smaller a dominator, the better it is suited as an explanation, since it requires fewer details to explain how the barrier is overcome. We therefore define the *minimal dominating set* (MDS) as follows.

$$\underline{\Delta}(A, B) = \{D \mid D \subseteq \Delta(A, B) \wedge D' \subset D \Rightarrow D' \notin \Delta(A, B)\}$$

Note that $\underline{\Delta}$ may contain multiple elements, which means that minimal dominators are not unique. In other words, a decision may have different minimally sized explanations. Again, due to the small size of our example, the only dominator is also the MDS in this case. Nevertheless, it captures the explanation that Y is preferred over X due to the extreme price difference.

---

[1] This definition allows dominators to contain negative components, which are counter-productive to the goal of dominators. However, the definition of minimal-size dominators will never produce a dominator with a negative component, so that the general definition does not hurt.

3 Dynamic Programming with Semirings

We show how to represent dynamic programming (DP) algorithms by semirings in Sect. 3.1 and how such a representation can automatically generate efficient implementations from recursive specifications in Haskell in Sect. 3.2. We illustrate the use of the library with an example in Sects. 3.3 and 3.4.

3.1 Semirings and Dynamic Programming

A semiring is an algebraic structure $(S, \oplus, \otimes, \mathbf{0}, \mathbf{1})$, which consists of a nonempty set S with binary operations for addition ($\oplus$) and multiplication ($\otimes$) plus neutral elements zero ($\mathbf{0}$) and one ($\mathbf{1}$) [7]. Figure 1 lists the axioms that a semiring structure has to satisfy and several semiring examples.

$$a \oplus (b \oplus c) = (a \oplus b) \oplus c$$
$$a \oplus b = b \oplus a$$
$$a \oplus \mathbf{0} = \mathbf{0} \oplus a = a$$
$$a \otimes (b \otimes c) = (a \otimes b) \otimes c$$
$$a \otimes \mathbf{1} = \mathbf{1} \otimes a = a$$
$$a \otimes (b \oplus c) = a \otimes b \oplus a \otimes c$$
$$(a \oplus b) \otimes c = a \otimes c \oplus b \otimes c$$
$$a \otimes \mathbf{0} = \mathbf{0} \otimes a = \mathbf{0}$$

Semiring	Set	$\oplus$	$\otimes$	$\mathbf{0}$	$\mathbf{1}$
Boolean	$\{true, false\}$	$\vee$	$\wedge$	$false$	$true$
Counting	$\mathbb{N}$	$+$	$\times$	0	1
Tropical (Min-Plus)	$\mathbb{R}^+ \cup \{\infty\}$	$\min$	$+$	∞	0
Arctic (Max-Plus)	$\mathbb{R}^+ \cup \{-\infty\}$	$\max$	$+$	$-\infty$	0
Viterbi	$[0, 1]$	$\max$	$\times$	0	1

Fig. 1. Semiring axioms and examples.

A semiring $(S, \oplus, \otimes, \mathbf{0}, \mathbf{1})$ with a partial order $\leq$ over S is *monotonic* if $\forall s, t, u \in S, (s \leq t) \Rightarrow (s \otimes u \leq t \otimes u)$ and $(s \leq t) \Rightarrow (u \otimes s \leq u \otimes t)$. A monotonic semiring ensures the so-called *optimal subproblem property*, which says that the optimal solution of a dynamic programming problem contains the optimal solutions of the subproblems into which the original problem was divided. This can be seen as follows [8]. Suppose the values s and t correspond to two solutions of a subproblem such that s is a better solution than t (that is, $s \leq t$). Further, suppose that u is the optimal solution of a set of subproblems that does not include the subproblems producing the values s and t. The monotonicity property ensures that s combined with u (and not t combined with u) always results in the optimal solution when the aforementioned subproblem is combined with the set of subproblems.

Dynamic programming algorithms can be described by recursive equations that use operations of a particular kind of semiring, and since monotonic semirings satisfy the optimal substructure property, the computations produce correct solutions. Note that we can slightly weaken the requirements for the optimal subproblem property. Since monotonicity doesn't depend on the absorption rule (which requires $a \otimes \mathbf{0} = \mathbf{0} \otimes a = \mathbf{0}$), the optimal subproblem property holds for DP algorithms that are based on what we call *quasi-semirings*, which are semirings for which the absorption rule doesn't hold. We will make use of this property later in Sect. 3.4 where we define a quasi-semiring for computing values "alongside" the values of a semiring.

3.2 A Haskell Library for Dynamic Programming

We have implemented a library for dynamic programming and semirings that is based on the DP library by Sasha Rush.[2] The first component is a representation of semirings. The semiring structure can be nicely captured in a Haskell type class. Of course, the required laws cannot be expressed in Haskell; it's the programmer's obligation to ensure that the laws hold for their instance definitions.

```
class Semiring a where
  zero, one :: a
  (<+>), (<.>) :: a -> a -> a

sconcat :: Semiring a => [a] -> a
sconcat = foldr (<+>) zero
```

Several Haskell packages exist that already define a `Semiring` type class (some of which are defunct). In general, previous approaches have the advantage that they integrate the `Semiring` class more tightly into the existing Haskell class hierarchy. For example, `zero` and `<+>` are essentially `mempty` and `mappend` of the class `Monoid`. Mainly for presentation reasons we decided to define the `Semiring` type class independently, since it allows the definition of instances through a single definition instead of being forced to split it into several ones.

To see how this library is used, consider the following implementation for computing Fibonacci numbers, which uses the Counting semiring, obtained by defining a number type as an instance of the `Semiring` class in the obvious way.[3]

```
instance Semiring Integer where
  {zero = 0; one = 1; (<+>) = (+); (<.>) = (*)}
```

The semiring recurrence representation is very similar to the well-known recursive definition, except for two notable differences are: First, recursive calls are made by a function `memo` to indicate when intermediate results of recursive calls should be stored in a table. Second, the implementation consists of two parts, (a) the definition of the recurrence relation that denotes a table-based, efficient implementation (`fibT`), and (b) an interface that simply executes the table-based implementation (`fib`).

---

[2] See http://hackage.haskell.org/package/DP. The code has not been maintained in some time and doesn't seem to work currently. Our implementation is available at https://github.com/prashant007/XDP.

[3] Note that the Counting semiring is *not* monotonic. The implementation of Fibonacci numbers is still correct, since the $\oplus$ function isn't used to select among different alternatives.

```
fibT :: DP Integer Integer
fibT 0 = zero
fibT 1 = one
fibT n = memo (n-1) <+> memo (n-2)

fib :: Integer -> Integer
fib n = runDP fibT n
```

This examples illustrates some of the major building blocks that are provided by the dynamic programming library.

- The functions `<+>` and `<.>` correspond to semiring addition ($\oplus$) and multiplication ($\otimes$), respectively.
- The type `DP t r` represents a dynamic programming computation. Parameter `t` represents the argument, corresponding to the table index on which recursion occurs, and `r` represents the result type of the computation.
- The function `memo` takes an index as input. The index can be thought of as the input to the smaller subproblems that need to be solved while solving a dynamic programming problem; it is the quantity on which the algorithm is recursively invoked. With `memo` a subproblem for a given input value is solved only once, and the result is stored in a table for potential reuse.
- The function `inj` (used later) turns any semiring value (different from **0** and **1**) into a `DP` value.
- The function `runDP` executes a dynamic programming specification `DP t r` that works on tables indexed by a type `t` by producing a function that computes results of type `r` from an initial value of type `t`.

3.3   Computing the Lengths of Shortest Paths

In its simplest form, a shortest path algorithm takes a graph together with a source and destination node as inputs and computes the length of the shortest path between the two nodes.

In the following, we show how a program for computing shortest paths can be systematically extended to support the generation of explanations in addition to the computed answers. We use the *Bellman-Ford* algorithm [9], which can be concisely described by the following recurrence relation in which SP denotes the length of the shortest path in a graph between the start node s and any other v with at most i number of edges. This algorithm works only for graphs with non-negative edge weights. We directly show the definition using the operations from the Min-Plus semiring (see Fig. 1): $\oplus$ represents min, $\otimes$ represents numeric addition, and the constants **0** and **1** represent the additive and the multiplicative identity and stand for ∞ and 0, respectively.

$$SP(v,i) = \begin{cases} \mathbf{1} & i = 0 \wedge v = s \\ \mathbf{0} & i = 0 \wedge v \neq s \\ SP(v, i-1) \oplus \bigoplus_{(u,v)\in E}(SP(u, i-1) \otimes w(u,v)) & \text{otherwise} \end{cases}$$

Here E is the set of edges in the graph, and $w(u, v)$ denotes the weight of edge (u, v). This algorithm incrementally updates connection information between nodes. When all edge labels in a graph with n nodes are positive, the shortest path contains at most $n-1$ edges. Therefore, the shortest path to a node t can be obtained by the expression $SP(t, n)$. In each step the algorithm considers nodes that are one more edge away from the target node and updates the distance of the currently known shortest path.

Note that this formulation of the algorithm is actually more general than the original, since the operations can be taken from different semirings to express different computations. We will later take advantage of this generality by generating, in addition to the shortest path value, decomposed values, the path itself, and explanations.

Next we show how the shortest path algorithm can be expressed as a dynamic programming algorithm in our library. The Min-Plus semiring is implemented in Haskell through a class instance definition for the type constructor **Large** that adds ∞ to a number type. We need ∞ to represent the case when there isn't a path between two nodes.

```
data Large a = Finite a | Infinity deriving (Eq,Ord)

instance (Num a,Ord a) => Semiring (Large a) where
  {zero = Infinity; one = Finite 0; (<+>) = min; (<.>) = (+)}
```

The instance definitions for **Functor**, **Applicative**, and **Num** are all straightforward (they are basically the same as for **Maybe**), and we omit them here for brevity. One subtle, but important, difference between **Large** and **Maybe** is that **Infinity** is defined as the second constructor in the data definition, which makes it the largest element of the **Large** data type when an **Ord** instance is derived.

For the Haskell implementation of the algorithm, we represent edges as pairs of nodes and a graph as a list of edges paired with their lengths, see Fig. 2. We use a multi-parameter type class **SP** to facilitate a generic implementation of the shortest path function that works for different edge label types (type parameter **l**) and types of results (type parameter **r**). As in the Fibonacci example, the implementation consists of two parts: (a) a recurrence specification of the DP algorithm (the function **sp**) and (b) the function **shortestPath** for actually running the described computation. Both functions have a default implementation that doesn't change for different class instances. The class consists of an additional member **result** that turns labeled edges into values of the DP result type **r**. The definition of the **sp** function is directly derived from the semiring representation of the Bellman-Ford recurrence relation. Note that the **memo** function in the definition of **sp** takes pairs as input and effectively denotes a recursion of the **sp** function, memoizing the output of each recursive call for later reuse. The second argument of the **<+>** function in the recursive case of the **sp** function implements the part $\bigoplus_{(u,v)\in E}(SP(u, i - 1) \otimes w(u, v))$ of the recurrence relation. The function **sconcat** takes a list of values, namely all incoming edges at node **v**, and combines these using the semiring addition function **<+>**. Finally, the actual computation of a shortest path between two nodes is initiated by the function shortestPath through calling sp and passing the number of nodes of the graph as an additional parameter (computed by the helper function noNodes).

```
type Node = Int
type Edge = (Node,Node)
type Graph l = [(Edge,l)]

noNodes :: Graph l -> Int
noNodes = length . nub . concatMap (\((p,q),_) -> [p,q])

class Semiring r => SP l r where
  result :: (Edge,l) -> r

  sp :: Graph l -> Node -> DP (Node,Int) r
  sp g s (v,0) = if s==v then one else zero
  sp g s (v,i) = memo (v,i-1) <+> sconcat
                   [memo (u,i-1) <.> (inj.result) e | e@((u,v'),_)<-g, v'==v]

shortestPath :: Graph l -> Node -> Node -> r
shortestPath g s t = runDP (sp g s) (t,noNodes g-1)
```

Fig. 2. Generic shortest path implementation.

To execute the shortestPath function for producing path lengths for graphs with non-decomposed edge labels, we need to create an instance of the SP type class with the corresponding type parameters. Since the functions sp and shortestPath are already defined, we only need a definition for result.

```
instance SP Double (Large Double) where
  result (_,l) = Finite l
```

The result of running the shortest-path algorithm on the non-decomposed graph shown on the left of Fig. 3 produces the following output.

```
> shortestPath g 1 4 :: Large Double
30.0
```

Specifying the result type (r) to be Large Double selects the implementation in which the result function maps a labeled edge to the DP result type as shown. In addition to the length of the shortest path we may also want to know the path itself. We develop a solution based on semirings next.

3.4 Computing Shortest Paths

To compute shortest paths in addition to their lengths, we need an instance of Semiring for the type (Large Double,[Edge]). A first attempt could be to define pairs of semirings as semirings. This would require both components to be semirings themselves, but since there is not a straightforward instance of lists as semirings, we have to adopt a different strategy.

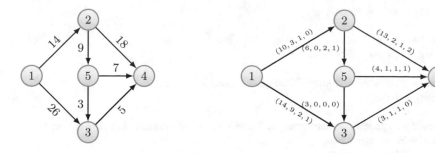

Fig. 3. An edge-labeled graph (g) and its version with decomposed edge-labels (g^d).

If we look at this example more closely, we can observe that the DP computation of a shortest path is solely driven by the first component of the pair type and that the paths are computed alongside. This means that the path type doesn't really need to support the **Semiring** structure. We can exploit this fact by defining a semiring instance for pairs that relies for its semiring semantics only on the semiring instance of its first component. To handle the combination of values in its second component, we require that the type be a monoid and use the binary operation in the instance definition for the `<.>` function. The `<+>` function acts as a selector of the two values, and the selection is controlled by a selection function that the first type parameter has to support through a corresponding instance definition for the class **Selector**. The function **first** implements a selection decision between two values; it returns **True** if the first argument is selected and **False** otherwise. The code is shown in Fig. 4.

Note that **View** is *not* a semiring, because the absorption rule ($a \otimes \mathbf{0} = \mathbf{0} \otimes a = \mathbf{0}$) doesn't hold. However, that is not a problem, since the monotonicity property, which ensures the correctness of DP implementation, is not affected by that.

With the help of this view quasi-semiring structure we can now obtain a DP algorithm that computes the paths alongside the lengths. To this end, we represent a path **P** and its length **l** as a value **View l p** so that the length provides a view on the path on which the DP computation operates.

    type Path l = View l [Edge]

The shortest path algorithm results from an instance of the **SP** type class for the result type **Path (Large Double)**, which again only requires the definition of the **result** function to map labeled edges to the DP result type.

    instance SP Double (Path (Large Double)) where
      result (e,l) = View (Finite l) [e]

The result of running the shortest-path algorithm on the non-decomposed graph produces the following output. Again, we specify the result type of the DP computation to select the appropriate implementation of **result** and thus **sp**.

```
data View a b = View a b

class Selector a where
  first :: a -> a -> Bool

instance Ord a => Selector (Large a) where
  first = (<=)

instance (Selector a,Semiring a,Monoid b) => Semiring (View a b) where
  zero = View zero mempty
  one  = View one mempty
  l@(View x _) <+> r@(View y _) = if first x y then l else r
  (View x a)   <.> (View y b)   = View (x <.> y) (mappend a b)
```

Fig. 4. The View quasi-semiring.

```
> shortestPath g 1 4 :: Path (Large Double)
View 30.0 [(1,2),(2,5),(5,4)]
```

This is the correct result, but we don't get an explanation why it is faster than, say, the more direct path [(1,3),(3,4)].

4   Explanations from Value Decomposition

To use the generic DP programming framework with value decompositions, we have to define a type for decomposed values and define its Ord and Eq type class instances. Both definitions use the sum of the elements of the lists contained in the Values constructors to perform the comparison.

```
newtype Decomposed a = Values {values :: [a]}

instance (Eq a,Num a) => Eq (Decomposed a) where
  (==) = (==) `on` sum.values

instance (Ord a,Num a) => Ord (Decomposed a) where
  (<=) = (<=) `on` sum.values
```

These definitions ensure that decomposed values are compared based on their sums.

To use value decompositions in the shortest path computation, we need a Num instance for the Decomposed data type, which is straightforward to define, except that we need a flexible interpretation of the semiring constants that depends on the number of value components. For example, in the Min-Plus semiring we expect 1 to denote $[0,0]$ in the context of $[1,2] \otimes 1$, while it should denote $[0,0,0]$ in the context of $[1,2,3] \otimes 1$. We can achieve this behavior by defining the Num instance to be singleton lists by default that will be padded to match the length of potentially longer arguments.

Next we can obtain two more versions of the shortest path algorithm as an instance of the SP type class, one for computing lengths only, and one for computing paths alongside lengths. The type of the edge labels is [Double] to reflect the decomposed edge labels in the input graphs. The result types for the DP computations are either the path lengths represented as decomposed edge labels or the view of paths as decomposed values. Here are the corresponding instance definitions.

```
instance SP [Double] (Large (Decomposed Double)) where
    result (_,l) = Finite (Values l)
```

```
instance SP [Double] (Path (Large (Decomposed Double))) where
    result (e,l) = View (Finite (Values l)) [e]
```

The shortest-path algorithms use the graph gd with decomposed edge labels.

```
> shortestPath gd 1 4 :: Large (Decomposed Double)
[20.0,4.0,4.0,2.0]
```

```
> shortestPath gd 1 4 :: Path (Large (Decomposed Double))
View [20.0,4.0,4.0,2.0] [(1,2),(2,5),(5,4)]
```

We can compute valuation differences and minimally dominating sets to compare the results with alternative solutions. For example, the decomposed length of the alternative path $(1,3),(3,4)$ between nodes 1 and 4 is [17,10,3,1]. Since Decomposed and Large are Num instances, we can compute the valuation difference with respect to the shortest path to be [3.0,-6.0,1.0,1.0]. To implement a function for computing minimally dominating sets, we have to extract the decomposed values (of type Decomposed Double) from the semiring values (of type Large (Decomposed Double)) produced by the shortest path function. Moreover, when sorting the components of the valuation difference into positive and negative parts, we need to decide which parts constitute the barrier and which parts are supporting components of the computed optimal value. This decision depends on the semiring on which the computation to be explained is based. In the shortest path example, we have used the Min-Plus semiring for which positive value differences constitute barriers and negative values overcome the barrier. In general, a value s is a *supporting value* (for overcoming a barrier) if $s \oplus 1 = s$. We can realize both requirements through a (multi-parameter) type class Decompose that relates semiring types with the types of values used in decompositions, see Fig. 5.[4]

With this type class we can directly implement the definition of Δ from Sect. 2 as a function for computing the smallest sublist of supporting values whose (absolute) sum exceeds the sum of the barrier, in this case it's the singleton list [-6.0]. Since the number itself doesn't tell us what category provides this dominating advantage, we assign meaning to the bare numbers through a data

---

[4] The additional argument of type a for supportive is required to keep the types in the multi-parameter type class unambiguous. Moreover, we can't unfortunately simply give the generic definition for supportive indicated by the equation, since that would also lead to an ambiguous type.

```
class Semiring a => Decompose a b | a -> b where
  dec :: a -> Decomposed b
  supportive :: a -> b -> Bool

instance Decompose (Large (Decomposed Double)) Double where
  dec Infinity = Values []
  dec (Finite vs) = vs
  supportive _ x = x<0

data Labeled a = Label String a

unlabel :: Labeled a -> a
unlabel (Label _ x) = x

withCategories :: Decomposed a -> [String] -> Decomposed (Labeled a)
withCategories d cs = Values (map Label cs) <*> d

explainWith :: (Decompose a b,Ord b,Num b) =>
               [String] -> a -> a -> Decomposed (Labeled b)
explainWith cs d d' = Values $ head $ sortBy (compare `on` length) doms
    where (support,barrier) = partition sup $ values delta
          doms = [d | d <- sublists support, abs (sum d) > abs (sum barrier)]
          delta = dec d `withCategories` cs - dec d' `withCategories` cs
          sup = supportive d . unlabel
```

Fig. 5. Minimal dominators and explanations.

type Labeled that pairs values with strings. Creating a Num instance for Labeled allows us to assign labels to the individual numbers of a Decomposed value and apply the computation of dominating sets to work with labeled numbers, resulting in the function explainWith. If P is the result of the shortest path function shown above and P' is the corresponding value for the alternative path considered, then we can explain why P is better than P' by invoking the function.

```
> explainWith ["Distance","Traffic","Weather","Construction"] p p'
[Traffic:-6.0]
```

The result says that, considering traffic alone, P has an advantage over P', since the traffic makes the path of P faster by 6.

The generation of explanation for other DP algorithms works in much the same way: First, identify the appropriate semiring for the optimization problem. The View quasi-semiring facilitates variety of computations that produce results on different levels of detail. Second, implement the DP algorithm as a type class that contains the main recurrence, a wrapper to run the described computation, plus the function result that ties the DP computation to different result types. Finally, define a value decomposition for the result type. The function explainWith can then compare optimal results with alternatives and produce explanations based on value categories.

5 Proactive Generation of Explanations

At this point, a user who wants an explanation has to supply an alternative as an argument for the function `explainWith`. Sometimes such examples can be automatically generated, which means that user questions about solutions can be anticipated and proactively answered.

In the case of finding shortest paths, a result may be surprising—and therefore might prompt the user to question it—if the suggested path is not the shortest one in terms of traveled distance. This is because the travel distance retains a special status among all cost categories in that it is always a determining factor in the solution and can never be ignored. This is different for other categories, such as traffic or weather, which may be 0 and in that case play no role in deciding between different path alternatives.

In general, we can therefore distinguish between those categories that always influence the outcome of the computation and those that only *may* do so. We call the former *principal categories* and the latter *minor categories*. We can exploit knowledge about principal and minor categories to anticipate user questions by executing the program with decomposed values but keeping only the values for the principal categories. If the result is different from the one produced when using the complete value decomposition, it is an alternative result worthy of an explanation, and we can compute the minimal dominating set accordingly.

Unfortunately, this strategy doesn't work as expected, because if we remove minor categories to compute an alternative solution, the values of those categories aren't aggregated alongside the computation of the alternative and thus are not available for the computation of minimal dominating sets. Alternatively, instead of changing the underlying decomposition data, we can change the way their aggregation controls the DP algorithm. Specifically, instead of ordering decomposed values based on their sum, we can order them based on a primary category (or a sum of several primary categories). In Haskell we can achieve this by defining a new data type `Principal`, which is basically identical to `Decomposed` but has a different `Ord` instance definition.

```
instance (Ord a,Num a) => Ord (Principal a) where
    (<=) = (<=) `on` head.pvalues
```

We also need a function that can map `Principal` data into `Decomposed` data within the type of the semiring to get two `Decomposed` values that can be compared and explained by the function `explainWith`. To compute the main result (calculated using all the categories), and the alternative result (calculated using just the principal categories) simultaneously we can use a *pair* semiring, which is defined component-wise in the obvious way. With these preparations we can define the function `explain` that takes an instance of the function to be explained. The function outputs a pair of `Decomposed` and `Principal` values whenever they differ, which can then be explained as before using the function `explainWith` (Fig. 6).

To use `explain` in our example, we have to create another instance for the `SP` class that works with the pair of `Decomposed` and `Principal` types, captured

```
newtype Principal a = PValues {pvalues :: [a]}

class FromPrincipal f where
  fromPrincipal :: f (Principal a) -> f (Decomposed a)

explain :: (FromPrincipal f,Decompose (f (Decomposed a)) b,
            Eq (f (Decomposed a)),Ord b,Num b) =>
           (i -> (f (Decomposed a), f (Principal a))) -> [String] -> i ->
           (f (Decomposed a),Maybe (f (Decomposed a),Decomposed (Labeled b)))
explain f cs i | o1==o2    = (o1,Nothing)
               | otherwise = (o2,Just (o2,explainWith cs o1 o2))
               where  (o1,o') = f i
                      o2      = fromPrincipal o'
```

Fig. 6. Generating automatic explanations.

in the type synonym `LPair`. We also have to create an instance for the function `fromPrincipal` so that we can turn `Principal` data into `Decomposed` data inside the `Large` type.

```
type LPair = (Large (Decomposed Double),Large (Principal Double))

instance SP [Double] LPair where
  result (e,l) = (Finite (Values l),Finite (PValues l))

instance FromPrincipal Large where
  fromPrincipal = fmap (Values . pvalues)
```

Finally, to be able to apply `explain` we have to normalize the argument type of the shortest path function into a tuple.

```
type SPInput = (Graph [Double],Node,Node)

spPair :: SPInput -> LPair
spPair (g,v,w) = shortestPath g v w
```

When we apply `explain`, it will in addition to computing the shortest path also automatically find an alternative path and explain why it is not a better alternative.

```
> explain spPair ["Distance","Traffic","Weather","Construction"] (gd,1,4)
([20.0,4.0,4.0,2.0],Just ([17.0,10.0,3.0,1.0],[Traffic:-6.0]))
```

Of course, the output could be printed more prettily.

6   Related Work

In [10,11] we proposed the idea of preserving the structure of aggregated data and using it to generate explanations for reinforcement learning algorithms based on so-called *minimum sufficient explanations*. That work is less general than what we describe here and strictly situated in a machine learning context that is tied to the framework of *adaptation-based programming* [12]. Value decomposition and minimal dominating sets are a general approach to the generation of explanations for a wider range of algorithms. A different concept of "minimal sufficient explanations" was also used in related work on explanations for optimal Markov Decision Process (MDP) policies [13]. That work is focused on automated planning and on explaining the optimal decision of an optimal policy. Those explanations tend to be significantly larger than explanations for decisions to select between two alternatives. Also, that work is not based on value or reward decompositions.

Debugging can be viewed as a specific form of explanation. For example, *Delta debugging* reveals the cause-effect chain of program failures, that is, the variables and values that caused the failure [14]. Delta debugging needs two runs of a program, a successful one and an unsuccessful one. It systematically narrows down failure-inducing circumstances until a minimal set remains, that is, if there is a test case which produces a bug, then delta debugging will try to trim the code until the minimal code component which reproduces the bug is found. Delta debugging and the idea of MDSs are similar in the sense that both try to isolate minimal components responsible for a certain output. An important difference is that delta debugging produces program fragments as explanations, whereas an explanation based on value decompositions is a structured representation of program inputs.

The process of debugging is complicated by the low-level representation of data processed by programs. *Declarative debugging* aims to provide a more high-level approach, which abstracts away the evaluation order of the program and focuses on its high-level logical meaning. This style of debugging is discussed in [15] and is at the heart of, for example, the Haskell debugger Buddha. *Observational debugging* as used in the Haskell debugger Hood [16] allows the observation of intermediate values within the computation. The programmer has to annotate expressions of interest inside the source code. When the source code is recompiled and rerun, the values generated for the annotated expressions are recorded. Like value decomposition, observational debugging expects the programmers to identify and annotate parts of the programs which are relevant to generate explanations. A potential problem with the approach is that the number of intermediate values can become large and not all the intermediate values have explanatory significance.

The *Whyline* system [17] inverts the debugging process, allowing users to ask questions about program behavior and responding by pointing to parts of the code responsible for the outcomes. Although this system improves the debugging process, it can still only point to places in the program, which limits its explanatory power. In the realm of spreadsheets, the *goal-directed debugging* approach [18] goes one step further and also produces change suggestions that would fix errors. Change suggestions are a kind of counter-factual explanations.

Traces of program executions can explain how outputs are produced from inputs. While traces are often used as a basis for debugging, they can support more general forms of explanations as well. Since traces can get quite large, focusing on interesting parts poses a particular challenge. Program slicing can be used to filter out irrelevant parts of traces. Specifically, *dynamic slicing* has been employed to isolate parts of a program that potentially contribute to the value computed at a point of interest [19]. Using dynamic slicing for generating explanations of functional program execution is described in [20]. This approach has been extended to imperative functional programs in [21]. Our approach does not produce traces as explanations. Instead, value decompositions maintain a more granular representation of values that are aggregated. Our approach requires some additional work on the part of the programmers in decomposing the inputs (even though in our library we have tried to minimize the required effort). An advantage of our approach is that we only record the information relevant to an explanation in contrast to generic tracing mechanisms, which generally have to record every computation that occurs in a program, and require aggressive filtering of traces afterwards.

7   Conclusions and Future Work

We have introduced an approach to explain the execution of dynamic programs through value decompositions and minimal dominating sets: Value decompositions offer more details about how decisions are made, and minimal dominating sets minimize the amount of information a user has to absorb to understand an explanation. We have put this idea into practice by integrating it into a Haskell library for dynamic programming that requires minimal effort from a programmer to transform a traditional, value-producing program into one that can also produce explanations of its results. The explanation component is modular and allows the explanations for one DP algorithm to be specialized to different application domains independently of its implementation. In addition to producing explanations in response to user requests, we have also shown how to anticipate questions about results and produce corresponding explanations automatically.

In future work, we will investigate the applicability of our approach to more general algorithmic structures. An open question is how to deal with the aggregation of data along unrelated decisions. Our approach works well for dynamic programming algorithms because all the decisions involved in the optimization process are compositionally related through a semiring. For algorithms that don't fit into the semiring structure, the data aggregation for producing explanations must be achieved in a different way.

References

1. Roehm, T., Tiarks, R., Koschke, R., Maalej, W.: How do professional developers comprehend software? In: 34th International Conference on Software Engineering, pp. 255–265 (2012)
2. Murphy, G.C., Kersten, M., Findlater, L.: How are Java software developers using the eclipse IDE? IEEE Softw. **23**(4), 76–83 (2006)
3. Vessey, I.: Expertise in debugging computer programs: an analysis of the content of verbal protocols. IEEE Trans. Syst. Man Cybern. **16**(5), 621–637 (1986)

4. Parnin, C., Orso, A.: Are automated debugging techniques actually helping programmers? In: International Symposium on Software Testing and Analysis, pp. 199–209 (2011)

5. Marceau, G., Cooper, G.H., Spiro, J.P., Krishnamurthi, S., Reiss, S.P.: The design and implementation of a dataflow language for scriptable debugging. Autom. Softw. Eng. **14**(1), 59–86 (2007)

6. Khoo, Y.P., Foster, J.S., Hicks, M.: Expositor: scriptable time-travel debugging with first-class traces. In: ACM/IEEE International Conference on Software Engineering, pp. 352–361 (2013)

7. Golan, J.S.: Semirings and their Applications. Springer, Dordrecht (1999). https://doi.org/10.1007/978-94-015-9333-5

8. Huang, L.: Advanced dynamic programming in semiring and hypergraph frameworks. In: Advanced Dynamic Programming in Computational Linguistics: Theory, Algorithms and Applications - Tutorial Notes, pp. 1–18 (2008)

9. Bellman, R.: On a routing problem. Q. Appl. Math. **16**(1), 87–90 (1958)

10. Erwig, M., Fern, A., Murali, M., Koul, A.: Explaining deep adaptive programs via reward decomposition. In: IJCAI/ECAI Workshop on Explainable Artificial Intelligence, pp. 40–44 (2018)

11. Juozapaitis, Z., Fern, A., Koul, A., Erwig, M., Doshi-Velez, F.: Explainable reinforcement learning via reward decomposition. In: IJCAI/ECAI Workshop on Explainable Artificial Intelligence, pp. 47–53 (2019)

12. Bauer, T., Erwig, M., Fern, A., Pinto, J.: Adaptation-based program generation in Java. In: ACM SIGPLAN Workshop on Partial Evaluation and Program Manipulation, pp. 81–90 (2011)

13. Khan, O.Z., Poupart, P., Black, J.P.: Minimal sufficient explanations for factored Markov decision processes. In: 19th International Conference on Automated Planning and Scheduling, pp. 194–200 (2009)

14. Zeller, A.: Isolating cause-effect chains from computer programs. In: 10th ACM SIGSOFT Symposium on Foundations of Software Engineering, pp. 1–10 (2002)

15. Pope, B.: Declarative debugging with Buddha. In: Vene, V., Uustalu, T. (eds.) AFP 2004. LNCS, vol. 3622, pp. 273–308. Springer, Heidelberg (2005). https://doi.org/10.1007/11546382_7

16. Gill, A.: Debugging Haskell by observing intermediate data structures. Electron. Notes Theoret. Comput. Sci. **41**(1), 1 (2001)

17. Ko, A.J., Myers, B.A.: Finding causes of program output with the Java Whyline. In: SIGCHI Conference on Human Factors in Computing Systems, pp. 1569–1578 (2009)

18. Abraham, R., Erwig, M.: GoalDebug: a spreadsheet debugger for end users. In: 29th IEEE International Conference on Software Engineering, pp. 251–260 (2007)

19. Ochoa, C., Silva, J., Vidal, G.: Dynamic slicing based on redex trails. In: ACM SIGPLAN Symposium on Partial Evaluation and Semantics-based Program Manipulation, pp. 123–134 (2004)

20. Perera, R., Acar, U.A., Cheney, J., Levy, P.B.: Functional programs that explain their work. In: 17th ACM SIGPLAN International Conference on Functional Programming, pp. 365–376 (2012)

21. Ricciotti, W., Stolarek, J., Perera, R., Cheney, J.: Imperative functional programs that explain their work. Proc. ACM Program. Lang. **1**, 14:1–14:28 (2017)

A DSL for Integer Range Reasoning: Partition, Interval and Mapping Diagrams

Johannes Eriksson[1]([✉])[iD] and Masoumeh Parsa[2][iD]

[1] Vaadin Ltd., Turku, Finland
joheriks@vaadin.com
[2] Department of Information Technologies, Åbo Akademi University, Turku, Finland
mparsa@abo.fi

Abstract. Expressing linear integer constraints and assertions over integer ranges—as becomes necessary when reasoning about arrays—in a legible and succinct form poses a challenge for deductive program verification. Even simple assertions, such as integer predicates quantified over finite ranges, become quite verbose when given in basic first-order logic syntax. In this paper, we propose a domain-specific language (DSL) for assertions over integer ranges based on Reynolds's *interval* and *partition diagrams*, two diagrammatic notations designed to integrate well into linear textual content such as specifications, program annotations, and proofs. We extend intervalf diagrams to the more general concept of *mapping diagrams*, representing partial functions from disjoint integer intervals. A subset of mapping diagrams, *colorings*, provide a compact notation for selecting integer intervals that we intend to constrain, and an intuitive new construct, the *legend*, allows connecting colorings to first-order integer predicates. Reynolds's diagrams have not been supported widely by verification tools. We implement the syntax and semantics of partition and mapping diagrams as a DSL and theory extension to the Why3 program verifier. We illustrate the approach with examples of verified programs specified with colorings and legends. This work aims to extend the verification toolbox with a lightweight, intuitive DSL for array and integer range specifications.

1 Introduction

Deductive program verification is the activity of establishing correctness by mathematically proving verification conditions (VCs) extracted from a program and its specification. If all VCs are proved, the program is guaranteed to terminate in a state satisfying its postcondition for all inputs satisfying the precondition. While much of the mechanics of program verification is automated by VC generators and automatic theorem provers, the construction of correct programs by this method remains a largely interactive task. In the case of total correctness verification of sequential programs, VC generation relies on supplying a pre- and postcondition specification of each subroutine (procedure, method), and verification of a subroutine in turn requires intermediate assertions and loop invariants to be inserted into the routine. Producing these assertions requires both familiarity with a formal state description language and the ability to express the assertions in it succinctly. Such languages are usually based on first- or

© Springer Nature Switzerland AG 2020
E. Komendantskaya and Y. A. Liu (Eds.): PADL 2020, LNCS 12007, pp. 196–212, 2020.
https://doi.org/10.1007/978-3-030-39197-3_13

higher-order logic, and like programming languages general-purpose. While concise at expressing basic mathematical relations, constraints over arrays and integer ranges tend to require verbose expressions, obfuscating the original notion. Indeed, for array constraints, pictures often provide a more intuitive grip on the problem. For instance, given the textbook verification exercise of specifying the loop invariant of a binary search routine that determines the presence of the value x in a sorted array a (indexed from 0 to $n-1$), we may start by jotting down a box diagram similar to the following:

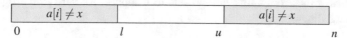

This diagram captures the pertinent assertions over the mutable state of binary search: that the loop variables l and u partition the array into three disjoint subarrays, and that the value x is not present in the leftmost or rightmost subarray. Once these relationships have been understood, we may then refine the diagram into a logic formula. A possible rendition of the above in first-order predicate logic is:

$$0 \leq l \leq u+1 \leq n \wedge \forall i (0 \leq i < l \vee u < i < n \Rightarrow a[i] \neq x)$$

It is easy to see that the formula lacks the legibility of the diagram, but is it actually more *formal*, as to make us accept this tradeoff? If we stipulate that the juxtaposition of the indexes (0, l, u and n) and the vertical lines denotes order constraints, and that the propositions written inside the shaded ranges are universally quantified over the corresponding subarrays, the diagram becomes semantically equivalent to the predicate logic formula. Hence, if the diagram incurs no loss of information, but appears more closely connected to our understanding of the domain, reasoning with the diagram directly could benefit both precision and legibility. As Dijkstra notes, "the purpose of abstraction is not to be vague, but to create a new semantic level in which one can be absolutely precise" [8]. However, unlike diagrams, predicate logic carries with it a collection of formula manipulation rules. Only given similar rules for diagrams like the above, may we consider them a worthy alternative to predicate logic for writing specifications and proofs. This is precisely the motivation behind Reynolds's *interval* and *partition diagrams*, introduced 40 years ago [16] together with a set of abstractions for reasoning about arrays. Reynolds argues "Of course, an equivalent assertion can be given in the predicate calculus, but this sacrifices the intuitive content of the diagram [...] A better approach is to formalize and give rigorous meaning to the diagram itself."

Approaching diagrams as formal specifications in their own right rather than as stepping stones, we do observe some rough edges in the box diagram: multiple occurrences of the expression $a[i] \neq x$ and the *ad hoc* assumption that i is quantified over the indexes of the shaded subarrays, while a and x, on the other hand, are free. To avoid the redundancy and clarify variable binding in the shaded subarrays, we redraw the diagram as follows:

$$i \ : a[i] \neq x \qquad \boxed{\ 0 \ \ \ |\ \ l \ \ \ |\ \ u \ \ \ |\ \ n\ }$$

The revised diagram consists of two components: a *legend* asserting $a[i] \neq x$ over a single shaded element at index i, and a box diagram specifying the constraints on l, u

and n as well as the extent of the shading. Following Reynolds, we also place the partition bounds inside the boxes rather than below them, as this convention both conserves space and increases legibility of a bound's position relative to its adjacent vertical line. Our intention with this example so far has only been to demonstrate that box diagrams are sufficiently precise for formal specification. As we will see through examples in the sequel, legends extend naturally to properties involving multiple indexes, such as sortedness (which we omitted for brevity in the above example). We give a detailed syntax and semantics of these diagrams, and present tool support for verifying programs specified with such diagrams.

Reynolds's Diagrams as a DSL. Domain-specific languages (DSLs), mini-languages tailored for a particular application, are commonly used in software engineering to raise the level of abstraction. The degree of sophistication range from substitution macros to rich high-level languages. A DSL should be easy to both use and opt out of if not deemed beneficial. Following the DSL approach, we decided to add diagram support to an existing language satisfying the following desiderata:

– Established in the verification community and supported by state-of-the-art, open-source tooling for VC generation and automatic theorem proving.
– Able to lexically combine box diagrams with the language's own syntax.
– Able to represent diagrams as data types, avoiding error-prone lexical translation stages and enabling use of diagrams in proofs.
– Tooling supports automatic reduction of VCs containing diagrams into their logical equivalences, e.g., by rewrite rules.

Consequently, we chose Why3 [11], an open-source platform[1] for deductive program verification consisting of a specification language, an ML-like programming language, and a common interface to multiple automatic theorem provers—including SMT solvers, the workhorses of modern program verification.

Contribution. We generalize Reynolds's interval diagrams to *mapping diagrams*, formally partial functions from a set of disjoint integer intervals to any type. *Colorings* constitute a subset of mapping diagrams, labeling intervals from a finite set ("palette") of colors. We introduce the *legend* construct for attaching interpretation to colorings. Intuitively, colorings specify labeled selections, e.g., "all integers between 0 and l are red" and "all indexes in the array are green", while legends express quantified predicates like "x is not among the red elements", "all red elements are greater than all green elements" and "all green elements are sorted". We show that colorings and legends are automatically reducible to universally quantified predicates. We have implemented an extension to the Why3 theorem prover to support diagrams similar to those shown in the introduction. The extension consists of a DSL allowing partition and mapping diagrams to be used in Why3 theories and programs, and a Why3 theory encoding partition and mapping diagrams as a data type together with the functions and predicates defining their semantics. The diagram syntax is character-based and does not require sophisticated editor support. All properties have been mechanically proved in Why3 using its underlying theorem provers. We demonstrate the DSL by verified code examples.

---

[1] Binary, source, and documentation available at https://why3.lri.fr.

Notational Conventions. We give the semantics of diagrams in first-order predicate logic with partial expressions. While the Why3 logic is total and requires a parametric data type (option) for expressing partiality, we describe the general semantics using partial expressions for brevity. We denote by the operator def definedness of a partial expression, and by $=_\exists$ the existential equality relation between two partial expressions e_1 and e_2 satisfying

$$e_1 =_\exists e_2 \triangleq \mathsf{def}\ e_1 \wedge \mathsf{def}\ e_2 \wedge e_1 = e_2$$

In syntax definitions we adopt the convention that the meta-variables A and B stand for integer expressions, Q stands for Boolean expressions (predicates), E and F stand for expressions of other types, and X stands for identifiers. Subscript variables (e.g., A_1, A_2) are considered separate meta-variables of the same class. For sequences of identifiers, we write $\bar{X}$. We write $E^?$ to indicate that an expression may be omitted in a syntactic context, and we semantically handle absence by partiality. We indicate by $E[X]$ that X is a free variable in E. When $E[X]$ occurs as a subexpression we assume that adjacent subexpressions do not contain free occurrences of X; for instance, in the syntax definition $Q_1[X] \wedge Q_2$, the Boolean expression Q_1 may contain free occurrences of X whereas Q_2 may not. We write $\lambda X(E[X])$ for the anonymous function of variable X to value E. Other logic and arithmetic operators are the standard ones.

Overview of Paper. The rest of the paper is structured as follows. Section 2 describes interval and partition diagrams. Section 3 generalizes interval diagrams to mapping diagrams and colorings. Section 4 introduces the legend notation for assertions over colored intervals. Section 5 describes a tool extension allowing diagrams to be used in Why specifications. We illustrate use of this tool by example in Sect. 6. We review related work in Sect. 7 and conclude the paper with a discussion of lessons learned so far and possible future research directions in Sect. 8.

2 Interval and Partition Diagrams

Reynolds [16] introduces two interpretations for the pictogram $A_1\ \boxed{}\ A_2$: as an *interval diagram*, standing for the (possibly empty) integer interval $\{x \mid A_1 < x \leq A_2\}$, and as a *partition diagram*, standing for the predicate $A_1 \leq A_2$. This dual interpretation reflects the close semantical relationship between intervals and partitions. As diagrams are formulas, the intended meaning can in practice always be determined from the context: in a set-theoretic context it is an interval diagram, whereas in a logical context it is a partition diagram. Note that when $A_1 = A_2$ the partition diagram is universally true and the interval diagram represents the empty interval.

The form $A_1\ \boxed{}\ A_2$ is called the *normal form* of an interval or partition diagram, where both bounds are written to the left of the corresponding adjacent vertical lines, called *dividing lines*. Alternatively, either or both bounds of a diagram may be written to the right of the dividing line to offset the bound by 1. This means that the bound "$A - 1|$" can be equivalently written as "$|A$". Below we list the alternative forms together with the corresponding normal forms and meanings as interval and partition predicate:

diagram	equiv. normal form	integer interval	partition predicate
A_1 ▢ A_2	A_1 ▢ A_2-1	$\{x \mid A_1 < x < A_2\}$	$A_1 < A_2$
A_1 ▢ A_2	A_1-1 ▢ A_2-1	$\{x \mid A_1 \leq x < A_2\}$	$A_1 - 1 \leq A_2 - 1$
A_1 ▢ A_2	A_1-1 ▢ A_2	$\{x \mid A_1 \leq x \leq A_2\}$	$A_1 - 1 \leq A_2$

Note that when interpreted as partition diagrams, A_1▢A_2 and A_1▢A_2 are equivalent, whereas when interpreted as interval diagrams, they represent different intervals. As a shorthand, we may write $\boxed{A}$ to denote the *singleton* interval containing only A:

$$\boxed{A} \qquad A-1\;\boxed{A} \qquad \{x \mid x = A\} \qquad A - 1 \leq A$$

When considered a partition diagram, $\boxed{A}$ is a tautology. However, the singleton form is still useful as a component of *general partition diagrams*. These consist of multiple chained partition diagrams that share dividing lines so that the right bound of the predecessor becomes the left bound of the successor. The following definition formalizes this notion.

Definition 1. *A general partition diagram is a sequence of n (where $n \geq 1$) component partition diagrams, with $n+1$ integer bounds $A_0, \ldots, A_n$, asserting that these partition the total interval A_0▢A_n into n disjoint and connected component intervals:*

$$A_0 \boxed{\;\;A_1\;} \boxed{\;\;A_2\;} \cdots A_{n-1} \boxed{\;\;A_n\;} \;\; \triangleq \;\; \bigwedge_{j=0}^{n-1} \left(A_j \leq A_{j+1} \right)$$

(Here the fragment A_2┆ $\cdots$ A_{n-1}┆ is meta-syntax standing for any number of intermediate component intervals; it is not part of the actual diagram syntax).

While each component diagram in Definition 1 is given on normal form (where each component interval bound is written to the left of the dividing line), as with the basic partition diagrams, a bound may be written on the opposite side of the dividing line to offset it by 1. We illustrate this with two examples.

Example 2.1. The partition diagram corresponding to the partial binary search invariant discussed in Sect. 1, 0 ▢ l ▢ u ▢ n, has the equivalent normal form -1 ▢ $l-1$ ▢ u ▢ $n-1$ and stands for the predicate $0 \leq l \leq u + 1 \leq n$ (equivalently $-1 \leq l - 1 \leq u \leq n - 1$).

Example 2.2. The partition diagram 0 ▢ k ▢ n has the equivalent normal form -1 ▢ $k-1$ ▢ k ▢ n and stands for the predicate $0 \leq k \leq n$ (equivalently $-1 \leq k - 1 \leq k \leq n$).

We note that Definition 1 is stricter than Reynolds's original definition, which considers the diagram true also when $A_0 \geq A_1 \geq \cdots \geq A_n$. I.e, in the original notation an empty partition may be specified with a left bound exceeding the right bound (i.e., $A_i > A_{i+1}$). Reynolds calls such diagrams *irregular* representations of the empty interval. Our definition allows only for what Reynolds refers to as *regular* representations of empty intervals (i.e., $A_i = A_{i+1}$), and a partition diagram is always false if any $A_i > A_{i+1}$. The stricter interpretation has the advantages that the basic partition diagram with two bounds $A_1 \boxed{} A_2$ constitutes a meaningful assertion by itself (rather than a tautology), and that the cardinality of an interval diagram is $A_2 - A_1$ when its corresponding partition diagram is true. Unlike for partition diagrams, Reynolds does not define a chained form for interval diagrams.

3 Mapping Diagrams and Colorings

Next we introduce *mapping diagrams*, a generalization of interval diagrams to partial functions from the integers. A mapping diagram consists of a sequence of *mapping components*. A mapping component $X \to A_1 \boxed{{}^{\#}E[X]\; A_2}$, where E is a total expression over the integer parameter X to some type T, stands for the function $\lambda X(E)$ from the domain $A_1 \boxed{} A_2$ to the range T.

Definition 2. *A general mapping diagram is a sequence of mapping components that stands for the union of the corresponding functions:*

$$X \to A_0 \boxed{{}^{\#}E_0[X]^?\; A_1} \;\cdots\; A_{n-1} \boxed{{}^{\#}E_{n-1}[X]^?\; A_n}$$
$$\triangleq$$
$$\bigcup_{i=0}^{n-1} \left\{ (x, \lambda X(E_i)(x)) \mid x \in A_i \boxed{} A_{i+1} \wedge \operatorname{def} E_i \right\}$$

We note that when the corresponding partition diagram $A_0 \boxed{} A_1 \cdots A_{n-1} \boxed{} A_n$ is true, the union of tuples is a partial function (as the domains of the component functions are disjoint). This is a side condition of the definition that we always verify when introducing a mapping diagram. In the diagram, an expression E_i may be omitted to indicate that the mapping is undefined on the interval $A_i \boxed{} A_{i+1}$.

Property 3.1. A mapping diagram with bounds $A_0, \ldots, A_n$ and expressions $E_0, \ldots E_{n-1}$ is well-defined in each point of each interval i where E_i is present, and undefined in each point on each interval j where E_j is absent as well as in each point outside of the total interval $A_0 \boxed{} A_n$.

Example 3.1. The mapping diagram $k \to a \boxed{{}^{\#}-k\; b} \quad c \boxed{{}^{\#}k\; d}$ stands for the following partial piecewise defined function: $\lambda k \begin{cases} -k & \text{if } a < k \le b \\ k & \text{if } c < k \le d \end{cases}$. The function is undefined on the interval $b \boxed{} c$.

Definition 3. *A coloring is a mapping diagram where each component interval is either unmapped, or mapped to a member of a set of labels (colors) C:*

$$A_0 \boxed{{}^{\#}E_0^?\; A_1} \;\cdots\; A_{n-1} \boxed{{}^{\#}E_{n-1}^?\; A_n}$$

In the above, each $E_i \in C$ if $\operatorname{def} E_i$.

The term *coloring* reflects the use of colors for marking intervals of interest in box diagrams. In particular, we will use colorings to assert a given predicate (specified with the *legend* construct described in the next section) over one or more intervals.

Property 3.2. A coloring *col* with component bounds $A_0,\ldots,A_n$ maps each point in an interval with a defined color to that value. That is, for each interval j, $0 \le j < n$:

$$\forall k \left(A_j < k \le A_{j+1} \wedge \operatorname{def} E_j \Rightarrow col(k) = E_j\right)$$

Example 3.2. The coloring $\boxed{0 \quad {}^{\#}\mathrm{R} \quad l \quad u \quad {}^{\#}\mathrm{R} \quad n}$ stands for the following piece-

wise defined partial function: $\lambda k \begin{cases} \mathrm{R} & \text{if } 0 \le k < l \\ \mathrm{R} & \text{if } u < k < n \end{cases}$.

4 Legends

A *legend* defines the interpretation of a coloring by a parametric, universally quantified assertion over all intervals colored in accordance with the legend.

Definition 4. *A legend is a binding expression over a sequence of integer variables $\bar{X}$ associating a coloring with bounds $A_0[\bar{X}],\ldots,A_n[\bar{X}]$ and colors $E_0,\ldots,E_{n-1}$ of type C to a predicate $Q[\bar{X}]$:*

$$\bar{X} : A_0[\bar{X}] \boxed{{}^{\#}E_0^? \quad A_1[\bar{X}]} \quad \cdots \quad A_{n-1}[\bar{X}] \boxed{{}^{\#}E_{n-1}^? \quad A_n[\bar{X}]} \rightarrow Q[\bar{X}]$$

It stands for the following parametric predicate where the parameter $r \in \mathbb{Z} \rightarrow C$:

$$\forall \bar{X} \left(\bigwedge_{j=0}^{n-1} \left(A_j \boxed{\quad} A_{j+1} \wedge (\operatorname{def} E_j \Rightarrow \forall k (k \in A_j \boxed{\quad} A_{j+1} \Rightarrow r(k) =_\exists E_j)) \right) \Rightarrow Q \right)$$

Informally put, the legend states that Q is true for a partitioning if the parameter function r returns the prescribed color value in every point of each colored component (on uncolored component intervals, the value of r is ignored).

Example 4.1. The legend "$i : \boxed{i\,{}^{\#}\mathrm{R}} \rightarrow a[i] \ne x$" stands for the following parametric predicate over r:

$$\forall i \, (i-1 < i \wedge (\operatorname{def} \mathrm{R} \Rightarrow \forall k (i-1 < k \le i \Rightarrow r(k) =_\exists \mathrm{R})) \Rightarrow a[i] \ne x)$$
$$\equiv \{ \text{ tautology elimination, singleton quantification domain } \}$$
$$\forall i \, (r(i) =_\exists \mathrm{R} \Rightarrow a[i] \ne x)$$

Example 4.2. The legend "$i \, j : \boxed{i\,{}^{\#}\mathrm{B} \quad j\,{}^{\#}\mathrm{B}} \rightarrow a[i] \le a[j]$" is equivalent to the fol-lowing parametric predicate over r (the predicate has been simplified):

$$\forall i \, j \, (i < j \wedge r(i) =_\exists \mathrm{B} \wedge r(j) =_\exists \mathrm{B} \Rightarrow a[i] \le a[j])$$

Informally, Example 4.1 states that x is not among the elements of the array a colored R, while Example 4.2 states that the elements of a at ordered index pairs i, j colored B are sorted in nondecreasing order (regardless of coloring of interjacent indexes). To use a legend in expressing a state assertion, we apply it to a coloring function over the state space of the program we are specifying.

Example 4.3. Applying the legend given in Example 4.1 to the coloring $\boxed{0 \quad ^\#\text{R} \quad}l$
reduces to an assertion that the subarray $a[0],\ldots,a[l-1]$ does not contain the value x:

$$(i: \boxed{i\,^\#\text{R}} \to a[i] \neq x)(\boxed{0 \quad ^\#\text{R} \quad}l)$$
$$\equiv \{ \text{ Definition 4, } \beta\text{-reduction } \}$$
$$\forall i\, ((\boxed{0 \quad ^\#\text{R} \quad}l)(i) =_\exists \text{R} \Rightarrow a[i] \neq x)$$
$$\equiv \{ \text{ definition of } =_\exists \}$$
$$\forall i\, (0 \leq i < l \Rightarrow a[i] \neq x)$$

An important design consideration has been that using legends and colorings when
writing assertions should not result in formulas that make automatic verification more
difficult compared to equivalent assertions written in traditional quantifier notation. As
the inner quantification in the legend definition and the color type C are syntactic artifacts of the DSL, they should preferably be eliminated from the correctness formula
before applying SMT solvers or other ATPs. To achieve this, our tool applies to each
formula an elimination rule that rewrites terms of the form $lgd(col)$, where lgd is a
legend and col is a coloring. The following proposition formalizes the elimination rule.

Proposition 1. *Given the legend*

$$lgd = \bar{X} : A_0[\bar{X}]\boxed{\begin{array}{cc} ^\#E_0^? & A_1[\bar{X}] \end{array}} \quad \cdots \quad A_{n-1}[\bar{X}]\boxed{\begin{array}{cc} ^\#E_{n-1}^? & A_n[\bar{X}] \end{array}} \to Q[\bar{X}]$$

and the coloring

$$col = B_0\boxed{\begin{array}{cc} ^\#F_0^? & B_0 \end{array}} \quad \cdots \quad B_{m-1}\boxed{\begin{array}{cc} ^\#F_{m-1}^? & B_m \end{array}}$$

the following equivalence holds for the application $lgd(col)$:

$$lgd(col) \equiv \forall \bar{X} \left(\bigwedge_{j=0}^{n-1} (A_j \leq A_{j+1} \wedge (\text{def } E_j \Rightarrow \text{contains } (A_j, E_j, A_{j+1}, col))) \Rightarrow Q \right)$$

where contains *is defined recursively on the structure of mapping diagrams:*

$$\text{contains } (a,e,b, \wedge \boxed{\begin{array}{cc} ^\#E\ D \end{array}}) \triangleq \qquad\qquad (rec.\ case)$$
$$b \leq a$$
$$\vee\ (A \leq a \leq B \wedge (A = B \vee e =_\exists E) \wedge \text{contains } (B, e, b, B_1'))$$
$$\vee\ \text{contains } (a, e, b, B_1')$$

$$\text{contains } (a,e,b, A \boxed{\begin{array}{cc} ^\#E\ B \end{array}}) \triangleq \qquad\qquad (base\ case)$$
$$b \leq a$$
$$\vee\ (A \leq a \leq B \wedge (A = B \vee e =_\exists E))$$

Proof. $\Leftarrow$ by structural induction on col and Property 3.2, $\Rightarrow$ by transitivity of contains
and induction over an integer interval.

Note that the definition of contains involves only Boolean connectives, integer comparison, and color terms of the form $e =_\exists E$. When e and E are literal color values (or
absent), the equality $e =_\exists E$ can be immediately evaluated, reducing the inner quantification of the legend to a propositional formula where the atoms are linear integer
constraints.

5   Diagram Extension to the Why3 Verification Platform

We have developed a prototype extension Why3 supporting mechanically proving meta-properties like Proposition 1 as well as specifying programs with partition and mapping diagrams. We first briefly present relevant features of the Why3 platform and then describe our implementation. The implementation is available in source form at https:// gitlab.com/diagrammatic/whyp.

The Why3 Platform. The Why3 specification language is a first-order logic extended with polymorphic types and algebraic data types. Theorems can be proved using over a dozen supported automatic and interactive theorem provers. Users interact with Why3 in batch mode through a command-line interface, or interactively through a graphical IDE. In addition to the purely logical specification language, programs with loops, mutable variables, and exceptions can be written in the WhyML language. Why3 generates VCs from WhyML programs based on weakest preconditions. A good example-driven tour of Why3 is given by Bobot et al. [6]. Why3 provides a set of transformations on verification tasks, including definition inlining, application of rewrite rules and logical inference rules. The Why3 drivers for external theorem provers employ these to transform the sequent into a form amenable to automation, for instance by eliminating language features that are not supported by the target prover (e.g. algebraic data types). Other transformations are intended to be used interactively to reduce a goal into one or more subgoals, e.g., proof-by-cases, instantiation, and induction. Why3 is designed to both be a backend for other tools as well as an extensible verification platform. It comes with a standard library of theories which can be reused through an importing mechanism. The platform itself can be extended with different kinds of plug-ins adding new input formats, prover drivers and other extensions. The core of Why3 is implemented in OCaml and is offered as a software library for programmatic access to all platform functionality, including parsing, typing, transformations, and invocation of external theorem provers.

Extension Architecture. The extension to Why3 consists of two components: a set of Why3 theories formalizing partition diagrams and mappings, and a syntactic preprocessor (written in OCaml) that translates the concrete diagram syntax into Why3 terms. Figure 1 shows the data flow when the user asks the tool to check a theory containing diagrams (indicated by the theory existing in a file with the suffix .whyp). The preprocessor parses the input theory and translates all partition diagrams, mapping diagrams and legends into normal form and then into instances of a data type defined in the theory extension. The resulting AST is dispatched to Why3 for typing, inclusion of standard library theories, task generation, and external theorem prover execution. From here onwards the data flow is identical to that of checking a normal Why3 theory. Next, we describe the concrete diagram syntax and the embedding of the diagrams in the Why3 logic.

DSL Syntax and Semantics. The DSL follows the ASCII-based lexical rules of Why3 [5]. A partition diagram must be enclosed in square brackets '[' and ']', and vertical dividing lines are written as '|'. The leftmost or rightmost vertical line may be omitted

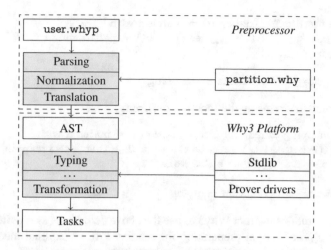

Fig. 1. Processing pipeline of Why3 extension

when it would be adjacent to a square bracket. The bounds themselves follow the syntax of Why3 terms. Mapping diagrams must be enclosed in '[X→[' and ']]' (the binder X may be omitted for colorings). The ellipsis '...' separates bounds inside a component, and in mapping diagrams may be followed by '#' and an expression. The following are examples of accepted ASCII partition and mapping diagrams and their diagrammatic equivalents:

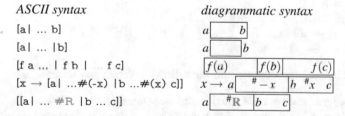

Partition and mapping diagrams may occur in a Why3 theory anywhere a term is expected. After parsing, both types of diagrams are translated into instances of the polymorphic data type diag:

type diag α = P int (option α) (diag α) | L int (option α) int

The data type represents partition diagrams in normal form; the preprocessing hence includes a normalization stage, converting each '|e'-fragment into 'e-1|' and each '|e|'-fragment into 'e-1|...e|', before finally converting the result into an instance of the above data type. The option data type from Why3s standard library is used to handle partiality. It has two constructors, None and Some α. For partition diagrams, the second parameter is always None. For mapping diagrams, it is Some α for each interval associated with an expression of type α, otherwise None. The semantics of partition diagrams is given by the predicate partitioning:

```
predicate partitioning (d:diag α) = match d with
  | P a _ ((P b _ _ | L b _ _) as r) → a≤b ∧ partitioning r
  | L a _ b → a≤b
  end
meta "rewrite_def" predicate partitioning
```

and for mapping diagrams by the function mapping:

```
function mapping (d:diag α) (i:int) : option α = match d with
  | P a e ((P b _ _ | L b _ _) as r) → if a<i≤b then e else mapping r i
  | L a e b → if a<i≤b then e else None
  end
meta "rewrite_def" function mapping
```

The **meta** declarations instruct Why3 to use the above definitions as rewrite rules when transforming a proof task in preparation for sending it to an external theorem prover. The rewrites are applied recursively and exhaustively, viz. partitioning is rewritten into a conjunction sequence and mapping into a nested **if-else**-expression. This is normally desirable when using diagrams for specification; only when proving meta-theorems about partition and mapping diagrams may we want to suppress automatic rewriting.

A legend is declared with the **legend** keyword followed by an identifier, a sequence of parameters and a semicolon-separated list of coloring-to-predicate mappings. The preprocessor translates the legend into a conjunction of universally quantified statements according to Definition 4. For example, the legend:

```
type col = R | G
legend lgnd(a: array int)(x:int) of col =
  i : [[i≠R]] → a[i]≠x;
  i,j : [[i| ... ≠G j]] → a[i]≤a[j]
```

is translated by the preprocessor into the following Why3 predicate:

```
predicate lgnd(a:array int)(x:int)(~r:int→option col) =
  (forall i:int. i-1≤i ∧ (forall ~k:int. i-1<~k≤i → ~r ~k = Some R) → a[i]≠x) ∧
  (forall i,j:int. i≤j ∧ (forall ~k:int . i<~k≤j → ~r ~k = Some G) → a[i]≤a[j])
```

For automatic elimination of the inner quantification and color-typed terms in a legend applied to a coloring, as described in Sect. 4, the partitioning theory includes the following lemma declared as a rewrite rule:

```
lemma mapping_to_contains [@rewrite]:
  forall a,b:int, c:α, d: diag α.
    (forall k:int. a<k≤b → mapping d = Some c) ↔ contains a b c d
```

Here contains is defined as in Proposition 1. The rewrite is automatically applied (from left to right) by Why3 when executing the compute_specified and compute_in_goal transformations on a goal. The default strategy of the extended Why3 verifier applies these transformations prior to invoking the user's back-end theorem prover of choice.

Listing 1. Dutch National Flag

```
type col = B | W | R

legend flag(a: array col) =
    i: [[i#B]] → a[i] = B;
    i: [[i#W]] → a[i] = W;
    i: [[i#R]] → a[i] = R;


let dutch_national_flag (a: array col) : unit
    ensures { exists b r: int . flag a [[0 ...#B |b ...#W |r ...#R |length a]] }
    ensures { permut_all (old a) a }
=
    let b = ref 0 in
    let i = ref 0 in
    let r = ref (length a) in
    while !i < !r do
        invariant { [0 ... |!b ... |!i ... |!r ... |length a] }
        invariant { flag a [[0 ...#B |!b ...#W |!i ... |!r ...#R |length a]] }
        invariant { permut_all (old a) a }
        variant { !r - !i }
        match a[!i] with
        | B → swap a !b !i;  b := !b + 1; i := !i + 1
        | W → i := !i + 1
        | R → r := !r - 1; swap a !r !i
        end
    done
```

6 Verified Code Examples

In this section we present three formally specified and verified procedures where the pre- and postconditions and loop invariants are expressed as diagrams. The procedures are specified in the WhyML language with the diagram extensions described in Sect. 5, and all VCs were proved automatically by a combination of Z3 [7], CVC4 [3] and Alt-Ergo [4] after preprocessing by our tool.

A classical example of using the coloring analogy in verification is the *Dutch National Flag* problem introduced by Dijkstra [9]. It is a simplified sorting problem: an array containing, in random order, any number of each of the three values blue (B), white (W), and red (R) should be rearranged so that the blue elements precede all the white elements, which in turn precede all the red elements (i.e., the final order is B, W, R). Listing 1 shows an adaptation of an existing Why3 solution[2], in which we have replaced the textual postcondition (ensures clauses) and loop invariant (invariant clauses) with diagrammatic equivalents. The procedure executes in time linear to the size of the array and mutates the array by pairwise compare and swap. The loop invariant consists of three components: a partition diagram constraining the values

[2] Part of a gallery of verified programs available at http://toccata.lri.fr/gallery/why3.en.html.

Listing 2. Binary search

```
type sorted_col = SO

legend sorted (a: array int) of sorted_col =
    i,j: [[i#SO| ... |j#SO]] → a[i] ≤ a[j] ;

type found_col = NE | EQ

legend found (a: array int) (x:int) of found_col =
    i: [[i#NE]] → a[i] ≠ x ;
    i: [[i#EQ]] → a[i] = x

let binary_search (a: array int) (x: int) : int
    requires { sorted a [[0 ...#SO |length a]] }
    ensures { [0 ... |result| ... |length a] }
    ensures { found a v [[result#EQ]] }
    raises { Not_Found → found a x [[0 ...#NE |length a]] }
=
    let l = ref 0 in
    let u = ref (length a - 1) in
    while !l ≤ !u do
        invariant { sorted a [[0 ...#SO |length a]] }
        invariant { [0 ... |!l] ∧ [!u ... |(length a)-1] }
        invariant { found a x [[0 ...#NE |!l ... !u| ...#NE |length a]] }
        variant {!u - !l}
        let m = !l + div (!u - !l) 2 in
        if a[m] < x then l := m + 1
        else if a[m] > x then u := m - 1
        else return m
    done;
    raise Not_Found
```

of the loop variables b, i and r; a coloring mapping the intervals `[0      ]`b, `[b      ]`i and `[r      ]`length a to B, W and R, respectively; and a (non-diagrammatic) assertion that the modified array is a permutation of the original. The swap operation and the permut_all predicate are imported from the Why3 array library together with the property that the former maintains the latter. The program is atypical in that the color values, represented by the datatype col, are not pure specification constructs but also occur in the computation itself. The legend flag is trivial due to the nature of the program; it simply asserts that a is elementwise equal to the coloring on the intervals on which the latter is defined.

Listing 2 shows a verified implementation of binary search with a diagrammatic postcondition and loop invariant similar to the invariant discussed in the introduction. The procedure binary_search determines the presence of the value x in the sorted input array a. It has two exits, one normal and one abnormal. If x is found in a, the procedure

Listing 3. Insertion sort

```
type col = SO | I

legend sorting (a: array int) of col =
    i,j: [[i#SO| ... |j#SO]] → a[i] ≤ a[j] ;
    i: [[i#I|i+1#SO]] → a[i] ≤ a[i+1]

let insertion_sort (a: array int)
    ensures { sorting a [0 ...#B |length a] }
    ensures { permut_all a (old a) }
=
    let m = ref 0 in
    while !m < length a do
        invariant { [0 ... |!m| ... length a] }
        invariant { sorting a [[0 ...#SO |!m]] }
        invariant { permut_all a (old a) }
        variant { length a - !m }
        let k = ref !m in
        while !k > 0 && a[!k-1] > a[!k] do
            invariant { [0 ... |!k| ... !m] }
            invariant { sorting a [[0 ...#SO |!k#I| ...#SO !m]] }
            invariant { permut_all a (old a) }
            variant { !k }
            swap a !k (!k - 1);
            k := !k - 1
        done;
        m := !m + 1
    done;
```

exits normally returning an index containing x (in Why3, normal return values are represented by the result variable in the postcondition specification). If x is not found in a, the procedure exits abnormally in the Not_Found exception carrying the associated postcondition that all elements of a are different from x. To express the specification and invariants diagrammatically, we introduce two legends for the specification of binary search: sorting, expressing sortedness of the SO-colored range; and found, expressing existence (EQ) or absence (NE) of the sought element x.

The final example, Listing 3 shows an implementation of a simple sorting algorithm, insertion sort. The procedure insertion_sort sorts the input array by maintaining two partitions, one sorted partition ranging from index 0 to m, followed by one unsorted partition ranging from m to the end of the array. Each iteration of the outer loop extends the sorted partition by one element, until the whole array is sorted. The outer loop invariant is expressed by the partition diagram `|0     |!m|    length a|` and the coloring `|0   #SO  |!m`. The first component of the legend sorting for SO-colored intervals is identical to the one introduced in Listing 2. In order to achieve sortedness of the first interval after incrementing m, the inner loop moves the element at index m backwards into its final position in the sorted partition by repeatedly swapping it with its predecessor using the loop counter k. During the execution of the inner loop, the outer loop invariant is temporarily invalidated: the interval $\boxed{0 \qquad !m}$ is almost sorted, but with the exception of a single potential inversion of elements at indexes k-1 and k. Diagrammatically, this is expressed by the index k being colored by I, and the second component of the sorting legend specifying that any I-colored element followed by an SO-colored element constitutes a sorted pair.

7   Related Work

Partition and interval diagrams were originally proposed by Reynolds [16], who used them extensively in the specification and verification of several array-manipulating programs in his textbook *The Craft of Programming* [17]. Notably, Reynolds gives a formal syntax and a set of manipulation rules for the diagrams to facilitate their use as terms in calculational correctness proofs. Reynolds writes universally quantified invariants using the standard ∀-operator and gives the quantification domain as an interval diagram, rather than making the quantification implicit in the diagrammatic notation itself. Many textbooks, e.g. [12, 18], use similar box diagrams (termed "array pictures" or "array diagrams") in the presentation of assertions over both array indexes and array elements, but most of them do not formalize their semantics fully. Astrachan [1] suggests diagram representations for arrays and linked lists, emphasizing the role of diagrams in comprehension. Generating visual representations from textual specifications has been addressed in the context of the Z language [14]. Similar diagrams have also been proposed for visualizing array VCs [13], as an aid to proof and debugging. Wickerson et al. [19] employ partition-like diagrams in the visual proof notation called ribbon proofs for separation logic. Pearce [15] explores through a number of examples how array-based programming is enhanced by languages which support specifications and invariants over arrays. Invariant-based programming [2] is a correct-by-construction formal method aimed at teaching in which programs and their proofs are constructed diagrammatically, often with the aid of partition diagram-like pictures during the initial stages of construction. The idea of colorings and legends also originates from the authors' previous joint work with R-J. Back [10]. We are not aware of existing work on integrating partition or interval diagrams into a general-purpose program verification platform.

8   Conclusions and Future Work

This paper approaches box diagrams from the viewpoint that they can serve as an expressive formal mini-language—a DSL—rather than being restricted to their traditional role of ephemeral pre-code sketches and post-code visualizations. We have introduced an extension to Reynolds's original partition and interval diagrams for piecewise definition of partial functions over integer intervals, and a legend construct for asserting a predicate over a sequence of labeled ("colored") intervals. We have extended Why3 to read diagrammatic syntax and formalized its semantics in a Why3 theory.

We believe that the value of a formal specification is largely dependent on its legibility, as the specification cannot be proved correct (only checked for internal consistency), but is instead subject to human assessment of fitness for purpose (validation). Also, although significant advances have been made in automatically synthesizing invariants from the code, such techniques cannot discover difficult invariants, meaning that the same requirement of legibility applies to these as well. Good notation makes writing readable assertions more tractable, and while notation by itself may not be the primary challenge of verification, it is nevertheless held in high regard among verification practitioners. In particular, we have observed a tendency among the experienced to write integer range and array predicates following idioms that serve similar organizational purposes as the diagrams proposed herein, such as chaining relational operators and maintaining increasing order of bounds from left to right, preferring the relations $<$ and $\leq$ over $>$ and $\geq$. Formalizing such idioms is where a DSL and tool support can be of value. However, diagrammatic languages requiring sophisticated tool support and considerable learning investments from users are hard to justify for niche domains. The authors believe that the DSL presented here achieves a sensible compromise between expressive power and ease of integration. During implementation of the tool support, we came to appreciate both the semantically rich Why3 and WhyML languages and the extensibility of the Why3 platform through its API. The one feature we missed was a way to extend the Why3 language in a modular fashion, e.g., by adding new term productions while leaving the rest of the grammar intact, rather than by modifying its parser.

Finally, we emphasize that our goal has not been to address all aspects of array reasoning. The authors have found the DSL useful when writing array invariants that involves partitioning, but do not make further claims regarding its general applicability. There are classes of array invariants for which the DSL is not a sensible choice: clearly, assertions not involving partitions may have little to gain, and assertions with multiple nested quantifications may find the legibility advantage being lost. A lightweight DSL has the advantage that we can restrict its use to specification tasks for which we deem it beneficial, and fall back to standard FOL notation in other cases Hence we believe the DSL's primary role is to ease writing of certain classes of array and integer range properties, viz. those that involve partitioning and universal quantification. We surmise that the class of programs involving such properties is large enough that a DSL like the one presented here could justify its place in the modern verification toolbox.

Future Work. There is scope for much further work on partition, interval and mapping diagrams, both in improving tool support and in generalizing the notation itself. The tool is in the first prototype stage and has so far only been tested on a small collection of toy examples. We have identified enhancements and optimizations that will be required to address real-world requirements. For instance, the diagram syntax is currently not supported in the Why3 IDE during interactive proofs. Also, the contains rewrite should be optimized, as it currently expands a diagram into a formula that is exponential in the length of the diagram chain (this has not been an issue in practice with typical diagrams, but prevents larger diagrams from being processed). More experiments will be needed to gain more experience with the notation and identify potential pitfalls, and a comparative study with real users is necessary to experimentally assess the merits of the DSL over regular FOL notation. Finally, we are also looking into extending the diagram notation beyond the domain of integers, in particular to non-linear structures in order to reason about multi-dimensional arrays, trees and graphs.

References

1. Astrachan, O.L.: Pictures as invariants. In: Dale, N.B. (ed.) Proceedings of the 22nd SIGCSE Technical Sympòsium on Computer Science Education, pp. 112–118. ACM (1991). https://doi.org/10.1145/107004.107026
2. Back, R.J.: Invariant based programming: basic approach and teaching experiences. Form. Asp. Comput. **21**(3), 227–244 (2009). https://doi.org/10.1007/s00165-008-0070-y
3. Barrett, C., et al.: CVC4. In: Gopalakrishnan, G., Qadeer, S. (eds.) CAV 2011. LNCS, vol. 6806, pp. 171–177. Springer, Heidelberg (2011). https://doi.org/10.1007/978-3-642-22110-1_14
4. Bobot, F., Conchon, S., Contejean, E., Iguernelala, M., Lescuyer, S., Mebsout, A.: The Alt-Ergo Automated Theorem Prover (2008). http://alt-ergo.lri.fr/
5. Bobot, F., Filliâtre, J.C., Marché, C., Melquiond, G., Paskevich, A.: The Why3 Platform (2019). Version 1.2.0. http://why3.lri.fr/manual.pdf
6. Bobot, F., Filliâtre, J.C., Marché, C., Paskevich, A.: Let's verifythis with why3. Int. J. Softw. Tools Tech. Transf. **17**(6), 709–727 (2015). https://doi.org/10.1007/s10009-014-0314-5
7. de Moura, L., Bjørner, N.: Z3: an efficient SMT solver. In: Ramakrishnan, C.R., Rehof, J. (eds.) TACAS 2008. LNCS, vol. 4963, pp. 337–340. Springer, Heidelberg (2008). https://doi.org/10.1007/978-3-540-78800-3_24
8. Dijkstra, E.W.: The humble programmer. Commun. ACM **15**(10), 859–866 (1972). https://doi.org/10.1145/355604.361591
9. Dijkstra, E.W.: A Discipline of Programming. Prentice-Hall, Upper Saddle River (1976)
10. Eriksson, J., Parsa, M., Back, R.-J.: A precise pictorial language for array invariants. In: Furia, C.A., Winter, K. (eds.) IFM 2018. LNCS, vol. 11023, pp. 151–160. Springer, Cham (2018). https://doi.org/10.1007/978-3-319-98938-9_9
11. Filliâtre, J.-C., Paskevich, A.: Why3—where programs meet provers. In: Felleisen, M., Gardner, P. (eds.) ESOP 2013. LNCS, vol. 7792, pp. 125–128. Springer, Heidelberg (2013). https://doi.org/10.1007/978-3-642-37036-6_8
12. Gries, D.: The Science of Programming, 1st edn. Springer, New York (1987)
13. Jami, M., Ireland, A.: A verification condition visualizer. In: Giannakopoulou, D., Kroening, D. (eds.) VSTTE 2014. LNCS, vol. 8471, pp. 72–86. Springer, Cham (2014). https://doi.org/10.1007/978-3-319-12154-3_5
14. Moremedi, K., van der Poll, J.A.: Transforming formal specification constructs into diagrammatic notations. In: Cuzzocrea, A., Maabout, S. (eds.) MEDI 2013. LNCS, vol. 8216, pp. 212–224. Springer, Heidelberg (2013). https://doi.org/10.1007/978-3-642-41366-7_18
15. Pearce, D.J.: Array programming in whiley. In: Proceedings of the 4th ACM SIGPLAN International Workshop on Libraries, Languages, and Compilers for Array Programming, pp. 17–24. ACM, New York (2017). https://doi.org/10.1145/3091966.3091972
16. Reynolds, J.C.: Reasoning about arrays. Commun. ACM **22**(5), 290–299 (1979). https://doi.org/10.1145/359104.359110
17. Reynolds, J.C.: The Craft of Programming. Prentice Hall PTR, Upper Saddle River (1981)
18. Tennent, R.D.: Specifying Software - A Hands-On Introduction. Cambridge University Press, Cambridge (2002)
19. Wickerson, J., Dodds, M., Parkinson, M.: Ribbon proofs for separation logic. In: Felleisen, M., Gardner, P. (eds.) ESOP 2013. LNCS, vol. 7792, pp. 189–208. Springer, Heidelberg (2013). https://doi.org/10.1007/978-3-642-37036-6_12

Variability-Aware Datalog

Ramy Shahin$^{(\boxtimes)}$ and Marsha Chechik

University of Toronto, Toronto, Canada
{rshahin,chechik}@cs.toronto.edu

Abstract. Variability-aware computing is the efficient application of programs to different sets of inputs that exhibit some variability. One example is program analyses applied to Software Product Lines (SPLs). In this paper we present the design and development of a variability-aware version of the Soufflé Datalog engine. The engine can take facts annotated with Presence Conditions (PCs) as input, and compute the PCs of its inferred facts, eliminating facts that do not exist in any valid configuration. We evaluate our variability-aware Soufflé implementation on several fact sets annotated with PCs to measure the associated overhead in terms of processing time and database size.

Keywords: Variability-aware programming · Product-line engineering · Soufflé

1 Introduction

A Datalog engine is used to infer knowledge from a set of facts given some inference rules. There are cases though where we need to apply the same rules to different sets of facts coming from different worlds, or different configurations. For example, the Doop [2] pointer analysis framework encodes its logic as Datalog rules, and applies them to facts extracted from Java programs. Doop can only work on a single software product at a time. However, it is common for software engineers to develop a whole family of products, a Software Product Line (SPL) [5], as one project, exploiting the commonality across those products. Different *variants* (products) implement different sets of *features*. Since each feature can be either present or not in a variant, the number of variants is usually exponential in the number of features.

To use a framework like Doop on an SPL, we need to apply it to each of the variants individually. This is infeasible in most cases because of the exponential number of variants. Also, it involves a lot of redundancy because it does not leverage the commonality across variants. To mitigate those drawbacks, some program analyses have been *lifted* to efficiently work on SPLs instead of single products [1,4,6,9–11,14]. This lifting process usually invovles reimplementing the analysis to be variability-aware.

Our prior work [12] outlines an approach to apply Doop (and similar frameworks) to the whole SPL at once, showing orders of magnitude of savings in

© Springer Nature Switzerland AG 2020
E. Komendantskaya and Y. A. Liu (Eds.): PADL 2020, LNCS 12007, pp. 213–221, 2020.
https://doi.org/10.1007/978-3-030-39197-3_14

```
Path(v1, v2) :- Edge(v1, v2).
Path(v1, v3) :-
        Edge(v1, v2), Path(v2, v3).
```

Listing (1.1) Path rules.

```
Edge(Athens, Rome)    @ Sea.
Edge(Rome, Toronto)   @ Air.
Edge(NYC, Athens)     @ !Land.
Edge(Toronto, NYC)    @ Land.
```

Listing (1.2) Variability-aware inputs.

```
Path(Athens, Rome)      @ Sea.
Path(Rome, Toronto)     @ Air.
Path(NYC, Athens)       @ !Land.
Path(Toronto, NYC)      @ Land.
Path(Athens, Toronto)   @ Sea /\ Air.
Path(Rome, NYC)         @ Air /\ Land.
Path(Toronto, Athens)   @ Land /\ !Land.
Path(NYC, Rome)         @ Sea.
```

Listing (1.3) Variability-aware outputs.

Fig. 1. Motivating example.

computation time and storage space compared to running on each variant separately. One building block of that work was modifying the Soufflé [8] Datalog engine to be variability-aware, i.e., taking fact variability into consideration when inferring new facts. One fundamental advantage of our approach is that lifting a Datalog engine to be variability-aware automatically lifts all analyses that use it. In addition, variability-aware inference can be widely applied beyond program analysis. In any application domain, it is possible for different facts to be present only in specific situations, configurations, or in some constrained worlds. Instead of modeling each of those variants separately, it makes sense to model them together since inference rules are orthogonal to variability.

The rest of this paper starts with some background definitions and a motivating example (Sect. 2), followed by the design of variability-aware Soufflé (Sect. 3). We then present the results of our evaluation experiments (Sect. 4), and finally conclude and suggest some future directions (Sect. 5).

2   Background and Motivating Example

In this section we define some Datalog and variability terms, illustrating them on the motivating example in Fig. 1. We then briefly introduce the architecture of the Soufflé Datalog engine.

2.1   Datalog and Variability

Datalog is a declarative data definition and query language that combines relational data manipulation and logical inference [3]. A *Datalog program* is a set of inference rules, collectively referred to as the *Intentional Dataabse (IDB)*. For example, the Datalog program in Listing 1.1 computes directed paths given graph edges.

A program takes *facts*, referred to as the *Extensional Database (EDB)*, as input, and by repeatedly applying the inferrence rules to the input facts new output facts are generated. Listings 1.2 and 1.3 are examples of input and output facts respectively.

Variability-aware computing is the ability to efficiently compute over values from different worlds at the same time. A set of worlds is defined in terms of a

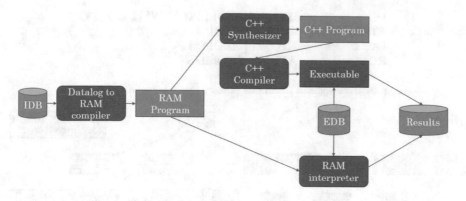

Fig. 2. Soufflé architecture.

set of *features* $\mathcal{F}$. A world is defined by a *configuration* ρ, where each feature can be either present or absent. A set of worlds is defined by a propositional formula over features.

Each software artifact can be labeled with a *Presence Condition (PC)*: a propositional formula specifying the set of worlds in which this artifact exists. Datalog facts are an example of artifacts. If we are modeling a set of worlds defined by three features: *Land, Air* and *Sea*, facts can be labeled by PCs as seen in Listing 1.2. The '@' symbol is syntactically used to separate the fact predicate from its PC. We use the symbols '!' for negation, '\/ ' for disjunction, and '/\ ' for conjunction. Parenthesis can be also used to override operator precedence.

Usually not all feature combinations are valid. For example, the expression (Land $\wedge$ Sea) states that we have an edge that is *both* overland and marine, which does not make sense. To rule out invalid feature combinations, a product line usually has a *feature model* $\mathcal{FM}$: a propositional formula over features specifying their valid combinations (valid worlds). A configuration ρ is valid only if $\rho \wedge \mathcal{FM}$ is satisfiable. Our example's feature model is

$$(Air \vee Land \vee Sea) \wedge \neg(Air \wedge Land) \wedge \neg(Land \wedge Sea) \wedge \neg(Sea \wedge Air)$$

Now a *variability-aware Datalog engine* needs to take both the feature model and the presence conditions of facts into consideration when inferring new facts. Whenever a new fact is inferred, its Presence Condition (PC) should be the conjunction of the PCs of its resolvent facts together with the feature model. If this PC is not satisfiable, the inferred fact does not belong to any valid configuration (world), and can be removed.

Listing 1.3 shows the results of applying our variability-aware Datalog engine to the program and facts aforementioned. Crossed-out facts are the ones removed because their presence conditions are not satisfiable (in general or with respect to the feature model).

Formal syntax and semantics of variability-aware Datalog, together with correctness criteria of the lifted inference algorithm, and proof of correctness are presented in [12].

$$PC \qquad ::= ID \mid !PC \mid (PC) \mid PC \bigvee PC \mid PC \bigwedge PC$$
$$ATOMLIST ::= ATOM \mid ATOM, ATOMLIST$$
$$FACT \qquad ::= ATOM \; . \mid ATOM @ PC \; .$$
$$RULE \qquad ::= ATOM :\text{-} ATOMLIST \; .$$

Fig. 3. BNF syntax of Soufflé clauses and presence conditions.

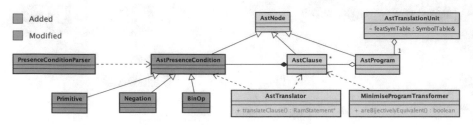

Fig. 4. Modifications and additions to Soufflé syntax and parsing classes.

2.2 Soufflé

Soufflé [8] is an optimized Datalog engine, with a Datalog interpreter in addition
to the option of compiling programs into native C++ code (Fig. 2). Soufflé first
compiles Datalog into Relational Algebra Machine (RAM) programs, which are
then either interpreted or compiled. RAM is a relational algebra language with
a fixpoint operator.

Soufflé employs a semi-naive Datalog evaluation algorithm to compile Datalog into RAM. Elaborate data indexing techniques and multi-threaded query
processing are then used to evaluate RAM programs. These techniques, in addition to the ability to compile RAM into C++, and subsequently into optimized
native machine code, result in high-performance exeuction of Datalog programs.

3   Variability-Aware Soufflé

We modified the Soufflé engine to support variability-aware Datalog inference.
Soufflé runs in two modes: interpreter mode and compilation (code synthesis)
mode. We only support the interpreter mode at this time.

3.1   Syntax Extension

We extend the Soufflé fact syntax (Fig. 3) with an optional *Presence Condition
(PC)* before the period ('.') at the end. A presence condition is prefixed with the
'@' symbol, and has the syntactic structure of a propositional formula.

The Soufflé grammar (Lex and Yacc files) is extended accordingly, and
Abstract Syntax Tree (AST) classes are added to the code-base for Presence
Conditions (Fig. 4). *AstPresenceCondition* is an abstract class inheriting from
AstNode. Concrete subclasses of *AstPresenceCondition* are *Primitive* (for True,
Falseand atomic propositional symbols), *Negation*, and *BinOp* (for conjunction
and disjunction).

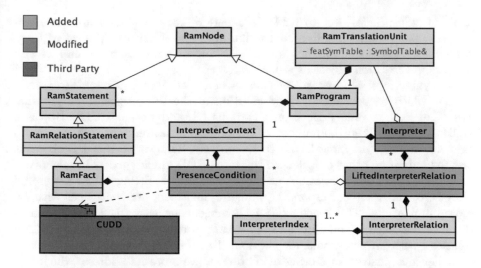

Fig. 5. Modifications and additions to RAM interpreter classes.

The syntactic category of presence conditions can appear in Soufflé programs, and also in CSV files. While the Soufflé parser takes care of programs, we had to implement a separate parser for PCs appearing in CSV files (the *PresenceConditionParser* class). It identifies a PC as an optional field prefixed with '@' coming at the end of a fact. If a PC exists, it is parsed into an *AstPresenceCondition* object.

The *AstClause* class is now extended with an *AstPresenceCondition* field. Unless a PC is provided for a clause, the default value is the *True*proposition (indicating that the fact is present in all configurations). *AstTranslator* has a method called *translateClause* that compiles an *AstClause* into a *RamStatement*. This method is modified to translate the PC of the clause as well.

The propositional symbols used in PCs come from a syntactic category different from that of Soufflé variables and constants. To avoid name collisions, we store those symbols in a separate symbol table (*featSymTable*). An *AstTranslationUnit* now has two symbols tables: one for Datalog symbols and the other for propositional symbols (feature names).

Soufflé performs some optimizations on the AST before it is translated into a RAM program. For example, in the *MinimiseProgramTransformer* class, *areBijectivelyEquivalent* is a method that checks if two clauses are bijectively equivalent. We extend this method to compare the PCs of the clauses as well. If the PCs are not syntactically the same, we consider the two clauses not equivalent.

3.2 RAM

The AST of a Soufflé translation unit is compiled into a *Relational Algebra Machine (RAM)* program, encapsulated in a *RamTranslationUnit* object (Fig. 5). Similar to *AstTranslationUnit*, we need to carry the feature symbol table (*featSymTable*) over to RAM as a part of the translation unit. A *Ram-Program* is contained within a translation unit, and it consists of a set of *Ram-Statement* objects. A *RamFact* is a special kind of *RamStatement*, and we add a *PresenceCondition* object as a field to it.

A syntactic *AstPresenceCondition* is compiled into a *PresenceCondition* object, which encapsulates a representation of the PC propositional formula. We store PCs as Binary Decision Diagrams [7], and we use CUDD [13] as a BDD engine. To keep the number of PC objects at a minimum, we also maintain a hash-table mapping BDDs to PC objects. This way a new PC object is created only if no other object with the same BDD already exists in memory.

Soufflé stores RAM relations as tables of numbers. String values are stored elsewhere, and their corresponding numeric identifiers are the values actually stored in relations. This keeps relations homogeneous, easy to access and index. Since we now need to add a PC for each RAM record, the easiest way is to extend relations with an extra field for the PC. To keep the relation data-structure homogeneous, instead of storing a PC object, we store its address, which is a 64-bit numeric value, pretty much like other fields. This way our extra PC field is opaque to the rest of the RAM subsystem. We had to take special care of *nullary relations*, i.e., relations of zero fields. They have special semantics in Soufflé, and to preserve the semantics, we consider a relation of a single field (the PC) to be nullary.

3.3 Interpreter

The Soufflé interpreter runs a program on the fly, keeping a context of type *InterpreterContext*, and manipulating a set of RAM relations. To avoid getting into the details of how relations are stored, and how data indices are maintained, we decided not to modify *InterpreterRelation* and *InterpreterIndex*. Instead, we wrap *InterpreterRelation* in *LiftedInterpreterRelation*. The wrapper maintains the same interface, but adds the semantic manipulation of the PC field.

Another significant difference between *LiftedInterpreterRelation* and *InterpreterRelation* is existence checking of records. In Soufflé checking if a record exists in a relation is straightforward using the full index of the relation, returning true if the record exists in the index and false otherwise. With PCs existence checking is more subtle because the record we are looking for might exist but with a different PC. To accommodate for this, we add a PC output parameter to *exists*, the existence checking method of *LiftedInterpreterRelation*. Now instead of just returning a boolean indicating whether a record exists in a relation, we also return a pointer to the stored PC of the record (if the record exists).

Now whenever two records are resolved by the interpreter, their PCs need to be conjoined, and the conjunction (if satisfiable) becomes the PC of the resulting record. If on the other hand the conjunction is not satisfiable, the result can be safely ignored because an unsatisfiable PC indicates an empty set of configurations in which this record exists. Satisfiability checking is a constant-time operation on BDDs (although BDD construction might take exponential time

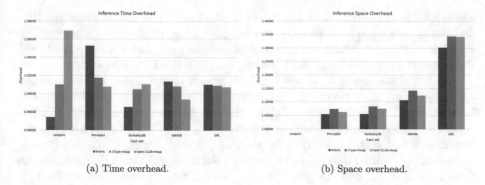

(a) Time overhead.   (b) Space overhead.

Fig. 6. Time and space overhead due to variability-aware inference for five different fact sets and three sets of rules.

Table 1. Inference time for three different Datalog programs applied to five different fact sets. For each fact base we report the number of features (R), number of facts with PCs other than True (FPC), inference time (T), database size (S), non-variability-aware inference time (TN), and non-variability-aware database size (SN). Time is reported in milliseconds, and space is reported in Kilobytes.

Fact-base	R	FPC	insens				1Type+Heap				taint-1Call+Heap			
			T(ms)	S(KB)	TN(ms)	SN(KB)	T(ms)	S(KB)	TN(ms)	SN(KB)	T(ms)	S(KB)	TN(ms)	SN(KB)
Lampiro	18	343	8,111	41,170	8,324	41,160	20,725	149,686	20,522	149,661	45,996	230,370	43,014	230,329
Prevayler	5	6,507	5,334	4,407	5,066	4,177	6,013	8,630	5,908	8,035	9,717	5,534	9,640	5,203
BerkeleyDB	42	49,062	10,810	49,725	10,966	47,071	17,273	122,922	17,186	113,346	21,474	112,060	21,247	104,137
MM08	27	6,811	4,720	3,259	4,656	2,944	5,142	6,990	5,099	6,114	9,306	7,829	9,360	6,960
GPL	21	3,353	4,517	409	4,471	314	4,718	593	4,675	441	8,861	462	8,795	344

in the number of variables). Because clause resolution might take place recursively, we add a PC field to *InterpreterContext*, which keeps track of the PCs of intermediate results.

When inserting a record into a relation, again we need to take the PC into consideration. If that record already exists in the relation with the same PC, then we do not need to add it again. If on the other hand it exists with a different PC, we now need to disjoin that with the new PC because we are expanding the set of configurations where this record exists into that of the union of the two PCs. If the record does not exist at all, we just add it with its new PC.

We had to modify the I/O subsystem of Soufflé to make sure we correctly read and write PCs together with records from/to CSV files. *PresenceConditionParser* is used to parse PCs on input, and logic for serializing PCs is added to the *PresenceCondition* class. At this point, we do not support storing facts to SQLite databases.

4   Evaluation

We evaluate the performance of our implementation of variability-aware Soufflé in terms of time and space overhead. In particular, the research question we are trying to answer is how much of an overhead in terms of inference time and database size is attributed to our modifications to Soufflé. To answer this question, we compare the performance of Soufflé on a fact set annotated with PCs against its performance on the same set with the PCs removed.

We use the same dataset used in [12], which is comprised of five fact sets extracted from Java programs, and three program analyses (implemented as Datalog rules) applied to each of them. Table 1 summarizes the number of features (R) and number of facts annotated with PCs (FPC) for each of the five benchmark fact sets. In addition, for each of the three Datalog rule sets (insens, 1Type+Heap, taint-1Call+Heap) it outlines the inference time (T), database size after inference (S), and the corresponding values when the fact set with no PC annotations is used (TN and SN respectively). Time is measured in milliseconds, and space is measured in Kilobytes.

Figure 6a shows the inference time overhead when applying each of the three Datalog programs to each of the five fact sets. Overhead is calculated as a ratio between the time taken by variability-aware inference to standard Datalog inference. There are a few cases of overhead values less than 1.0, which can be considered as outliers due to other factors affecting overall processing time (e.g., I/O). From this graph, we can conclude that the overhead is relatively small (7% was the maximum reported for taint-1Call+Heap on Lampiro). We still can not see a direct correlation between the time overhead and fact set attributes (e.g., feature count, percentage of facts annotated with PCs).

Similarly, Fig. 6b shows the database size overhead when applying the same Datalog programs to the fact sets, where the ratio here is between database sizes. Soufflé databases are stored as text files, and since variability-aware facts (including inferred ones) might have PCs, and those PCs are stored as text, it is natural that a variability-aware fact database takes more space than a plain databse with no PCs. We can see from this graph that the database size overhead grows roughly with the percentage of PC-annotated input facts. This overhead reaches almost 34% for GPL, where about 60% of the input facts are PC-annotated.

Please recall that the rationale behind variability-aware computing is to run a program only once on values from all configurations, as opposed to running the program on each configuration separately. Since the number of configurations is typically exponential in the number of features, the marginal overhead we see here is negligible compared to the savings due to running the program only once. More details on our experiment setup and evaluation results can be found in [12].

5   Conclusion and Future Work

In this paper we presented the design and development of the variability-aware Soufflé Datalog engine. The engine can take Datalog facts annotated with presence conditions as input, and compute the presence conditions of its inferred facts, eliminating facts that do not exist in any valid configuration.

We evaluated the overhead of our variability-aware Datalog inference in terms of inference time and size of the fact database, showing that time overhead is marginal, and space overhead grows with the percentage of PC-annotated input facts. This overhead is acceptable compared to the brute force approach (each configuration running separately), where the number of configurations, and accordingly the overhead, is exponential in the number of variability features.

For future work, we plan to extend our variability-aware inference implementation to the Soufflé C++ code generator. We also plan to extend our theoretical foundations and implementation to support presence conditions on rules. This would allow for variability of inference logic in addition to data.

References

1. Bodden, E., Tolêdo, T., Ribeiro, M., Brabrand, C., Borba, P., Mezini, M.: SPLL-IFT: statically analyzing software product lines in minutes instead of years. In: Proceedings of PLDI 2013, pp. 355–364. ACM (2013)
2. Bravenboer, M., Smaragdakis, Y.: Strictly declarative specification of sophisticated points-to analyses. In: Proceedings of the 24th ACM SIGPLAN Conference on Object Oriented Programming Systems Languages and Applications, OOPSLA 2009, pp. 243–262. ACM, New York (2009)
3. Ceri, S., Gottlob, G., Tanca, L.: What you always wanted to know about datalog (and never dared to ask). IEEE Trans. Knowl. Data Eng. **1**(1), 146–166 (1989). https://doi.org/10.1109/69.43410
4. Classen, A., Heymans, P., Schobbens, P.Y., Legay, A., Raskin, J.F.: Model checking lots of systems: efficient verification of temporal properties in software product lines. In: Proceedings of the 32Nd ACM/IEEE International Conference on Software Engineering, ICSE 2010, vol. 1, pp. 335–344. ACM, New York (2010)
5. Clements, P., Northrop, L.: Software Product Lines: Practices and Patterns. Addison-Wesley Professional, Boston (2001)
6. Gazzillo, P., Grimm, R.: SuperC: parsing all of C by taming the preprocessor. In: Proceedings of PLDI 2012, pp. 323–334. ACM (2012)
7. Huth, M., Ryan, M.: Logic in Computer Science, 2nd edn. Cambridge University Press, Cambridge (2004)
8. Jordan, H., Scholz, B., Subotić, P.: SOUFFLÉ: on synthesis of program analyzers. In: Chaudhuri, S., Farzan, A. (eds.) CAV 2016. LNCS, vol. 9780, pp. 422–430. Springer, Cham (2016). https://doi.org/10.1007/978-3-319-41540-6_23
9. Kästner, C., Apel, S., Thüm, T., Saake, G.: Type checking annotation-based product lines. ACM Trans. Softw. Eng. Methodol. **21**(3), 14:1–14:39 (2012)
10. Midtgaard, J., Dimovski, A.S., Brabrand, C., Wąsowski, A.: Systematic derivation of correct variability-aware program analyses. Sci. Comput. Program. **105**(C), 145–170 (2015)
11. Salay, R., Famelis, M., Rubin, J., Di Sandro, A., Chechik, M.: Lifting model transformations to product lines. In: Proceedings of the 36th International Conference on Software Engineering, ICSE 2014, pp. 117–128. ACM, New York (2014)
12. Shahin, R., Chechik, M., Salay, R.: Lifting datalog-based analyses to software product lines. In: Proceedings of the 2019 27th ACM Joint Meeting on European Software Engineering Conference and Symposium on the Foundations of Software Engineering, ESEC/FSE 2019, pp. 39–49. ACM, New York (2019)
13. Somenzi, F.: CUDD: CU decision diagram package release 2.2.0, July 1998
14. Thüm, T., Apel, S., Kästner, C., Schaefer, I., Saake, G.: A classification and survey of analysis strategies for software product lines. ACM Comput. Surv. **47**(1), 6:1–6:45 (2014)

Author Index